Derek Tidball (Bible Themes)

The Message of Women

The Bible Speaks Today: Bible Themes series

The Message of the Living God
His glory, his people, his world
Peter Lewis

The Message of the Resurrection
Christ is risen!
Paul Beasley-Murray

The Message of the Cross
Wisdom unsearchable, love indestructible
Derek Tidball

The Message of Salvation
By God's grace, for God's glory
Philip Graham Ryken

The Message of Creation
Encountering the Lord of the universe
David Wilkinson

The Message of Heaven and Hell
Grace and destiny
Bruce Milne

The Message of Mission
The glory of Christ in all time and space
Howard Peskett and Vinoth Ramachandra

The Message of Prayer
Approaching the throne of grace
Tim Chester

The Message of the Trinity
Life in God
Brian Edgar

The Message of Evil and Suffering
Light into darkness
Peter Hicks

The Message of the Holy Spirit
The Spirit of encounter
Keith Warrington

The Message of Holiness
Restoring God's masterpiece
Derek Tidball

The Message of Sonship
At home in God's household
Trevor Burke

The Message of the Word of God
The glory of God made known
Tim Meadowcroft

The Message of Women
Creation, grace and gender
Derek and Dianne Tidball

The Message of Women

Creation, grace and gender

Derek Tidball

Visiting Scholar, Spurgeon's College, London
formerly Principal of London School of Theology

Dianne Tidball

Regional Minister (Team Leader),
East Midlands Baptist Association

Inter-Varsity Press

InterVarsity Press
P.O. Box 1400, Downers Grove, IL 60515-1426
Internet: www.ivpress.com
Email: email@ivpress.com

InterVarsity Press® is the book-publishing division of InterVarsity Christian Fellowship/USA®, a movement of students and faculty active on campus at hundreds of universities, colleges and schools of nursing in the United States of America, and a member movement of the International Fellowship of Evangelical Students. For information about local and regional activities, write Public Relations Dept., InterVarsity Christian Fellowship/USA, 6400 Schroeder Rd., P.O. Box 7895, Madison, WI 53707-7895, or visit the IVCF website at www.intervarsity.org.

ISBN 978-0-8308-2436-6

Printed in the United States of America ∞

Library of Congress Cataloging-in-Publication Data
A catalog record for this book is available from the Library of Congress.

P 22 21 20 19 18 17 16 15 14 13 12 11 10 9 8 7 6 5 4 3 2 1

Y 31 30 29 28 27 26 25 24 23 22 21 20 19 18 17 16 15 14 13

Dedicated to women growing in faith:
Jenny, Rachel, Natalie, Abi, Emily, Becky and Sarah

Contents

Part 4. Women in the new community

GENERAL PREFACE

THE BIBLE SPEAKS TODAY describes three series of expositions, based on the books of the Old and New Testaments, and on Bible themes that run through the whole of Scripture. Each series is characterized by a threefold ideal:

- to expound the biblical text with accuracy
- to relate it to contemporary life, and
- to be readable.

These books are, therefore, not 'commentaries', for the commentary seeks rather to elucidate the text than to apply it, and tends to be a work rather of reference than of literature. Nor, on the other hand, do they contain the kinds of 'sermons' that attempt to be contemporary and readable without taking Scripture seriously enough. The contributors to *The Bible Speaks Today* series are all united in their convictions that God still speaks through what he has spoken, and that nothing is more necessary for the life, health and growth of Christians than that they should hear what the Spirit is saying to them through his ancient – yet ever modern – Word.

ALEC MOTYER
JOHN STOTT
DEREK TIDBALL
Series editors

Authors' preface

The debts owed in writing a book like this are immense, far too numerous to mention. We wish to particularly acknowledge the women who taught us at bible college and the many female colleagues we have had both in our work in ministry and in theological education. They have been persuasive and humble arguments for egalitarianism even if, as one said to one of us recently, 'I'm no feminist!' Perhaps that, in fact, makes the case even more powerfully.

As always we would like to thank Jenny Aston of London School of Theology for her willingness to continue to read and edit the manuscript. Lish Eves and Sandra Byatt also read and commented on the manuscript, for which we were grateful. It is always good to work with Philip Duce at IVP and we were particularly grateful to him for his special editorial interest in this volume. Needless to say, the published work represents our views rather than those who helpfully offered critique.

We are aware that the subject of this book is contentious but we would hope not to lose friends because of what we have written. We have no desire to add to the conflict or adopt a political agenda of any kind. Rather we hope it will contribute to unity in the body of Christ and the encouragement of both women and men to use to the full their gifts for the glory of Christ and for making him known.

DEREK AND DIANNE TIDBALL
Leicester

Abbreviations

AB	Anchor Bible
AUSS	*Andrews University Seminary Studies*
BibInt	*Biblical Interpretation*
BTB	*Biblical Theology Bulletin*
BNTC	Black's New Testament Commentaries
BST	The Bible Speaks Today
CBQ	*Catholic Biblical Quarterly*
DBE	*Discovering Biblical Equality: Complementarity without Hierarchy,* ed. Ronald W. Pierce and Rebecca Merrill Groothuis (Downers Grove: IVP and Leicester: Apollos, 2005)
DJG	*Dictionary of Jesus and the Gospels,* ed. Joel B. Green, Scot McKnight, I. Howard Marshall (Downers Grove and Leicester: IVP, 1992)
DLNTD	*Dictionary of Later New Testament Writings and its Developments,* ed. Ralph P. Martin and Peter H. Davids (Downers Grove and Leicester: IVP, 1997)
DOTWPW	*Dictionary of Old Testament Wisdom, Poetry and Writings,* ed. Temper Longman III and Peter Enns (Downers Grove and Leicester: IVP, 2008)
ESV	English Standard Version
Fresh Analysis	*Women in the Church: A Fresh Analysis of 1 Timothy 2:9-15,* eds. Andreas J Köstenberger, Thomas R. Schreiner and H. Scott Baldwin (Grand Rapids: Baker Books, 1995)
Int	Interpretation Commentaries
ICC	International Critical Commentary
JAAR	*Journal of the American Academy of Religion*
JETS	*Journal of the Evangelical Theological Society*
JSOT	*Journal for the Study of the Old Testament*
KJV	King James' Version

11

NIB	*The New Interpreters' Bible*, 12 vols. (Nashville: Abingdon Press, 1994-98)
NCB	New Century Bible
NDBT	*New Dictionary of Biblical Theology,* ed. T. D. Alexander and Brian S. Rosner (Downers Grove and Leicester: IVP, 2000)
NIBC	New International Biblical Commentary
NIGTC	New International Greek Testament Commentary
NICOT	New International Commentary on the Old Testament
NICNT	New International Commentary on the New Testament
NIV	New International Version (2011 edn.)
NRSV	New Revised Standard Version
NTS	*New Testament Studies*
OTL	Old Testament Library
PNTC	Pillar New Testament Commentary Series
RBMW	*Recovering Biblical Manhood and Womanhood,* ed. John Piper and Wayne Grudem (Wheaton: Crossway, 2006)
RSV	Revised Standard Version
SNTSMS	Society for New Testament Studies Monograph Series
TDNT	*Theological Dictionary of the New Testament,* ed. G. Kittell and G. Friedrich, translated G. W. Bromiley, 10 vols. (Grand Rapids: Eerdmans, 1964-76)
TOTC	Tyndale Old Testament Commentaries
TrinJ	Trinity Journal
Two Views	*Two Views on Women in Ministry,* Craig S. Keener, Linda L. Belleville, Thomas R. Schreiner and Craig L. Blomberg, Counterpoints (Grand Rapids: Zondervan, 2005)
WBC	Word Bible Commentary
ZECNT	Zondervan Exegetical Commentary on the New Testament

Select bibliography

Abraham, J., *Eve: Accused or Acquitted? A Reconsideration of Feminist Readings of the Creation Narrative Texts in Genesis 1–3* (Carlisle: Paternoster, 2002).

Arnold, C. E., *Ephesians*, ZECNT (Grand Rapids: Eerdmans, 2010).

___, 'Jesus Christ: "Head" of the Church', in M. M. B. Turner and J. B. Green (eds.), *Jesus of Nazareth: Lord and Christ: Essays on the Historical Jesus and New Testament Christology* (Grand Rapids: Eerdmans, 1983), pp. 346–366.

Ascough, R. S., *Lydia: Paul's Cosmopolitan Hostess*, Paul's Social Network (Collegeville: Liturgical Press, 2009).

Atkinson, D., *The Message of Genesis 1 – 11*, BST (Leicester: IVP, 1990).

Bailey, K. E., *Jesus Through Middle Eastern Eyes: Cultural Studies in the Gospels* (London: SPCK, 2008).

___, *Paul Through Mediterranean Eyes* (London: SPCK, 2011).

___, *Through Peasant Eyes* (Grand Rapids: Eerdmans, 1980).

___, 'Women in the New Testament: A Middle Eastern Cultural View', *Anvil* 11 (1994), pp. 7–24.

Bartlett, D. L., *Ministry in the New Testament* (Minneapolis: Fortress Press, 1993).

Bauckham, R., *Gospel Women: Studies in the Named Women in the Gospels* (London: T & T Clark, 2002).

Baugh, S. M., 'A Foreign World: Ephesus in the First Century', in *Fresh Analysis*, pp. 14–50.

Belleville, L. L., 'Teaching and Usurping Authority: 1 Timothy 2: 11–15, *DBE*, pp. 205–223.

___, 'Women in Ministry: A Egalitarian Perspective', *Two Views*, pp. 19–104.

Blomberg, C., 'Women in Ministry: A Complementarian Perspective', *Two Views*, pp. 121–184.

Bockmuehl, M., *The Epistle to the Philippians*, BNTC (London: A & C Black, 1998).

Briggs, R., *Gender and the New Testament* (Grove: Cambridge, 2001).

Brown, H. O. J., 'The New Testament against itself: 1 Timothy 2:9–15 and the "Breakthrough" of Galatians 3:28', in *Fresh Analysis*, pp. 197–208.

Brown, R. E., *The Gospel According to John XIII–XXI*, AB (Doubleday: New York, 1970).

Bruce, F. F., *The Book of Acts*, NICNT (Grand Rapids: Eerdmans, 1988).

____, *Commentary on Galatians*, NIGTC (Exeter: Paternoster, 1982).

Brueggemann, W., *Genesis*, Int (Atlanta: John Knox Press, 1982).

Bush, F., *Ruth, Esther*, WBC (Dallas: Word, 1996).

Butler, T., *Judges*, WBC (Nashville: Nelson, 2009).

Camp, C. V., *Wisdom and the Feminine in the Book of Proverbs* (Decatur: Almond Press, 1985).

Campbell, J. C., *Phoebe: Patron and Emissary*, Paul's Social Network (Collegeville: Liturgical Press, 2009).

Carson, D. A., *The Gospel According to John*, PNTC (Grand Rapids: Eerdmans and Leicester: IVP, 1991).

____, 'Silent in the Churches: On the role of women in 1 Corinthians 14:33b–36', *RBMW*, pp. 140–153.

Ciampa, R. E. and Rosner, B. S., *The First Letter to the Corinthians*, PNTC (Grand Rapids: Eerdmans and Nottingham: Apollos, 2010).

Clarke, A. D., *Serve the Community of the Church: Christians as Leaders and Ministers* (Grand Rapids: Eerdmans, 2000).

Clark, S. B., *Man and Woman in Christ: An Examination of the Roles of Men and Women in Light of Scripture and the Social Sciences* (Ann Arbor: Servant, 1980).

Clines, D., *What Does Eve Do to Help?* JSOT Sup 94 (Sheffield: Sheffield Academic Press, 1990).

____, 'Why is There a Song of Songs and What Does It Do to You If You Read It?', *Jian Dao* 1 (1994), pp. 1–27.

Cole, G., 'Women teaching Men the Bible: What's the Problem?', *Zadok Perspectives* 95 (December 2007).

Craddock, F. B., *Luke*, Int (Louisville: John Knox Press, 1990).

Cranfield, C. E. B., *The Epistle to the Romans,* vol. 2, ICC (Edinburgh: T & T Clark, 1979).

Davids, P. H., *The First Epistle of Peter*, NICNT (Grand Rapids: Eerdmans, 1990).

____, 'A Silent Witness in Marriage: 1 Peter 3:1–7', *DBE*, pp. 224–238.

Davidson, R. M., 'Theology of Sexuality in the Song of Songs: Return to Eden', *AUSS* 27 (1989), pp. 1–19.

Dawes, G. W., *The Body in Question: Metaphor and Meaning in the Interpretation of Eph. 5:21–33*, BibInt 30 (Leiden: Brill, 1998).

Delling, G., 'hypotassō', *TDNT*, vol. 8, pp. 39–46.

deSilva, D. A., *Honor, Patronage, Kinship and Purity: Unlocking New Testament Culture* (Downers Grove: IVP, 2000).

Dunn, J. D. G., *The Epistle to the Galatians*, BNTC (London: Hendrickson, 1993).

____, *Romans 9-16*, WBC (Dallas: Word, 1988).

Edwards, J. R., *The Gospel According to Mark*, PNTC (Grand Rapids: Eerdmans and Leicester: Apollos, 2002).

Ellis, E. E., *Pauline Theology: Ministry and Society* (Grand Rapids: Eerdmans and Exeter: Paternoster, 1989).

English, D., *The Message of Mark*, BST (Leicester: IVP, 1992).

Evans, M., *Woman in the Bible* (Exeter: Paternoster Press, 1983).

Eves, A., 'Judges', in C. C. Kroeger and M. J. Evans (eds.), *IVP Women's Bible Commentary* (Downers Grove: IVP, 2002).

Fee, G. D., *The First Epistle to the Corinthians*, NICNT (Grand Rapids: Eerdmans, 1987).

____, 'Male and Female in the New Creation: Galatians 3:26–29', *DBE*, pp. 172–185.

____, *Paul's Letter to the Philippians*, NICNT (Grand Rapids: Eerdmans, 1995).

____, 'Praying and Prophesying in the Assemblies', *DBE*, pp. 149–155.

____, *1 and 2 Timothy, Titus*, NIBC (Peabody: Hendrickson, 1984).

Fitzmeyer, J. A., 'Another look at *Kephalē* in 1 Corinthians 11:3', *NTS* 35.4 (1989), pp. 503–511.

Forster, F. and Forster, R., *Women and the Kingdom* (London: Push Publishing and Ichthus Christian Fellowship, 2010).

France, R. T., *The Gospel of Mark*, NIGTC (Grand Rapids: Eerdmans, 2002).

____, *The Gospel of Matthew*, NICNT (Grand Rapids: Eerdmans, 2007).

____, *Women in the Church's Ministry: A Test-Case for Biblical Hermeneutics*, The Didsbury Lectures (Carlisle: Paternoster, 1995).

Fretheim, T. E., 'The Book of Genesis', *NIB*, vol. 1 (Nashville: Abingdon, 1994).

Fontaine, C., 'Proverbs', in C. A. Newsom and S. Ringe (eds.), *The Women's Bible Commentary* (London: SPCK and Louisville: Westminster/John Knox Press, 1992).

Fung, R. Y. K., *The Epistle to the Galatians*, NICNT (Grand Rapids: Eerdmans, 1988).

Gafney, W. G., *Daughters of Miriam: Women Prophets in Ancient Israel* (Minneapolis: Fortress Press, 2008).

Gaiser, F. J., *Healing in the Bible: Theological Insights for Christian Ministry* (Grand Rapids: Baker, 2010), pp. 165–176.

Giles, K., *The Trinity and Subordinationism: The Doctrine of God and the Contemporary Gender Debate* (Downers Grove: IVP, 2002).

Gehring, R. W., *House Church and Mission: The Importance of Household Structures in Early Christianity* (Peabody: Henrickson, 2004).

Gledhill, T., *The Message of the Song of Songs*, BST (Leicester: IVP, 1994).

Goldingay, J., *Models for Interpretation of Scripture* (Grand Rapids: Eerdmans, 1995).

Gombis, T. G., 'A Radically New Humanity: The Function of the *Haustafel* in Ephesians', *JETS* 48 (2005), pp. 317–330.

Green, J., *The Gospel of Luke*, NICNT (Grand Rapids: Eerdmans, 1997).

Grenz, S. J., *Theology for the Community of God* (Carlisle: Paternoster, 1994).

Grenz, S. J. and Kjesbo, D. M., *Women in the Church: A Biblical Theology of Women in Ministry* (Downers Grove: IVP, 1995).

Groothius, R., 'Equal in Being, Unequal in Role', *DBE*, pp. 301–333.

Grudem, W., 'Does *Kephalē* mean "Source" or "Authority Over" in Greek Literature?', *TrinJ* 6 (1985), pp. 38–59.

____, *Evangelical Feminism and Biblical Truth: An Analysis of 118 Disputed Questions* (Leicester: IVP, 2005).

____, *The Gift of Prophecy* (Eastbourne: Kinsgway, 1998).

____, 'The Meaning of *Kephalē* ("Head"): A Response to Recent Studies', *RBMW*, pp. 425–468.

____, 'Wives Like Sarah, and Husbands Who Honour Them', *RBMW*, pp. 194–208.

Guelich, R. A., *Mark 1–8:26*, WBC (Dallas: Word, 1989).

Hamilton, V. P., *The Book of Genesis, Chapters 1–17*, NICOT (Grand Rapids: Eerdmans, 1990).

Hansen, G. W., *The Letter to the Philippians*, PNTC (Grand Rapids: Eerdmans and Nottingham: Apollos, 2009).

Hawthorne, G. F., *Philippians*, WBC (Waco: Word, 1983).

Hays, R., *The Moral Vision of the New Testament: A Contemporary Introduction to New Testament Ethics* (London and New York: T & T Clark, 1996).

Heine, S., *Women and Early Christianity* (SCM: London, 1987).

Henry, M., *Commentary on the Whole Bible*, 6 vols. (London: Marshall, Morgan and Scott, 1953).

Hess, R. S., 'Equality without Innocence. Genesis 1–3', *DBE*, pp. 79–95.

Hock, R. F., *The Social Context of Paul's Ministry: Tentmaking and Apostleship* (Philadelphia: Fortress Press, 1980).

Hooker, M., 'Authority on her Head: An examination of 1 Cor. 11:10', *NTS* 10 (1964), pp. 410–416.

Horrell, D. G., *The Social Ethos of the Corinthian Correspondence* (Edinburgh: T & T Clark, 1996).

Hubbard Jr, R. L., *The Book of Ruth*, NICOT (Grand Rapids: Eerdmans, 1988).

Hull, G. G., *Equal to Serve: Women and Men in the Church and Home* (London: Scripture Union, 1989).

Hurley, J. B., *Man and Woman in Biblical Perspective* (Leicester: IVP, 1981).

James, C. C., *The Gospel of Ruth: Loving God Enough to Break the Rules* (Grand Rapids: Zondervan, 2008).

Jewett, P. K., *Man as Male and Female* (Grand Rapids: Eerdmans, 1975).

Johnson, A. F. (ed.), *How I Changed my Mind about Women in Leadership* (Grand Rapids: Zondervan, 2010).

Jones, G. H., *1 and 2 Kings*, vol. 2, NCB (Grand Rapids: Eerdmans and London: Marshall, Morgan and Scott, 1984).

Judge, E. A., 'The Impact of Paul's Gospel on Ancient Society', in P. Bolt and M. Thompson (eds.), *The Gospel to the Nations: Perspectives on Paul's Ministry* (Downers Grove: IVP and Leicester: Apollos, 2000).

Keener, C. S., 'Learning in the Assemblies', *DBE*, pp. 161–171.

____, *Paul, Women and Wives* (Peabody: Hendrickson, 1992).

____, 'Women in Ministry: Another Complementarian Perspective', *Two Views*, pp. 203–248.

Keener, C. S., Belleville, L. L., Schreiner, T. R. and Blomberg, C. L, *Two Views on Women in Ministry*, Counterpoints (Grand Rapids: Zondervan, 2005).

Kidner, D., *Genesis*, TOTC (London: Tyndale House, 1967).

Knight III, G. W., 'Husbands and Wives as Analogues of Christ and the Church: Ephesians 5:21–33 and Colossians 3:18–19', *RBMW*, pp. 165–178.

____, *The New Testament Teaching on the Role Relationships of Men and Women* (Grand Rapids: Baker, 1977).

____, *The Pastoral Epistles*, NIGNT (Grand Rapids: Eerdmans, 1992).

____, 'Role distinctions in the Church: Galatians 3:28', *RBMW*, pp. 154–164.

Köstenberger, A., Schreiner, T. R. and Baldwin H. S. (eds.), *Women in the Church: A Fresh Analysis of 1 Timothy 2:9–15* (Grand Rapids: Baker Books, 1995).

Kroeger, R. and Kroeger, C. C., *I Suffer not a Woman: Rethinking 1 Timothy 2:11–15 in the Light of Ancient Evidence* (Grand Rapids: Baker, 1992).

LaCocque, A., *Romance She Wrote: A Hermeneutical Essay on the Song of Songs* (Harrisburg: Trinity Press, 1988).

Liefeld, W., 'Women, Submission and Ministry in 1 Corinthians', in A. Micklesen (ed.), *Women, Authority and the Bible* (Downers Grove: IVP, 1986), pp. 134–155,

Lincoln, A., *Ephesians*, WBC (Dallas: Word, 1990).

Longeneker, R. N., *Galatians*, WBC (Waco: Word, 1990).

Longman III, T., *Song of Songs*, NICOT (Grand Rapids: Eerdmans, 2011).

____, 'Woman Wisdom and Woman Folly', *DOTWPW*, pp. 912–916.

MacDonald, M. Y., 'Women Holy in Body and Spirit: The Social Setting of 1 Corinthians 7', *NTS* 36 (1990), pp. 161–180.

McKane, W., *Proverbs: A New Approach,* OTL (London: SCM Press, 1970).

McCann, J. C., *Judges*, Int (Louisville: John Knox Press, 2002).

McKnight, S., *Junia is Not Alone: Breaking our Silence about Women in the Bible and the Church Today* (Englewood: Patheos Press, 2011).

Malina, B. J., *The New Testament World: Insights from Cultural Anthropology* (Louisville: John Knox Press, 2001).

Marshall, I. H., 'The Gospel Does Not Change but our Perception of It May Need Revision', in A. F. Johnson (ed.), *How I Changed my Mind about Women in Leadership* (Grand Rapids: Zondervan, 2010), pp. 143–152.

____, *The Gospel of Luke*, NIGTC (Exeter: Paternoster, 1978).

____, 'Mutual Love and Submission in Marriage: Colossians 3:18-19 and Ephesians 5:21-33', *DBE*, pp. 106–204.

____, *The Pastoral Epistles*, ICC (Edinburgh: T & T Clark, 1999).

____, *I Peter*, IVP New Testament Commentary (Downers Grove and Leicester: IVP, 1991).

Meeks, W., *The First Urban Christians: The Social World of the Apostle Paul* (New Haven: Yale University Press, 2003).

Meyers, C., *Discovering Eve: Ancient Israelite Women in Context* (New York and Oxford: Oxford University Press, 1988).

Michaels, R. M., *1 Peter*, WBC (Waco: Word, 1988).

Micklesen, A. (ed.), *Women, Authority and the Bible* (Downers Grove: IVP, 1986).

Moo, D., *The Epistle to the Romans*, NICNT (Grand Rapids: Eerdmans, 1996).

____, 'What Does It Mean Not to Teach or Have Authority Over Men?', *RBMW*, pp. 179–193.

Morris, L. (with A. Cundall), *Judges, Ruth*, TOTC (London: Tyndale Press, 1968).

Mounce, W. D., *Pastoral Epistles*, WBC (Nashville: Thomas Nelson, 2000).

Murphy, R. L., *Proverbs*, WBC (Nashville: Thomas Nelson, 1998).

Murphy-O'Connor, J., 'Sex and Logic in 1 Cor. 11:2–16', *CBQ* 42 (1980), pp. 482–500.

Newsom, C. A. and Ringe, S. H. (eds.), *Women's Bible Commentary* (London: SPCK and Louisville: Westminister/John Knox, 1992).

Neufeld, D. and DeMaris, R. E. (eds.), *Understanding the Social World of the New Testament*, (London and New York: Routledge, 2010).

Nolland, J., *Luke 1–9:20*, WBC (Word: Dallas, 1985).

O'Brien, P. T., *The Letter to the Ephesians*, PNTC (Grand Rapids: Eerdmans and Nottingham: Apollos, 1999).

O'Day, G. R., 'John', in C. A. Newsom and S. H. Ringe (eds.), *Women's Bible Commentary* (London: SPCK and Louisville: Westminister/John Knox, 1992).

Olson, D. T., 'The Book of Judges', *NIB*, vol. 2 (Nashville: Abingdon, 1998).

Ortlund, R. C., 'Male-Female Equality and Male Headship. Genesis 1–3', *RBMW*, pp. 95–112.

Osiek, C., MacDonald, M. Y. and Tulloch, J. H., *A Woman's Place: House Churches in Earliest Christianity* (Minneapolis: Fortress Press, 2006).

Otwell, J. H., *And Sarah Laughed: The Status of Woman in the Old Testament* (Philadelphia, Westminster Press, 1977).

Packer, J. I., *The Proceedings of the Conference on Biblical Interpretation* (Nashville: Broadman, 1988).

Patterson, D., 'The High Calling of Wife and Mother in Biblical Perspective', *RBMW*, pp. 364–377.

Pawson, D., *Leadership is Male* (Crowborough: Highland Books, 1988).

Payne, P. B., *Man and Woman: One in Christ* (Grand Rapids: Zondervan, 2009).

Perdue, L. G., Blenkinsopp, J., Collins, J. J. and Meyers, C., *Families in Ancient Israel* (Louisville: Westminster Press, 1997).

Perriman, A., *Speaking of Women: Interpreting Paul* (Leicester: Apollos, 1998).

Peterson, D. G., *The Acts of the Apostles*, PNTC (Grand Rapids: Eerdmans and Nottingham: Apollos, 2009).

Peterson, E. H., *Five Smooth Stones for Pastoral Work* (Grand Rapids: Eerdmans, 1980).

Pierce, R. W. and Groothuis, R. M. (eds.), *Discovering Biblical Equality: Complementarity Without Hierarchy* (Downers Grove: IVP and Leicester: Apollos, 2005).

Piper, J. and Grudem, W. (eds.), *Recovering Biblical Manhood and Womanhood* (Wheaton: Crossway, 2006).

Phipps, W. E., 'The Plight of the Song of Songs', *JAAR* 42 (1974), pp. 82–100.

von Rad, G., *Genesis: A Commentary*, OTL (Philadelphia, Westminster, 1972).

Ryan, R., 'The women from Galilee and discipleship in Luke', *BTB* XV (1985), pp. 56–59.

Scholer, D. M., 'Women', *DJG*, pp. 880–881.

Schneider, T. J., *Judges*, Berit Olam: Studies in Hebrew Narrative and Poetry (Collegeville: Liturgical Press, 2000).

_____, *Mothers of Promise: Women in the Book of Genesis* (Grand Rapids: Baker, 2008).

Schreiner, T. R., 'Head Coverings, Prophecies and the Trinity', *RBMW*, pp. 124–139.

_____, 'An interpretation of 1 Timothy 2:9–15: A Dialogue with Scholarship', in *Fresh Analysis*, pp. 105–154.

_____, 'The Valuable Ministries of Women in the Context of Male Leadership', *RBMW*, pp. 209–224.

_____, 'Women in Ministry: Another Complementarian View', *Two Views*, pp. 263–323.

Schüssler Fiorenza, E., *In Memory of Her: A Feminist Theological reconstruction of Christian Origins* (10th anniversary edn, New York: Crossroad, 1994).

Snodgrass, K. R., 'Galatians 3:28: Conundrum or solution?', in A. Micklesen (ed.), *Women, Authority and the Bible* (Downers Grove: IVP, 1986), pp. 161–181.

Spurgeon, C. H., *Till He Come: A Collection of Communion Addresses* (Fearn: Christian Focus Publications, 2011).

Stagg, E. and Stagg, F., *Woman in the World of Jesus* (Philadelphia: Westminster Press 1978).

Stark, R., *The Rise of Christianity: A Sociologist Reconsiders History* (Princeton: Princeton University Press, 1996).

Stewart, E. C., 'Social Stratification and Patronage in Ancient Mediterranean Society', in D. Neufeld and R. E. DaMaris (eds.), *Understanding the Social World of the New Testament,* (London and New York: Routledge, 2010), pp. 156–166.

Storkey, E., *Created or Constructed? The Great Gender Debate* (Carlisle: Paternoster, 2000).

Thisleton, A. C., *The First Epistle to the Corinthians*, NIGTC (Grand Rapids: Eerdmans and Carlisle: Paternoster, 2000).

Thurston, B. B., *The Widows: A Women's Ministry in the Early Church* (Minneapolis: Fortress Press, 1989).

Tidball, Dianne, *Esther: A True First Lady. A Post-Feminist Icon in a Secular World* (Fearn: Christian Focus Publications, 2001).

Tidball, Derek, *Ministry by the Book: New Testament Patterns for Pastoral Leadership* (Nottingham: Apollos, 2008).

Tolbert, M. A., 'Mark', in C. A. Newsom and S. H. Ringe (eds.), *Women's Bible Commentary* (London: SPCK and Louisville: Westminister/John Knox, 1992).

Towner, P. H., 'Household Codes', *DLNTD*, pp. 513–520.

____, *The Letters to Timothy and Titus*, NICNT (Grand Rapids: Eerdmans, 2006).

Trepedino, A. M. and Brandao, M. L. R., 'Women and the Theology of Liberation', in I. Ellacuria and J. Sobrino (eds.), *Mysterioum Liberationis: Fundamental Concepts of Liberation Theology* (Maryknoll: Orbis Books, 1993).

Trible, P., 'Depatriarchalizing in Biblical Interpretation', *JAAR* 41 (1973), pp. 30–48.

____, *God and the Rhetoric of Sexuality* (London: SCM, 1992).

____, *Texts of Terror: Literary-Feminist Readings of Biblical-Narratives* (London: SCM, 1992).

Turner, M., *The Holy Spirit and Spiritual Gifts: Then and Now* (Carlisle: Paternoster, 1996).

Twelftree, G. H., 'Spiritual powers', *NDBT*, pp. 796–797.

Van Leeuwen, R., 'Proverbs', *NIB*, vol. 5 (Nashville: Abingdon Press, 1997).

Waltke, B. K., *Proverbs 15-31*, NICOT (Grand Rapids: Eerdmans, 2005).

Webb, B. G., *The Book of Judges: An Integrated Reading*, JSOT Sup (Sheffield: JSOT Press, 1987).

Webb, W. J., 'A Redemptive-Movement Hermeneutic: The Slavery Analogy', *DBE*, pp. 382–400.

____, *Slaves, Women and Homosexuals: Exploring the Hermeneutics of Cultural Analysis* (Downers Grove: IVP, 2001).

Weems, R. J., 'The Song of Songs', *NIB*, vol. 5 (Nashville: Abingdon Press, 1997).

Wenham, G., *Genesis 1-15*, WBC (Waco: Word, 1987).

____, *Genesis 16-50*, WBC (Dallas: Word, 1994).

Wilcock, M., *The Message of the Judges*, BST (Leicester: IVP, 1992).

Winter, B. W., *After Paul left Corinth: The Influence of Secular Ethics and Social Change* (Grand Rapids: Eerdmans, 2001).

____, *Roman Wives, Roman Widows: The Appearance of New Women and the Pauline Communities* (Grand Rapids: Eerdmans, 2003).

Witherington III, B., *The Acts of the Apostles: A Socio-Rhetorical Commentary* (Grand Rapids: Eerdmans and Carlisle: Paternoster, 1998).

____, *Conflict and Community in Corinth: A Socio-Rhetorical Commentary on 1 and 2 Corinthians* (Grand Rapid: Eerdmans, 1995).

____, *Letters and Homilies for Hellenized Christians: A Socio-Rhetorical Commentary on 1–2 Peter, vol. 2* (Downers Grove, IVP and Nottingham: Apollos, 2007).

____, 'Rite and Rights for Women – Galatians 3:28', *NTS* 27.5 (1981), pp. 593–604.

____, *Women and the Genesis of Christianity* (Cambridge: CUP, 1990).

____, *Women in the Ministry of Jesus*, SNTSMS 51 (Cambridge: Cambridge University Press, 1984).

Wright, N. T., *Simply Jesus* (London, SPCK, 2011).

Introduction

When playing Monopoly the unfortunate player may be instructed
to 'Go to Jail. Do not pass Go. Do not collect £200'. Regrettably we
fear that many who read this volume will fall into the equivalent trap
and go straight to the chapter on women in leadership, bypassing all
the other chapters en route. We beg you not to do so. One of the
most interesting reflections on writing this book is how many people
have assumed in conversation that it was about women in leadership
rather than women in Scripture. While the issue of women in leadership cannot be ignored, Scripture has much more to say about
women than whether they can be ordained or not. Moreover, we
would contend that it is by isolating this issue from the rest we are
liable to misunderstand what Paul was teaching.

Style of the book

More than most BST volumes, the nature of the chapters in this
volume vary not only because of the different genres of Scripture
involved but because doing justice to the topic demands we handle
them in different ways. Consequently, some chapters engage in
in-depth exegesis of a few verses whereas others cover a whole book,
or take, as in the case of the Gospel chapters, a thematic approach.

We have sought to let each chapter stand alone, which has necessarily led to some repetition and overlap, although we have tried to
keep this to a minimum and to make use of cross-referencing where
helpful.

We were both responsible for writing separate chapters initially
but then revising them after discussion and editing them into a
common style. Since the book comes from us both we see no reason
to identify who wrote what. Although we come from different backgrounds and have come to the positions expressed in this book via
different routes, we now take a common stance on the issues, which
gives an added reason for not identifying the writer of individual

chapters. We have chosen to use 'I' and 'my' rather than 'we' and 'our' when relevant, such as in using a personal illustration, since we believe this permits greater fluency in writing.

Content of the book

The book is divided into four sections. First we lay some crucial foundations about women in creation and in the new creation. Then we survey the rich Old Testament material concerning women, which was certainly a journey of some surprising discoveries for us as we sought to go where the evidence took us. The third section examines the Gospels and, given their nature as they record the life, works and teaching of Jesus, is inevitably more thematic than other chapters. The final section deals with both the practice and the teaching of the early church and fully examines some of the more controversial (and misunderstood?) writings of Paul. Apart from the Afterword, we end in a somewhat curious place, discussing widows. We do so because this is Scripture's own final major discussion on the topic. But it has the great advantage of reminding us that, after all the momentous events, radical teaching and debatable issues have been considered, most women (like most men) live very ordinary lives, dealing with circumstances that are not of their choosing, and God proves to be a compassionate God in the humdrum days and ordinary experiences as well as in the heady days of spiritual breakthrough.

Issues of interpretation

When we approach Scripture with integrity we find it speaks on the issue of women in ways which are diverse, complex and particular. Diversity demands we look to the range of the Bible's teaching and do not merely select those passages which suit our particular viewpoint. Complexity demands we study the text carefully, attempting to hear what it says, rather than reading into it what we think or have predetermined it says. Particularity means we must locate the text in its original cultural setting and the issues that were around then, and take due account of the purpose for which it was originally written, before we consider how it applies to our very different cultural context and questions today.

Anyone who wishes to write or teach in this area faces some other immense challenges. In addition to the particular exegetical issues thrown up by the individual passages, which are many, there are three other principal challenges to be faced. First, we must ask whether the passages we are considering are prescriptive (setting out how we ought to behave) or merely descriptive (setting out how people once behaved, but without necessarily commending it as a pattern for others). Secondly, we must ask the related question as to whether the individual passages are intending to give direction for all times and cultures or are limited, even if prescriptive, to a particular time and culture. Many of the disagreements between people who are all committed to the authority of Scripture revolve around these questions. Thirdly, we must ask which texts we prioritize, since the Bible speaks with different voices. Do we make the apparently restrictive texts our foundation and interpret the apparently liberating texts to fit them, or vice versa?

Many look to the Bible to find a ready-made agenda on the role of women in the contemporary church, family and world. Traditionalists look to it to justify the enduring principle of the headship of men and the submission of women. Progressives look to it to establish that anything less than the total non-discrimination agenda of contemporary Western cultures is unacceptable in God's sight. But, as always, we should approach the Bible with care. The Bible was not written to serve our very particular and passing concerns and we should learn to serve its agenda rather than making it serve ours. We need to approach it with integrity, asking what it is teaching in its original context, and avoid forcing it (man-handling it?) to fit our questions and systems.

In his discussion on this issue in *Gender and the New Testament*, which manages to be judicious and provocative at the same time, Richard Briggs says, 'It has become a commonplace that if hermeneutics is to teach us anything it must teach us humility – humility before the text of scripture, and especially before our dogmatic claims . . . '.[1] An honest, rather than prejudicial, examination of women in the Bible will certainly engender humility but not, we believe, mean we end up devoid of clarity or confidence, unable to address one of the most pressing issues of our day.

Complementarians and egalitarians

Humility demands that we eschew calling one another names. Sadly a good deal of name-calling goes on in the church and some feel that labelling an opponent's view as 'feminist' or 'reactionary' is sufficient not to consider thoughtfully what they are saying. This is part of a wider cultural trend which finds moral discussion difficult and thinks all questions are resolved by labelling those with whom we disagree. Such a trend is deeply worrying for society's

---

[1] *Gender and the New Testament* (Cambridge: Grove Books, 2001), p. 9.

well-being but it is deeply unworthy of the followers of Jesus Christ whose lives are to be characterized by love, patience and mutual submission.

On the subject of women there are a range of views which cover a diverse spectrum. There are, however, two words that are often used, as we will do in this book, to identify two broad perspectives in approaching the question of women in the Bible: complement-arians and egalitarians.

Complementarians are those who argue that while men and women are of equal worth and enjoy equal status before God they were created to fulfil different roles and functions, in other words, to complement each other. Complementarians, like egalitarians, come in all shades and sizes but their perspective leads them to argue that God made the man to be head of the women in the family and the church (some would also say in society) and this leads them to have different functions. The differences, they argue, are inherent in creation. Men alone, then, should be leader-teachers in the church and women learners and active in other ways; and, for some, men should be breadwinners and women homemakers in the family. Neither Christ, nor the early church, contradicted this 'creation principle'. In previous times this position was often called heirarchal-ism. But the broadening views of its adherents combined with the negative overtones of that term has led to its replacement by the term complementarianism.

With complementarians, egalitarians affirm that while there are obvious distinctions between men and women, not least biologically, they enjoy full equality before God in Christ. However, this leads egalitarians to argue not only for an equality of spiritual status but also for an equality of function, and they deny, therefore, that women should be confined to a domestic role or denied positions of leader-ship, teaching or authority in the church. Apart from the incontrovertible sexual differences, consigning men and women to different roles in church or society on gender differences is, they argue, the result of the fall and the resulting curse, and mostly socially constructed, rather than inherent in creation. They also argue that Christ inaugurated a new age and a new community in which the results of the fall are challenged and overcome. The full reversal may await the coming again of Jesus Christ, but the church is called to tread that road now.

In this book we essentially adopt an egalitarian perspective but not, we hope, in any naive way. It may be helpful to know that this was not the original starting point of one of the authors, who has come over many years to change position through the reading of Scripture and observation of what God is doing in his church. At all times, readers are encouraged to read the texts for themselves and pay diligent attention to what they say.

Bibliography and footnotes

The literature on women in Scripture is vast and multi-layered. Much of it is written from a strong ideological position. It has been impossible to read it all, but we have sought to be abreast of the main arguments and to have read carefully the main works that represent those various positions. If we had read it all, the bibliography alone could have been as long as the book itself. What we have included is selected from the full list of works found in the footnotes.

One book to which we have not referred is especially worth commending. *The Gender Agenda*, written by Lis Goddard and Clare Hendry,[2] is an excellent read and model for how disputes should be handled. It consists of an exchange of emails between two women, both of whom are in ministry, but who nonetheless take different stances on the issue of women and authority in the church. Written at a more popular level than the current book, it is in no way superficial in its discussion of the biblical and theological issues. And it has the added bonus of giving an insight as to how two women might engage with the topic.

Footnotes are important for more than simply identifying the source of a quotation. They also point to where a deeper discussion of the arguments we touch on are found and reveal the reasons why we have adopted certain interpretations. At crucial moments we also use them to point to representative literature on the various sides of the argument as a way of managing what would have become an unwieldy book otherwise. Occasionally we have used them as well to provide fuller information that would interrupt the flow of the main text.

[2] Nottingham: IVP, 2010.

Part One
Foundations

Genesis 1:26–30; 2:18–25
1. Women as the image of God

'"Begin at the beginning", the King said gravely, "and go on till you come to the end: then stop."'[1] The King's advice to the White Rabbit in *Alice's Adventures in Wonderland* is sound advice in undertaking an exploration of any theological theme, especially that of the role of women in the Bible. While we may despair of ever reaching the end, since the discussion of woman's role seems intractable among Christians, the chance of our doing so is greatly reduced unless we start in the right place. Many discussions of the role of women plunge into one scripture or another without any awareness of the unfolding biblical context in which they may be set. Or they take up the story halfway through and show ignorance of what has gone before or of other scriptures that are less convenient to the argument. Getting to one's destination is greatly helped by having the right starting point.

When discussing God's intention for women, the beginning comes very early in the Bible. The opening three chapters set the direction which is then followed through in the numerous twists and turns of the rest of Scripture. They teach us at least the essential truths about women in relation to God (1:26–27; 2:21–22), in relation to men (2:18–24) and in relation to our fallen humanity (3:1–24). This chapter deals with the first two of these foundation truths.

1. Created in God's image (1:26–30)

Genesis 1 provides the headlines that the following chapter is going to explore more fully. It presents God creating the world in a progressive and orderly fashion until he reaches the pinnacle of his work

---

[1] L. Carroll, *Alice's Adventure in Wonderland* (London: Penguin Classic, 2009), p. 105.

and brings humanity into being. In reporting this, the headline reads like this:

> Then God said, 'Let us make mankind in our image, in our likeness, so that they may rule over the fish in the sea and the birds in the sky, over the livestock and all the wild animals, and over all the creatures that move along the ground.'

> So God created mankind in his own image,
> in the image of God he created them;
> male and female he created them.

The essential truths flagged up in a preliminary way regarding men and women concern their identity (made in God's image), their unity (*mankind*), and their plurality (*male and female*). Both men and women are made in the *image of God*, with a job to do on earth, and the full meaning of humanity is to be found neither in the one nor the other but in both in relationship.

a. Identity: 'Let us make mankind in our image'

While creation in its totality is the handiwork of God, only humanity bears his *image* and *likeness*. God's majesty is seen 'in all the earth'[2] and yet human beings have a special place in that creation and God is mindful of them in a way that distinguishes them from all else.[3] So much can be (and has been) read into these words that the wonder of them is sometimes lost. Human beings bear the *image of God* as no other creature does.

Whatever else this means, it conveys the sense that humans are born to relate to God and, as his image, to reflect him in his world. *Image* means that we replicate and mirror God in his world, although we clearly do not do so in all respects since we are not creators *ex nihilo*, nor are we like him physically. It is generally thought that the word *likeness* was added to clarify this and remove any misunderstanding that humans are exact copies of the deity and that having done so in verses 26–27 the word is not used again.[4]

The meaning of 'made in God's image', besides placing humanity in a class all of its own, is hinted at in the surrounding verses. The

[2] Ps. 8:1.

[3] Ps. 8:4.

[4] On this and the numerous other issues which these verses throw up, see V. P. Hamilton, *The Book of Genesis, Chapters 1-17*, NICOT (Grand Rapids: Eerdmans, 1990), pp. 131–137 and G. Wenham, *Genesis 1-15*, WBC (Waco: Word, 1987), pp. 29–33.

claim is embedded in soil that is rich in the use of plural language. *Then God said, 'Let us . . . '* (26) and *in the image of God he created them, male and female he created them* (27). The *us* to whom God refers might mean he is talking with the angels, or a heavenly council, but there is good reason to think it is a reference to plurality in the Godhead, especially if 1:2 is saying 'the Spirit of God was hovering over the waters' and not merely 'the wind of God'.[5] The *image of God* then becomes an image about unity among diversity, harmony among difference in the Trinity.

The next phrase in verse 27 connects the image of this trinitarian God to the creation of *male and female*, as if this is intended to explain what the image means. Both are made in the one image. God's image is seen in *them*, not in him or her. Inherent in the image, then, is the idea that we are made for relationships, that we are only truly human when we are beings-in-fellowship[6] and will only become complete persons through others. 'Humanity', writes Paul Jewett, 'is in its deepest root, a shared humanity . . . Humanity that is not shared humanity is *in*humanity' because this is what the creator has implanted of himself within us.[7]

Another hint in the surrounding verses about what it means to be made in God's image is that the male and female are immediately commanded to *Be fruitful and increase in number; fill the earth and subdue it* and to *rule over* the creation (28). God instructs Adam and Eve to act as his representatives in creation, doing what he himself has done both in populating the earth and bringing order to it. Ruling over creation gives humanity no permission to exploit it, treat it abusively or become distant authoritarian overlords over it, since this is not how God rules over his creation. The objective of ruling is to bring peace, provide welfare and encourage prosperity, just as God does. Rule 'reflects royal language. But this rule is to be compassionate not exploitative'.[8] Given the context, some have argued that being in the image of God is essentially about our responsibility to the twin assignments of procreation and exercising dominion.

What is important for our purposes is that these commands are given to the man and the woman equally. While in filling out the details of the headline verses of 16–17 in 2:4–20, it appears that man rules over the creatures before the woman is created, 1:28 makes clear that these responsibilities were entrusted to *them*, not exclusively to him.

[5] See note above. The word *rûach* in 1:2 may be translated either Spirit or wind.

[6] I owe the term to S. J. Grenz, *Theology for the Community of God* (Carlisle: Paternoster, 1994), p. 233, who argues that the image of God is 'in the final analysis . . . a community concept'.

[7] P. K. Jewett, *Man as Male and Female* (Grand Rapids: Eerdmans, 1975), p. 36.

[8] Hamilton, *Genesis 1-17*, p. 138.

b. Unity: mankind

Some confusion exists because the word '*ādām* is used in two senses, as a generic word for humanity or mankind and also as the personal name of the first man, Adam. In fact, Adam is not used unambiguously as a personal name until Genesis 4:25.[9] We need to distinguish carefully between these two uses since when Adam is being used in its generic sense it is not used to indicate that humanity is primarily male.

The Hebrew language forces one to choose a masculine or feminine case since no neuter exists. Even if there were a suitable neuter it might import other disadvantages into the discussion by, say, detracting from the personal nature of human beings. The verse undermines the view that humans were first created as bisexual beings and only later were the sexes differentiated. Rather, verse 27 asserts that 'in the beginning' 'God created in his image a male '*ādām* and a female '*ādām*'.[10] Equally without foundation is the view that 'God's naming of the race "man" whispers male headship . . . '[11]. Neither the context nor the linguistic understanding of the use of '*ādām* gives any support to such a view.[12]

Man ('*ādām*), as the title for humankind as a whole, points to the way in which the human race, both male and female, are 'a single entity'[13] and are united equally as God's creatures.

c. Plurality: male and female

While the accent in this chapter may fall on the unity of men and women as made equally in God's image, what they have in common should not swallow up the equally important point that God made men and women to be different. The plurality of the Godhead is seen in the creation of male and female. Sexuality is a gift from the Creator. It is a biological necessity if children are to be born, but it is much more than this. It is a rich offering of God through which bonding takes place and human communities are created.[14] The existence of the two genders is the means by which through relationship each

[9] R. S. Hess, 'Equality without Innocence. Genesis 1-3', *DBE*, p. 80.

[10] Hamilton, *Genesis 1-17*, p. 138.

[11] R. C. Ortlund, 'Male-Female Equality and Male Headship. Genesis 1-3', *RBMW*, p. 98.

[12] The weakness of the argument is perhaps revealed in the choice of the word 'whisper' and not the choice of a stronger word.

[13] W. Brueggemann, *Genesis*, Int (Atlanta: John Knox Press, 1982), p. 34.

[14] On the key differences through which men and women complement each other, about which Elaine Storkey says 'the most reliable research . . . has yielded a surprising level of agreement', see *Created or Constructed? The Great Gender Debate* (Carlisle: Paternoster, 2000), pp. 64–66.

can become a more complete person. Physical differences are one aspect of the diversity of personhood which God has given, not in order that men and women can rival each other, still less denigrate each other, but through which each might become, through love and mutual service, through intimacy and respectful care, and even through their dependence on one another, fuller, deeper people, more alive to God and his world. No individual, let alone any one gender, is made to be self-sufficient but to belong in relationship.

2. Created as man's helper (2:18–20)

When Genesis returns to the creation of human beings, in 2:18–24, it does so with 'one basic thrust: to fill out the theme of man's creation as male and female. What was simply stated in the first creation account (Gen. 1:27) is now enlarged upon'.[15] It does so by way of explaining God's statement, *'It is not good for the man to be alone. I will make a helper suitable for him'* (18).

a. The need for a helper

The loneliness of Adam's existence on planet Earth would have been bad enough if it meant that at the end of the day he had no one to go home and share his day's work with, or no one to stimulate him with entertaining or intellectual conversation. But, in the context, Adam's loneliness is not about his emotional or psychological discomfort but of a more serious kind.

As the crown of God's creation, Adam had been entrusted with the responsibility of filling the earth and subduing it.[16] His twofold responsibility involved populating the planet with children and exercising stewardship over the sub-human creation. Both of these responsibilities served to emphasize Adam's loneliness. How could he fill the earth with his own kind, since as a male without a female companion procreation was impossible? As David Clines has said, tongue-in-cheek, 'Camels are all very well, and they can be a great help. But when it comes to the purpose God has in mind, camels are no help at all'.[17] As with the rest of the animal creation, procreation demands male and female.[18]

[15] Jewett, *Man as . . .* , p. 38.

[16] This does not prejudice the earlier statement of Gen. 1:28, where these responsibilities were given to the male and female who were created in God's image. It is rather to focus in more on the detail than that general introduction permitted.

[17] D. Clines, *What Does Eve Do to Help?* JSOT Sup. 94 (Sheffield: Sheffield Academic Press, 1990), p. 35.

[18] The point comes to the fore in Gen. 7:1–5.

His second responsibility only served to emphasis his isolation further. It was in fulfilling his responsibility to rule over the earth, that the difference between Adam, as a human being, and all other creatures became apparent. They shared much in common. Like the animals, Adam was created by God and formed *out of the ground.* Their material substance may have had similarities but their essential nature and callings were altogether different. Adam was in a unique relationship with God and only Adam is made in God's image and commissioned to administer God's rule on earth. As a sign of this authority over them, he is charged with naming them, not them him, and it has long been recognized that name-giving is 'an exercise of sovereignty, of command'.[19] The difference in nature, responsibility and in the order of creation meant that there was no equality between Adam and the animal creation. Perhaps they were helpers, as Eve was to be, but they could never be the companion and partner that she was. However much enjoyment they may have found in each other's company (as many people find enjoyment in their pets!) it would have been a delusion to think they could converse and act as equals. There would always be a distance between them.

For these reasons, God determined to create a *suitable helper* for Adam, one who would correspond to him on the same level and by nature be able to overcome the limitations the rest of the creation suffered.

b. The nature of the help

Any word association game would soon reveal that we tend to think of a helper as an assistant, junior or subordinate, giving support to someone who is superior. And that understanding has dogged our interpretation of Eve's role as Adam's helper. Taking our cue from this we soon muse on Adam coming home at the end of the day, expecting Eve to have his dinner on the table and slippers at the ready, as if she were some Edwardian housewife.

We must, however, rid ourselves of the idea that being a helper means being subordinate. The helper assists others in the achievement of their task by lending strength to them in their weakness as, for example, when the word is used to describe one nation assisting another in warfare.[20] On occasions it is certainly a superior power that comes to the assistance of a weaker one. But the most frequent use of the word *helper* in the Old Testament is in reference to God. Speaking from his personal experience, David says of God, 'you have

[19] G. von Rad, *Genesis: A Commentary*, OTL (Philadelphia, Westminster, 1972), p. 83. See, for example, Isa. 40:26.
[20] Josh. 10:33; 2 Sam. 8:5; 1 Kgs 20:16; 1 Chr. 12:21.

been my helper', and Israel as a whole confesses, 'The LORD is with me; he is my helper'.[21] Fifteen out of nineteen uses of the word *helper* apply to God in the Old Testament, with another three applying to men.[22] In the New Testament, Christ promises the Holy Spirit as a 'help' to the disciples.[23] It may be too much to claim, as some do, that the word necessarily implies the *helper* is the superior one, but certainly no case can be made that the word has any overtone of subordination or inferiority. To call Eve Adam's *helper* carries no overtones of her being the weaker partner in the relationship. Indeed, it implies she is every bit his equal in the role.

Her equality is further underlined by the use of the adjective *suitable* (18, 20), which describes the kind of *helper* God is going to create. The English translation suggests an appropriate fit, but the Hebrew involves more than this. '"Corresponding to him"', writes Craig Blomberg, 'is probably as good an idiomatic rendering as any'.[24] In a very real sense, Eve is going to be the counterpart, complement, companion and partner to Adam.

We are still left with the question of how Eve helps Adam. Many resist restricting her assistance to a particular role, in case it boxes Eve into some limited and therefore probably inferior role.[25] But, as David Clines somewhat amusingly points out, we are not told of Eve assisting Adam with the gardening or looking after the animals, mainly because we are not told of Adam doing that either. 'There is nothing,' he writes, 'that Eve actually *does* inside the garden except have a conversation with the snake and eat the forbidden fruit. It does not take a great deal of acumen to recognize that having theological conversations with snakes is not a great help . . . '[26] The context focuses on Eve assisting Adam to do what he cannot do on his own, namely to fulfil the call to 'be fruitful and increase in number' (1:28). The subsequent verses speak of their being *united* and becoming *one flesh*, and then refer to their being *both naked,* all of which draw attention to this physical aspect of their relationship.

There is a long history of Eve's help being understood in this way, even if it has not always been helpfully expressed. Augustine condescendingly wrote that he could not think why women were made unless for the purposes of procreation.[27] But, condescension aside, this seems to be the primary understanding of the help Eve was to

[21] Pss. 27:9; 118:7.
[22] M. Evans, *Women in the Bible* (Exeter: Paternoster, 1983), p. 16.
[23] John 14:16.
[24] C. Blomberg, *Two Views*, p. 130.
[25] See, for example, Evans, *Women*, p. 17.
[26] Clines, *What Does Eve Do?*, p. 34.
[27] Augustine, *On Genesis*, 9.5.9.

give Adam in the initial context of Genesis. The duality of male and female is important if the creation mandate for human beings is to be fulfilled. To pretend there is no distinction is to frustrate God's purposes and 'to neutralize the sexes is to dehumanise Man'.[28] Yet, even if it is the primary intention of this passage, there is no reason to restrict what it means to women being helpers only in childbirth, and the subsequent story of Scripture reveals the many other ways in which women partner men in fulfilling the purposes of God.

3. Created from Adam's side (2:21–23)

The creation of women from Adam's *rib* has often given rise to humorous jests that result in the meaning of the account of Eve's creation being thoroughly misunderstood. The description has been understood as saying that women are nothing more than a man's dispensable spare part, that women were created as an afterthought, and that they owe their existence to men. But nothing could be further from the writer's intention.

God is the active creator of both men and women. God performs the operation as anaesthetist and surgeon on a passive Adam.[29] Adam is emphatically not the creator of Eve and Eve's existence is not dependent on Adam's will or design but on God's, just as Adam's own creation was. Phyllis Trible incisively writes: 'Man has no part in making woman ... he is neither participant, nor spectator, nor consultant at her birth. Like man, woman owes her life solely to God.'[30] Neither sex has the priority in that regard, although it might be said that men were made from mere dust while women were crafted from the more valuable material of a living human being. 'The word *earth* never appears' in relation to the formation of Eve, making her unique in creation.[31] 'The man,' writes Matthew Henry, 'was dust refined, but the woman was dust double-refined, one remove further from the earth'.[32] The value of her creation is stressed further in verse 22 when we read *the LORD God made a woman from the rib he had taken out of the man. Made* is a slight translation and would be better translated by the weightier word *built,* drawing attention to the careful and robust crafting God undertook in bringing the woman into being.

[28] Jewett, *Man as . . .* , p. 28.
[29] P. Trible, *God and the Rhetoric of Sexuality* (London: SCM, 1992), pp. 95–96.
[30] P. Trible, 'Depatriarchalizing in Biblical Interpretation', *JAAR* 41 (1973), p. 37.
[31] Trible, *God and*, pp. 96, 102.
[32] M. Henry, *Commentary on the Whole Bible*, vol. 1 (London: Marshall, Morgan & Scott, 1953), p. 19.

The creation of woman from a man's side – 'side' is closer to the Hebrew than *rib*[33] – is a vividly poetic way of expressing the closeness of identity that men and women share in spite of the differences which each will bring to their common partnership. It is not intended to stress the superiority of a man to a woman as if she is some secondary creation – a mere spare rib – but rather their essential relatedness. Matthew Henry wrote somewhat sentimentally about this in his eighteenth-century Bible commentary and yet expressed what even some modern feminists still advocate as the essential meaning of this passage: 'The woman was *made of a rib out of the side of Adam;* not made out of his head to rule over him; nor out of his feet to be trampled upon; but out of his side to be equal with him, under his arm to be protected, and near his heart to be beloved.'[34]

Creation from Adam's side testifies to the solidarity, mutuality, equality and identity between the man and woman, rather than difference or any sense of authority and hierarchy. In the creation of Eve a brilliantly enriching as well as a biological necessary differentiation takes place. 'Gendered life is introduced, [but] the language describing it establishes the connection between female and male.'[35] And that is how Adam reacts when he wakes up from his sleep and first sets eyes on Eve. He does not see her as a rival but a partner. 'In ecstasy man bursts into poetry on meeting his perfect helpmeet.'[36] *'This is bone of my bones, and flesh of my flesh'* (23). In other words, this person I see before me is someone other than me, somewhat different from me, and yet recognizably the same as me. 'It is not the anatomical difference but the essential relatedness between the man and the woman that is emphasized.'[37] The very name 'woman' (*'iššâ*) expresses this and is chosen because of its closeness to 'man' (*'îš*).

Should we detect any significance in the order of creation, of man being made first and then woman? Many have thought Paul does so in 1 Timothy 2:13.[38] Eve is created after man and, it is sometimes assumed, is therefore somehow subordinate to him. But several factors weigh against that view. First, man is created after the animals not because he is inferior to them but for exactly the opposite reason. He is the pinnacle of creation. On this premise since women were

[33] Hess, 'Equality', p. 86; Hamilton, *Genesis 1-17*, p. 178.

[34] Henry, *Commentary*, p. 20. Hess comments that rib 'refers to the side of the man, a part of the body that is neither above or below him', *DBE*, p. 86.

[35] C. Meyers, *Discovering Eve: Ancient Israelite Women in Context* (New York and Oxford: Oxford University Press, 1988), p. 84.

[36] Wenham, *Genesis 1-15*, p. 70.

[37] Jewett, *Man as . . .* , p. 124.

[38] See pp. 253–254.

created subsequently they may arguably be seen as the crown of men. Secondly, while the woman was created out of the man on this occasion, the whole of subsequent human experience reverses that sequence and men are born out of women. This reversal only serves to stress the mutual dependence there is between men and women and undermines any idea that gender dependence flows exclusively in one direction. Paul is not embarrassed to say that 'God sent his Son, born of a woman . . . '.[39] 'Thus,' as Paul Jewett puts it, 'the score is evened up'.[40] Thirdly, Genesis never connects the fact that Adam was created before Eve with Adam having authority over Eve. Man is given authority over the garden but not over the woman. Richard Hess rightly concludes that, 'Genesis 2 nowhere suggests a hier-archical relationship between the man and the woman, and certainly not because of the "order of creation".'[41] The most that those who seek to find a justification for headship in these chapters can do is to imagine they hear a 'whisper' of it here.[42]

If the sequence of creation does not suggest that man has authority over the woman, does the fact that he names her, do so? After all, in talking of Adam naming the animals – a responsibility of ruling he shared with Eve according to 1:28, when God spoke not to him but to them – we acknowledged that this did indicate he was exercising authority over them. The attempts to argue that the vocabulary used when he 'calls' his new helper a woman is different from that used earlier when he 'names' the animals, and so distinguishes this act from the more official naming of the animals, are not wholly per-suasive.[43] Nonetheless, Adam must call her something and instinctively gives her not a personal name but initially a label that speaks of her gender. It is an act discerning of her nature rather than an exercise of authority.[44] It is only later that she is referred to by her personal name, Eve, when Adam 'names' her this (3:20). If we are to be consistent in arguing that 'naming' involves authority then this suggests he has authority over her.[45] But this second naming of Eve occurs after the fall, not prior to it. It may even be an example of Adam ruling over his wife (3:16) and no longer treating her as a person of equal worth, but reducing her to the level of the animals,

---

[39] Gal. 4:4.

[40] Jewett, *Man as . . .* , p. 113.

[41] Hess, 'Equality', p. 85.

[42] Ortlund, 'Male-Female Equality', p. 98.

[43] For examples see Trible, 'Depatriarchalizing', p. 38 and Evans, *Woman*, p. 16. For the problems with this see Clines, *What Does Eve Do?*, pp. 38–39.

[44] T. E. Fretheim, 'The Book of Genesis', *NIB*, vol. 1 (Nashville: Abingdon, 1994), p. 353.

[45] Wenham, *Genesis 1-15*, p. 81, argues this 'indicates his authority over her'.

rather than an exercise of God-intended authority.[46] Whatever the vocabulary, the circumstances of both references to Eve's name-calling appear different from those of the naming of the animals and do not seem to carry the same overtones of justified authority as that does.

4. Created for intimate partnership (2:24)

The focus remains on the way in which Adam is to fulfil the creation mandate to 'be fruitful and increase in number' (1:28), and so Genesis takes the next step and explains how Adam and Eve who share a common flesh (2:23) can graduate to becoming *one flesh*. The threefold process involves a leaving of the parental family, a joining with the partner, and then a consummation in the act of sexual intercourse. A rich theology of marriage is compressed into the simple words *leaves . . . is united . . . become one flesh*. God's pattern for marriage is undoubtedly established here as heterosexual. To forsake one's parents teaches that the husband now has a higher duty and loyalty than to them. To be united, or 'stick to' one's wife 'suggests both passion and permanence',[47] while becoming one flesh speaks of the closest bonding that occurs through sexual intimacy and union. Becoming one in this way transcends the differentiation that has occurred in the creation of male and female and restores a wholeness to human experience.[48] Our interest here, however, is confined to looking at what it teaches, if anything, about the role of women. And here there is at least one surprise.

In the patriarchal context that is often said to pervade the Old Testament, we might have expected to read that 'a woman leaves her father and mother and is united to her husband'. That, after all, is what we see a number of women doing in the stories that follow. But, significantly, Genesis 2:24 says the reverse. It is the man who leaves his parental home to be united with his wife. While some see in this the portrait of the man taking the initiative and functioning as the leader,[49] it is possible to read it in quite another way. He is the one called to cut ties with the familiar, break free from the *status quo*, and sacrifice the comfort of the home where he grew up, to make the move towards his wife. As Heinrich Baltenswiler has commented: 'He loves her so much; so much does the thought of her fill his mind, that he is ready to break the closest family ties which blood

---

[46] Trible, *God and*, p. 133. Eve means life although, as Trible writes, ironically 'he has just robbed her of life'.

[47] Wenham, *Genesis 1-15*, p. 71.

[48] Trible, *God and*, p. 104.

[49] Ortlund, 'Male-Female Equality', p. 103.

relationship can establish'.[50] That the move takes place in this direction may afford the wife a little protection, should she need it, from male authoritarianism, since she apparently remains close to her parental home. But that may be to read more into the text than Genesis intends. Even so, it is surprising that it is man who is called to pay the greatest cost in forming the marriage relationship.

The stress, so early in Scripture, on the union of the man and woman in marriage witnesses to its significance in the purposes of God. Sadly, this has sometimes resulted in those who remain single feeling, or being made to feel, second-class and in some respects not living up to God's creation intention. In view of this it is important to remember that when the creation of man and woman as male and female in the image of God was first mentioned, it was not exclusively tied to the question of marriage or procreation. Paul Jewett helpfully explains: 'While marriage is perhaps the *most intimate* form of human fellowship, it is not the *most basic*. Men and women may become related as husband and wife, and many do; but they are related as men and women by virtue of God's creative act.'[51] People have significance as men and women created in God's own image in their own right, not just because they become husbands or wives. And should that ever be doubted, one only has to remember that the most complete man who ever lived, Jesus, the perfect Son of God, remained single throughout his life.

5. Concluding comment

Wherever our journey takes us, when we begin at the beginning we start with a view of men and women created equally in the image of God and commissioned together to be fruitful and exercise dominion over the rest of creation. We find that the fuller account of Eve's creation does nothing to diminish this equality but serves to enhance it, with its stress on the close identity between Adam and Eve. We learn, further, that within the intimacy of marriage the differentiation of male and female is brought around full circle so that male and female become one flesh. The most people can discover in these chapters is a 'whisper', or 'quiet hues' and 'quiet overtones' of patriarchy.[52] Essentially, however, the creation accounts start with a picture of equality, unity and mutuality. The compass has been set

---

[50] Cited by Jewett, *Man as . . .* , p. 128.

[51] Jewett, *Man as . . .* , p. 24. Italics mine.

[52] These terms come from W. J. Webb, *Slaves, Women and Homosexuals: Exploring the Hermeneutics of Cultural Analysis* (Downers Grove: IVP, 2001), p. 131, who continues that 'Nevertheless [they] do not confirm the transcultural status of patriarchy' but may be limited to a particular time.

for the journey ahead. As the journey gets underway, however, men and women are thrown off course and, because of sin, deviate, sometimes grossly, from these ideal aspects of the creation which God had declared to be 'very good'.

Genesis 3:1–24
2. Women and the fall of humanity

Until recently, when the global positioning satellite (GPS) superseded it, the magnetic compass was the essential instrument of navigation. Aligning itself with the Earth's magnetic field, it indicated the direction of the magnetic north and having done so, made the calculation of other directions possible. Magnetic compasses, however, could be caused to deviate from true north by the interference of more local magnetic fields. The story of creation in Genesis 1 – 2 sets the direction of God's true north for humanity, but the story suddenly suffers from interference in Genesis 3, with the result that men and women deviate from the path God intended with catastrophic results.

1. The snake's subtle subversion (1–5)

Without introduction *the snake* appears in the garden and engages Eve in conversation. While he was one *of the wild animals the LORD God had made*, he is an alien presence, 'an intruder, unwelcome, incoherent, contrary to the story so far'[1] though not yet a cursed creature. We may speculate why a snake is chosen as the tempter, and we might find the way the snake was perceived elsewhere in the ancient word suggestive,[2] but Genesis only points to his craftiness as a creature of the field.[3] We may argue that the snake is a suitable disguise for Satan, the accuser and opponent of God to adopt, but

---

[1] C. J. H. Wright, *The God I Don't Understand* (Grand Rapids: Zondervan, 2008), p. 36.

[2] Details of such views are found in the standard commentaries, e.g., G. Wenham, *Genesis 1-15*, WBC (Waco: Word, 1987), pp. 72–73; V. P. Hamilton, *The Book of Genesis, Chapters 1–17* (Grand Rapids: Eerdmans, 1990), pp. 187–188.

[3] In the Hebrew the words 'more crafty' (*'ārûm*) may be a play on the word 'naked' (*'ărûmmîm*). The naked Adam and Eve are exposed to cunning and crafty elements of the world. T. E. Fretheim, 'The Book of Genesis', *NIB*, vol. 1 (Nashville: Abingdon, 1994), p. 359.

it is not until later that any clarity emerges about him.[4] Whenever the snake is mentioned he is associated with the enemies of God. Yet, as God's creation he is not an independent power, equal to God. The conflict between them is never going to be an even contest. His slithering style of motion is a perfect complement to his crafty character and as Gordon Wenham helpfully concludes, 'for any Israelite familiar with the symbolic values of different animals, a creature more likely than a serpent to lead man away from his creator could not be imagined'.

The source of temptation, then, is not to be found in God, who by nature 'cannot be tempted by evil, nor does he tempt anyone',[5] nor is it to be found originally within the human condition, since mankind was the pinnacle of God's 'very good' creation[6] and enjoyed an unclouded relationship with the Creator. The source of temptation, however, does lie within the world and will severely test human beings as creatures who had not only been entrusted with moral responsibility but also had wills of their own.

a. Who the snake addresses

The snake engaged Eve not Adam in his seductive conversation. Why did he choose her and not him? Tradition has often assumed that it is because women have a greater propensity for being deceived than men. A contemporary writer explains it this way: 'Generally speaking, women are more relational and nurturing and men given to more rational analysis and objectivity. Women are less prone than men to see the importance of doctrinal formulations . . .'.[7] Some think the key is that Satan is undermining Adam's role as the male head in the relationship.[8] 'The Genesis temptation,' Thomas Schreiner asserts, 'is a parable of what happens when male leadership is abrogated. Eve took the initiative in responding to the serpent and Adam let her do so'.[9] Paul's statement that 'Adam was not the one deceived; it was the woman who was deceived'[10] is often said to teach this.

Such arguments, however, are built on some very questionable assumptions. They stereotype men and women. They assume headship is clear in Genesis 1. And they import into Paul's statement

[4] See G. H. Twelftree, 'Spiritual powers', *NDBT*, pp. 796–797.

[5] Jas 1:13.

[6] Gen. 1:31.

[7] T. R. Schreiner, 'An interpretation of 1 Timothy 2:9-15: A Dialogue with Scholarship', *Fresh Analysis*, p. 145.

[8] Schreiner, 'An interpretation', pp. 142–145; R. C. Ortlund, 'Male-Female Equality and Male Headship. Genesis 1–3', *RBMW*, p. 107.

[9] Schreiner, 'An interpretation', p. 145.

[10] 1 Tim. 2:14.

what he does not say. In saying 'it was the woman who was deceived' Paul offers no explanation and attributes no motivation for what happened, but is merely making a factual observation.

Several other explanations are at least equally credible, if not more so. Naming the creatures, as Adam did, was not simply an exercise in ruling over them but in discerning their character, since names were chosen to identify character.[11] So if the snake had approached him, Adam would have immediately been on the alert, having already discerned that the snake was shrewd and, like a dodgy doorstep salesman, a not-quite-to-be-trusted creature. Eve was unlikely to have been forewarned in the way Adam was.

Or, perhaps just as significant, is the theme of wisdom that surfaces here. In the ancient world it was common to attribute wisdom to serpents. Since we know the outcome of the story, we assume the snake's cunning to be ominous, but the quality of shrewdness is not necessarily negative. In many contexts it is a commendable quality[12] and may be as much an exercise of the positive quality of diplomatic prudence as anything sinister. Moreover, in the conversation that ensues the snake offers Eve the possibility that by eating the forbidden fruit she could become as wise as God, *knowing good and evil.* Eve, verse 6 tells us, *saw the fruit* as *desirable for gaining wisdom.* Once we see this story through the lens of the wisdom writings, where wisdom is associated with the female gender, classically in Proverbs 8, it makes perfect sense that the snake should approach Eve, and not Adam.[13]

The truth is, no explanation is given as to why the snake approached Eve, so it is unwise of us to be dogmatic.

b. What the snake says

The snake's conversation is ample evidence of his shrewdness. He does not directly challenge God but raises a question about what God had said. In doing so, he flagrantly misquotes God and exaggerates his prohibition, since God had never said 'You must not eat from any tree in the garden', as he well knows. God had said quite the reverse: 'You are free to eat from any tree in the garden', excepting only 'the tree of knowledge of good and evil'.[14] But it was enough

---

[11] Gen. 2:20. For the justification of this statement see R. Hess, 'The roles of the woman and the man in Genesis 3', *Themelios* 18 (April, 1993), pp. 16, 18 n. 4; Fretheim, 'Genesis', p. 353.

[12] Matt. 10:16; Luke 16:8.

[13] C. Meyers, *Discovering Eve: Ancient Israelite Women in Context* (Oxford and New York: Oxford University Press, 1988), pp. 90–91.

[14] Gen. 2:16–17.

to engage Eve in the conversation, which he can exploit once she is hooked.

Eve's reply is a little more accurate than the snake's claim, but even so embellishes and distorts God's word. She identifies the tree as *in the middle of the garden* rather than by identifying it according to its nature, and so misses, or at least minimizes, the point of the prohibition. She adds that God had said *you must not touch it*, which he had not, and so turns a God of grace into a miserable God of law and turns his liberating wisdom into a cause of anxiety and fear. Then she makes light of God's warning, reducing the emphatic language of 'you will certainly die' in 2:16, to the less emphatic *or you will die*.

Furthermore, Eve's reply shows her colluding with the snake in a second respect. The tempter had abandoned the personal name for God ('Lord God') and spoke of him only by the more distant and impersonal term 'God'. So the relationship with God is undergoing a change. 'God is treated as a third person. God is not party to the discussion but is the involved object of the discussion . . . God has become objectified. The serpent is the first in the Bible to seem knowing and critical about God and to practice *theology* in the place of *obedience*'.[15] Creation itself has become the focus of their interest, not the Creator.[16]

Encouraged by her reply and taking up her reference to death, the snake becomes more daring and challenges God's claim and his motivation. *You will not certainly die . . . For God knows that when you eat from it your eyes will be opened, and you will be like God, knowing good and evil.* The snake's first claim is typically cunning since it is ambiguous. It is not clear if he means, 'It is not certain that you will die', or 'Certainly you will not die'. Whichever, subsequent events seem to confirm he was right to some degree. Adam and Eve do not physically die at the moment when they disobey God and are expelled from the garden. Yet, even though Adam lives until he is 930 years old,[17] God's judgment on Adam, *dust you are and to dust you will return* (19), is eventually fulfilled. They do, however, immediately die inwardly and having been rejected by God 'experience a living death'.[18] The snake speaks in half-truths rather than outright lies. He rightly asserts that *God knows*, even if they don't.[19] Yet, emboldened, he alleges that God has deceived them so that they

---

[15] W. Brueggemann, *Genesis*, Int (Atlanta: John Knox Press, 1982), p. 48.

[16] P. Trible, *God and the Rhetoric of Sexuality* (London: SCM, 1992), p. 109.

[17] Gen. 5:5. See Wenham, *Genesis 1-15*, p. 73.

[18] Wenham, *Genesis 1-15*, p. 90.

[19] 'In this, the serpent acts not as a deceiver but as a *truth-teller*' (Fretheim, 'Genesis', p. 361).

would be kept in their place as inferior and limited creatures, and not become God-like, knowing as God knows and being as 'wise' as him.[20]

Note that the snake does not actually invite Eve to eat the fruit. He merely unsettles her knowledge of what God has said and, having done so, plants the seed thought in her mind that the consequences of her eating the forbidden fruit may not be as dire as God has led her to expect. The serpent and the woman both go fundamentally adrift by their refusal to recall accurately and take seriously what God had spoken.

2. Eve's fateful decision (6–13)

a. Eve's action

The snake withdraws and speaks no more, while Eve's thoughts turn into actions. She *saw . . . took . . . ate . . . gave* (6).[21] Eve is subject to the enticements of our common humanity. Temptation, as so often, enters through her eyes. When she looked at the forbidden fruit she was not repelled by God's warning but enticed by its threefold attraction. It was *good for food and pleasing to the eye, and also desirable for gaining wisdom.* Surely, it seemed only sensible for her to satisfy her desires and avail herself of the full resources that God had placed within his world rather than exercise disciplined restraint.

So human wisdom supplanted God's wisdom and desire gave way to action. Fatefully, for herself and her husband, and for all humanity of whom she was the first mother, *she took some and ate.* It was just as James would later write, 'after desire has conceived, it gives birth to sin; and sin, when it is full-grown, gives birth to death'.[22]

b. Adam's complicity

Having eaten herself, *she also gave some to her husband, who was with her* (6). He has not figured in the account until this point but must have been near to hand and did nothing either to interrupt the

[20] There are various suggestions as to the meaning of 'knowing good and evil'. Since Adam and Eve are already moral creatures it must mean more than this. It has been taken to refer to immortality, omniscience, wisdom or merely that in eating the fruit they will know the good consequences of obedience and the evil consequences of disobedience. See Wenham, *Genesis 1-15*, pp. 62–65; D. Kidner, *Genesis*, TOTC (London: Tyndale House, 1967), p. 63.

[21] The reversal of this tragic 'meal' took place when the one fully obedient man anticipated his death in another 'meal' as he *took* bread, *gave* thanks and gave it to his disciples and commanded them to *eat* it (1 Cor. 11:23–26).

[22] Jas 1:15.

conversation with Satan or prevent her from taking the fruit. Rather he compounds her disobedience by his own complicity: *and he ate it.* 'The woman does not try to tempt the man', Victor Hamilton points out. 'She simply gives and he takes. He neither challenges nor raises questions. The woman allows her mind and her own judgement to be her guide; the man neither approves nor rebukes. Hers is a sin of initiative. His is a sin of acquiescence.'[23] Eve is not presented as the temptress; the snake alone tempts. Adam appears passive and ineffectual, and does nothing to resist the inroads of sin. The timing of Eve's fall is marginally prior to Adam's, just as when twins are born one comes out of the womb prior to the other, but the timing is insignificant. Adam and Eve are both caught up in the same moment, equally responsible and equally guilty.[24]

Any gender analysis of these verses builds on a flimsy foundation. On the one hand there are those who make much of Eve's role and argue that the whole fault lay in the subversion of Adam's role as head in the relationship. So, the snake intentionally went behind Adam's back to talk to Eve instead of going to Adam who was the primary moral agent in the family; and Eve equally disrespected Adam's headship by taking the fruit without consulting him first (although he does seem to have been at her side when it happened!). On the other hand, there are those who draw the opposite implications. Adam never steps up to the mark. He is 'bland'.[25] He never takes the initiative, assumes any responsibility, and, quite apart from any notion of headship, is happy for Eve to be the decisive, articulate action woman who acts as spokesperson for the family.[26] The man they say is inept in comparison to the woman.

New Testament reflections on this incident discourage us from apportioning the blame on the basis of gender. For the most part, Paul attributes the fall of humanity to Adam, explaining typically, 'just as sin entered the world through one man' bringing death to all, so, by God's grace, justification, righteousness and eternal life is made possible through 'the one man, Jesus Christ'.[27] Paul's attribution of 'blame' to Eve occurs only on one occasion[28] and is heavily outweighed by the responsibility he places on Adam's shoulders.

---

[23] Hamilton, *Genesis 1-17*, p. 191.

[24] Joseph Abraham, who has mounted a detailed and perceptive critique of various feminist interpretations of Genesis 1 – 3, including the views of Trible and Meyers, supports this equal attribution of guilt in *Eve: Accused or Acquitted? A Reconsideration of Feminist Readings of the Creation Narrative Texts in Genesis 1–3* (Carlisle: Paternoster, 2002), p. 69.

[25] Trible, *God and*, p. 113.

[26] Trible, *God and*, p. 113. Cf. Meyers, *Discovering Eve*, p. 91.

[27] Rom. 5:12, 16–17, 19; 1 Cor. 15:22.

[28] 1 Tim. 2:14.

c. Their discovery

In this single act of disobedience the compass is thrown off its true direction and all manner of evil follows. The outcome of their having acquired 'wisdom' by eating the forbidden fruit is the realization *that they were naked* (7). 'This,' as Hamilton observes, 'is hardly the knowledge for which they bargained'.[29] How ironic! Their nakedness had been mentioned positively in the footnote to the previous chapter after Eve was created and she and Adam became one flesh: they 'were both naked, and they felt no shame'.[30] Now their nakedness is negative. The immediate effect of their eyes being opened is a loss of innocence and intimacy between them and a sense of shame that leads them to make the most rudimentary of aprons and cover themselves up. The hiding from each other that began in the garden that day introduced a sense of alienation in relationships from which humanity has suffered ever since.

Adam and Eve are not only alienated from each other but alienated from God, as becomes movingly evident when he came to take his customary walk *in the garden in the cool of the day* (8). The unspoiled enjoyment of God's presence that they had experienced to this point had become a thing of the past as, aware of their nakedness, they hide from their Creator. Adam's response to God's plaintive '*Where are you?*' (9–10) raises more questions than it answers and only serves to initiate further interrogation. Their responses to God's questions show that the impact of their newly-acquired knowledge was far greater than the fact that they were naked. First Adam, then Eve, passes the buck. Their act of disobedience is not an isolated act. One sin leads to another as they seek to abdicate their privileges as moral human beings, excuse sin and blame their actions on others. The blame game is still one of the most practised sports in our contemporary world, as people seek to shift the guilt to 'society', 'the system', 'the government', 'them', 'my parents', 'my partner', or even 'the devil'.

3. God's enduring judgment (14–24)

Once God, the judge, has heard the case he pronounces sentence, first on the snake (14–15), then on Eve (16) and finally on Adam (17–19). Neither Adam nor Eve are cursed. The curse is reserved for the snake alone (14). They are sentenced to experience the painful consequences of their disobedience through the corruption and

---

[29] Hamilton, *Genesis 1-17*, p. 191.
[30] Gen. 2:15.

distortion of their original role in creation. Eve bears no greater sentence than her co-conspirator in sin, and the consequences for them both are severe.

Eve's sentence is twofold and affects her experience as a mother and a wife. As mother, Eve was created to partner Adam in the joy of procreation. Giving birth to new life would provide her with 'her highest sense of self-fulfilment',[31] but now it would be corrupted by severe labour pains. She was to *become the mother of all the living* (20) but giving birth was never to be the untarnished blessing God intended.[32]

Secondly, the unspoiled intimacy she and Adam had enjoyed, to which 2:23–24 had borne witness, was lost forever. *Your desire will be for your husband, and he will rule over you* (16). Just as desire was an element in Eve's downfall (6), so now desire plays its part in her judgment. The sentence seems straightforward.[33] Eve will long for intimacy with her husband but he will not reciprocate but rather will push her away and become domineering over her. So it is here that the element of hierarchy and headship comes into play for the first time, as part of the consequence of the fall, rather than being part of God's original intention at creation. Division and tension replace unity and shared delight. From this point on Adam becomes authoritarian and the beautiful harmony of mutuality and equality, experienced earlier, is but a memory. Phyllis Trible has termed it, 'a love story gone awry'.[34] Eros has been defiled. In Kidner's memorable words, '"To love and to cherish" becomes "To desire and to dominate"'.[35]

The enduring nature of this sentence is all too evident in the relationships which we witness (or sadly even experience) every day. But the original sentence gives rise to at least two questions. First, is this sentence God's prescription of what must take place in future or is it only his description of what will take place as a consequence of sin? Secondly, whether God's prescription or description, have we any liberty to combat it and seek to alleviate it, or are we, in doing so opposing God?

While some seek to lessen God's role in the sentencing of Eve and hold to the view that this is merely a description of what has become

---

[31] Hamilton, *Genesis 1-17*, p. 200.

[32] Gen. 4:1–26.

[33] A minority interpretation, based on the parallel use of 'desire' in Gen. 4:7, argues Eve's desire is to master Adam or seek independence from him. But the exegetical foundation is by no means certain and the end result is still a disruption of relationship in which Adam dominates Eve. See Fretheim, 'Genesis', p. 363; Hamilton, *Genesis 1-17*, pp. 201–202; Wenham, *Genesis 1-15*, pp. 81–82.

[34] Trible, *God and*, p. 72.

[35] Kidner, *Genesis*, p. 71.

inevitable as a consequence of sin, the opening words of God's address to Eve, *I will . . .* (16), makes this unlikely. The creator is here expressing his personal disapproval of her disobedience and has personal involvement in meting out the sentence. Even if the second half of the sentence may be read as a description, it is hard to read the first half in this way. Given this, the second question becomes more urgent. If we seek to alleviate God's judgment on sin, are we not opposing God?

This view was once put forward as a reason not to use any method of pain-reduction for women in labour. In 1847 James Simpson was accused of circumventing the divine will by using anaesthesia to deaden the pain of childbirth. Ironically, he won the argument by pointing out that God had caused Adam to fall into a 'deep sleep' when he conducted the first surgical operation in history and opened up his side in order to create Eve.[36] No-one, however, would now oppose the use of anaesthetics or drugs in order to relieve pain at such a time, and no-one would view it as seeking to subvert God's will. Similarly, no-one now takes God's cursing of the ground so that Adam experienced horticultural work as *painful toil* and produced food *by the sweat of [his] brow* as preventing the development of farm machinery and agricultural technology. Alleviating suffering and reducing the stress of work has not ultimately removed these symptoms of God's judgment. They remain in force. Alongside them though, improvements in medicine and farming witness to the creation mandate continuing. Men and women are still entrusted with ruling over the earth and this has not been removed by the fall, even if it has been corrupted by it.

Given this, why should it be considered, as some do, that the one line in God's judgment on Adam and Eve that it is wrong to ameliorate is that of the husband ruling over the wife? Wherever authoritarianism or twisted hierarchialism is evident, Christians, who have a vision of the new creation, should be the first to take steps to oppose it.[37] It is a mark of the fall that, while we will never eradicate it in this age, we should vigorously combat as we do the other marks of the fall, in anticipation of the new creation to which we are heading.

Genesis 3 ends with two contrasting notes. On the one hand, Adam names Eve (which means 'living'), *because she would become the mother of all living* (20). He has not named her before, but does so after the fall, exercising his newly acquired authority over her,

---

[36] I am indebted to P. K. Jewett, *Man as Male and Female* (Grand Rapids: Eerdmans, 1975), p. 122 for this.

[37] This will be developed more fully in ch. 18. See Eph. 5:25.

just as he has named the animals earlier.[38] On the other hand, we see God acting with extraordinary tender grace towards his now fallen and sentenced creatures. While God's reaction to their disobedience is severe and they are expelled from their home in Eden with their re-entry barred by cherubic guards, he nonetheless accommodates himself to their fallen state and demonstrates mercy in the midst of judgment. He makes *garments of skin* (21) for them and clothes them with more substantial and fitting garments than they had made to cover their shame for themselves.

4. Concluding comment

Genesis 3 reverses God's good intention for creation and undermines his intention for humankind. The contrasts between Genesis 2 and Genesis 3 are numerous. In Genesis 2:15, 'the LORD God took the man and put him in the Garden of Eden to work it'. In Genesis 3:23, *the LORD God banished him from the Garden of Eden to work the ground from which he had been taken.* In 2:17, Adam was told not to 'eat from the tree of the knowledge of good and evil'. In 3:6, responding to Eve's offer, *he ate it.* In 2:19, God brought the animals 'to the man to see what he would name them'. In 3:20, without God commanding him to do so, *Adam named his wife Eve.* In 2:23–24 Adam and Eve identify with each other and 'become one flesh'. In 3:16, they divide from each other and Adam begins to rule over Eve. In 2:25 they 'were both naked, and they felt no shame'. In 3:7, when their eyes had been opened by the consumption of the forbidden fruit, *they realised that they were naked; so they sewed fig leaves together and made coverings for themselves.*

Eve and Adam's disobedience throws the compass that had indicated the direction God intended human beings to follow out of alignment. The ideal state of their relationship was corrupted and, even though men and women are still capable of harmonious and even beautiful relationships, subsequent history testifies to the breakdown of the relationship between genders. The preponderance of tension, arrogance, hostility and even abuse between them is far from the Creator's plan.

---

[38] Trible, *God and*, p. 133. See fuller comment on pp. 40–41.

Galatians 3:26–28
3. Women and the new creation

Galatians 3:28 is the 'Magna Carta of Humanity' for both men and women in Christ.[1] God's good creation in which male and female were made in his image had been derailed by Eve's disobedience and Adam's fall. While parts of the track they should have followed continued to be travelled occasionally, men and women increasingly deviated from God's plan in their dealings with one another and their relationships became increasingly oppressive. During the intertestamental period, generally speaking, 'a deterioration seems to have taken place' to the detriment of women, although the picture is mixed. This resulted in a climate in which they were held to be more culpable for sin than men, were hemmed in by ritual laws, were comparatively uneducated in the law, confined to domestic duties, distrusted and considered of little value.[2] With the coming of Jesus and the in-breaking of God's kingdom, the derailed plan of God was brought back on track. Galatians 3:28 summarizes the 'liberating vision' of the gospel[3] and the restoration of authentic fellowship between the sexes.[4]

---

[1] P. K. Jewett, *Man as Male and Female* (Grand Rapids: Eerdmans, 1975), p. 142. The Magna Carta was a charter signed by King John in 1215 which enshrined the freedom of English citizens under the law.

[2] See K. E. Bailey, *Jesus Through Middle Eastern Eyes: Cultural Studies in the Gospels* (London: SPCK, 2008), pp. 189–190. Bailey points to the writings of Ben Sirach who wrote in the early second century, saying, 'Any iniquity is small compared to a woman's iniquity' (Eccles. 25:19, NRSV) and 'Better is the wickedness of a man than a woman who does good; it is woman who brings shame and disgrace' (Eccles. 42:14, NRSV). See also D. M. Scholer, 'Women', *DJG*, pp. 880–881; M. Evans, *Woman in the Bible* (Exeter: Paternoster 1983), pp. 33–37; B. Witherington III, *Women and the Genesis of Christianity* (Cambridge: Cambridge University Press, 1990), pp. 3–9.

[3] Jewett, *Man as . . .* , p. 12.

[4] Jewett, *Man as . . .* , p. 144.

There is unanimous agreement that this text means that men and women have equality before God as far as their salvation is concerned, just as Jews and Gentiles, slaves and free, do. Men have neither any superior standing in relation to God nor a different pathway to him. All are justified by faith. But there the agreement ends. Some say the equality of which the verse speaks is limited to a person's spiritual status, whereas others say the text inevitably has implications for a person's practical service in the church. England and the United States are often said to be two nations divided by a common language. In like manner those who accept the authority of the Bible fall into two camps divided by the common text of Galatians 3:28. The meaning of this charter of liberty has sadly become a matter of dispute and the liberating vision is in danger of being lost.

1. What does the text say?

The statement *There is neither Jew nor Gentile, neither slave nor free, nor is there male and female, for you are all one in Christ Jesus* (28) is introduced somewhat abruptly[5] and has a liturgical ring to it. This, together with the mention of baptism in the previous verse – a rite which is to become very significant to Paul's argument in Galatians – makes it 'quite likely that what we are dealing with is an early, perhaps pre-Pauline, baptismal formula'.[6] In baptism people of all backgrounds were united with Christ and incorporated into his body.[7]

The three great marks by which people in the ancient world distinguished themselves from others are mentioned here. The world was divided on the basis of ethnicity between Jews and Gentiles, social status between slaves and free, and gender between male and female. The first had to do with the cultural realm, the second with the economic and the third with the sexual. For the Christian, however, these distinctions were of no consequence. Only one distinction mattered: whether a person was in Christ or not. The passage is saturated with Christ. Christians are defined as being *in Christ . . . baptised into Christ . . . clothed with Christ . . . all one in Christ Jesus* and as those who *belong to Christ* (27–29). With Christ as the focus and orientation of one's life all the customary means by which a person measured another's worth become irretrievably irrelevant.

[5] J. D. G. Dunn, *The Epistle to the Galatians*, BNTC (London: Hendrickson, 1993), p. 205.

[6] B. Witherington III, 'Rite and Rights for Women – Galatians 3:28', *NTS* 27.5 (1981), p. 597; R. Y. K. Fung, *The Epistle to the Galatians*, NICNT (Grand Rapids: Eerdmans, 1988), p. 175.

[7] Rom. 6:1–7; 1 Cor. 12:13.

Did Paul choose these three distinctions deliberately to counter the three blessings that Jewish men prayed at the start of morning prayer: 'Blessed be He that He did not make me a Gentile; blessed be He that he did not make me a slave;[8] blessed be He that he did not make me a woman'? Perhaps. Paul may have been accustomed to pray this from an early age, although we have no firm evidence of the prayer being used as early as his time and comparable distinctions are found in Socrates and elsewhere.[9] Yet there is no need to find a particular reason for Paul's choice of couplets since they 'cover in embryonic fashion all the essential relationship of humanity'.[10]

Being in Christ did not obliterate the distinctions and cause Christians to be ethnically indistinguishable, culturally homogeneous, socially classless, economically equal, gender-neutral, or sexually androgynous. They remained identifiable as Jews or Greeks, slaves or free, males or females and were not required to deny their individuality. Indeed, in their everyday lives in the pagan world they would have still had to live and work within the legal and social constraints of their social position. Jews remained Jews; slaves, slaves; and women, women. But in Christ, such distinctions, so important to others, became entirely unimportant. Visiting another country usually involves exchanging money and trading in a currency that is not our own, since ours is not legal tender. So when entering the Christian community we are required to exchange the currency by which we value people, since what is in common circulation outside of Christ has no purchasing power among Christ's people. We trade by an altogether different coinage, that of being in him.

The three contrasting pairs that Paul uses here are both basic to the ancient world and, at the same time, are particularly appropriate to the argument he is advancing in the letter to Galatians. Elsewhere Paul employs a similar but not identical set of couplets. In both 1 Corinthians 12:13 and Colossians 3:11 he repeats the reference to ethnic and social distinctions but he does not repeat the division between male and female. In Colossians he adds two other pairs, 'circumcised or uncircumcised, barbarian, Scythian'. The particular contrasts employed seem carefully chosen for their relevance to his argument in each letter and so invites us to look closely at why he only mentioned male and female in Galatians.

Paul introduces each couplet by the same formula: there *is neither* (*ouk eni*). The only minor change to the way Paul words the contrasts is when he refers to *male and female* instead of 'male *or*

---

[8] The word used is 'brutish man' or 'boor', which is equivalent to 'slave'.

[9] F. F. Bruce, *Commentary on Galatians*, NIGTC (Exeter: Paternoster, 1982), p. 187; R. N. Longeneker, *Galatians*, WBC (Waco: Word, 1990), p. 157.

[10] Longeneker, *Galatians*, p. 157.

female'. The significance of this lies purely in the fact than the words *male and female* come from Genesis 1:27,[11] which Paul would quite naturally quote, while the other couples have no parallels in the Old Testament.

2. Why was the text written?

a. Where people agree

Understanding the meaning of the text requires more than an understanding of the words alone. Galatians 3:28 was not written as a clever sound bite to stand alone, disconnected from a wider argument, but is included because it contributes to the overall case that Paul is advancing. In general terms, the purpose of Galatians is well known. Some were teaching that in order to be a true Christian all people, Gentiles as well as Jews, were required to observe the Jewish law in addition to having faith in Christ. The debate particularly focused on the rite of circumcision,[12] an exclusively male rite, and the observance of Jewish food regulations. The apostle Peter's behaviour at Antioch seemed to lend credence to the importance of such customs.[13] Paul rebuts this view in the strongest of terms and argues vigorously that we are brought into and kept in a right standing with God ('justified') only 'by faith in Jesus Christ' and not 'by the works of the law'.[14] By definition, the gospel of God's grace means the old Jewish customs are no longer relevant. Indeed, there is no other gospel.[15]

Before explaining that justification by faith is no excuse for living an unholy life, since our freedom is a freedom to walk in step with the Spirit,[16] Paul validates his argument by retelling the story of Abraham. This story demonstrates that God had not changed his mind about the law, but has always worked on one and the same basis of faith. 'Abraham "believed God and it was credited to him as righteousness."'[17] He then appeals to the contrast between Sarah's son, the son of divine promise, and Hagar's son, the son of human wilfulness, for support. His concern is that Christian believers might experience the freedom of being God's genuine children, like Isaac, rather than living as slaves in their relation to God, still living under

[11] Also Matt. 19:4 and Mark 10:6.
[12] Circumcision is mentioned in 2:3, 7–9; 5:2–3, 6, 12; 6:12–13, 15.
[13] Gal 2:11–14.
[14] Gal. 1:6–9; 2:16.
[15] Gal. 1:1–9.
[16] Gal. 5:13 – 6:10.
[17] Gal. 3:6; see Rom. 4:1–25.

the whip of the law.[18] The great charter of Christian liberty in 3:28 serves to distil this truth.

As we mentioned earlier, all would agree that the gospel puts Jews and Greeks, slaves and free, males and females on a level playing field in their standing before God. None is in a privileged position vis-à-vis others. None enjoys a superior status. None have special advantages. All must come to God in the same way, since faith in Christ is the only way to become his child. Women no longer receive their spiritual status through their husbands.[19] That is why circumcision, which initiated Jewish males, but not females, into the family and gave them a privileged position in the practice of their faith, meant nothing.[20] Jew and Gentile, slave and free, male and female are on an equal footing, or, to enlist Peter's words, are joint heirs (synklēronomois) 'of the gracious gift of life'.[21]

b. Where people differ

Disagreement arises, however, over the application of this teaching. Does Galatians 3:28 apply only to a person's spiritual standing before God or has it practical implications for one's role in the church?

Some would restrict Paul's statement to a person's spiritual standing and say it has no implications for the way a woman may function in the church. Being in Christ does not obliterate one person's distinctiveness from another and equally, it is argued, distinctions remain in the roles and responsibilities people adopt within the church. This argument is supported by reference to other scriptures. George Knight III, for example, argues that Galatians 3:28 is about restoring the equality inherent in men and women being made in the image of God but that it does not remove the emphasis on difference found between them in Genesis 2:18–25. In his words, 'our spiritual equality as joint-heirs [does not] remove our maleness and femaleness and the role relationship which that created difference brings to the relation of man and woman . . . '[22] He applies this in the first instance to the role of men and women in marriage but later applies it to their roles within the church.[23] Other scriptures do seem to encourage the maintenance of role distinctions between men and

---

[18] Gal. 4:1–7.

[19] Witherington, 'Rite and Rights', pp. 600–602.

[20] Gal. 6:15.

[21] 1 Pet. 3:7.

[22] G. W. Knight III, *The New Testament Teaching on the Role Relationships of Men and Women* (Grand Rapids: Baker, 1977), pp. 20–21. See also his 'Role Distinctions in the Church: Galatians 3:28', *RBMW*, pp. 154–164.

[23] Knight, *New Testament Teaching*, pp. 29–53, esp. p. 40.

women and impose a severe qualification on this 'charter of liberty'. We shall briefly discuss this problem below but will largely reserve our discussion of the apparently restrictive passages until Part 4 of this volume.

The crucial question under consideration here is the question of the meaning of 3:28 in the context of the letter of Galatians itself. Seen in this context we might come to a somewhat different conclusion from those who argue for limiting its meaning only to a person's spiritual standing.

'The argument of Galatians,' writes Philip Payne, 'focuses on the conflicting practices of Paul and the Judaizers.'[24] Galatians is not only a profoundly theological document but also a profoundly practical one. Galatians 2:11–14 demonstrates this. Paul opposed Cephas (Peter) when he came to Antioch not because of what Cephas believed or taught, but because of what he did. By reverting to Jewish food customs and refusing to eat with Gentiles, Cephas 'was not acting in line with the truth of the gospel'.[25] His theology may have checked out but the practical implications of it had not been fully appreciated. Elsewhere it is the theology and practice of circumcision which raises Paul's ire.

Galatians, Payne says 'is a frontal attack against favored status or privileges being granted to Jews over Gentiles' who are being treated as second-class citizens.[26] Given this, why are slaves and females also mentioned? Gordon Fee has described this as 'a key exegetical question, seldom noted'.[27] The answer is that in the understanding of Paul's opponents the Jewish regulations, especially those to do with religious purity and full participation in the religious cult, discriminated against slaves and women as much as against Gentiles. Those laws made them, as much as Gentiles, second-class citizens not only in their relationship with God but also in their place in the worshipping community. The laws erected social barriers and prevented any but Jewish males from participating fully in the religious community.[28] Therefore, it would not make sense if the removal of these barriers had no social or cultural application.[29] 'To interpret Gal. 3:28 as affirming spiritual equality but as irrelevant

---

[24] P. B. Payne, *Man and Woman: One in Christ* (Grand Rapids: Zondervan, 2009), p. 82.

[25] Gal. 2:14.

[26] Payne, *Man and Woman*, p. 82.

[27] G. Fee, 'Male and Female in the New Creation: Galatians 3:26–29', *DBE*, p. 173.

[28] J. B. Hurley, *Man and Woman in Biblical Perspective* (Leicester: IVP, 1981), pp. 70–73 details the restrictive role they were permitted in religious life. Attendance at the synagogue was not required and most would not permit a woman to read the Scriptures, let alone ask questions.

[29] Payne, *Man and Woman*, p. 98.

to discrimination based on ethnic-religious background, economic status, or gender is to divorce it from the moral core of Paul's message in Galatians and of the gospel of Christ.'[30] All are now on the same footing without discrimination, and *are all one in Christ Jesus.*

Galatians sets out the vision of a new community formed, not on the basis of law, but on freedom in Christ. The church is the new 'Israel of God'[31] in which the fulfilment of the law is realized. A close examination of 3:27–28 underlines this. The effect of baptism, mentioned in verse 27, was 'so as to form one body'.[32] Circumcision discriminated between men and women but baptism united them. Circumcision was exclusive, baptism inclusive of all who had faith in Jesus. A precise reading of verse 28 shows that Paul's primary concern is not that each individual is justified by faith, irrespective of their social standing, 'but that all *constitute one people* (form one body) by their equal standing in Christ'.[33] That is why his *pièce de résistance* is *for you are all one in Christ Jesus.* Here Paul envisages the creation of a new humanity in which God's creation intention is restored. This community will only be fully realized in the age to come but is already breaking into our fractured and fragmented experience of life on earth. The only thing that matters, says Paul, is not human distinctions but 'the new creation'.[34] And while we await its consummation we govern our lives in the here and now as far as we can in the light of it. Therefore we do not measure anyone's value in the church by the currency of this age. So,

> even though our text does not explicitly mention roles and structures, its new creation theological setting calls these into question in a most profound way ... To give continuing significance to a male-authority viewpoint for men and women, whether at home or in the church is to reject the new creation in favour of the norms of a fallen world.[35]

Setting the text in its context in Galatians does seem to encourage us to view the abolition of human distinctions as applying to more than one's spiritual standing in Christ and to have practical implications for the way the church functions. This leads F. F. Bruce to affirm 'the denial of discrimination which is sacramentally affirmed in baptism holds good for the new existence "in Christ" in its

[30] Payne, *Man and Woman*, p. 101.
[31] Gal. 6:16.
[32] 1 Cor. 12:13.
[33] Fee, 'Male and Female', p. 176.
[34] Gal. 6:15.
[35] Fee, 'Male and Female', p. 185.

entirety'. Consequently, Bruce argues, just as Gentiles may become leaders in the church, no less than Jews, so too can slaves no less than free, and women no less than men.[36]

It is impossible to deny that Gentiles and slaves soon became leaders in the early church, thus apparently supporting the egalitarian interpretation of this text, nor would any question their legitimacy as leaders today. Yet some still wish to argue that the question of women is different and this text does not mean that they can become leaders in the church. Not only do they restrict the text (as we have seen) to the question of a person's spiritual status, and interpret it in the light of other apparently more restrictive New Testament texts (to which we will come), they also argue that the distinction between men and women is of a different kind than the other two distinctions here. Ethnicity and social status are not inherent in the creation order, whereas gender difference is.[37] Paul, however, is not seeking to deny the distinctions – our diversity within unity remains – but only to rise above the human structures that have been laid on top of that creation distinction.[38] So the question becomes not whether a woman may exercise leadership in the church, or what role they can adopt in the family, so much as what false interpretations and restrictions were laid on women in the religious community and family unit by the regulations and customs which arose in the practices of later Judaism. Once we approach the question from this perspective, the social and cultural barriers to women's full participation in the community of faith have to be jettisoned.

3. Where does the text sit?

Once we move out of Galatians into the wider teaching of the New Testament, the liberty that was championed there seems to be muted, if not silenced altogether. How can we explain the fact that 'this text appears implicitly or explicitly at odds with other things Paul said and taught'?[39] How does Galatians 3:28 fit with some of Paul's apparently more restrictive writings where the headship of men in church and home is asserted[40] and the silence of women in the church is enjoined?[41]

Several solutions to the apparent tensions have been offered.

[36] Bruce, *Galatians*, p. 190.
[37] Fung, *Galatians*, p. 176, n. 44.
[38] Fee, 'Male and Female', p. 177, n. 11.
[39] Hurley, *Man and Woman*, p. 127.
[40] 1 Cor. 11:2–15; Eph. 5:22–24; Col. 3:18.
[41] 1 Cor. 14:34–35; 1 Tim. 2:11–15.

61

First, some have argued that Paul is inconsistent on the question and it is impossible to find consistency in his writings.[42] This fits with a view of Scripture that sees it as merely a collection of human writings but is hard to reconcile with a high view of Scripture that believes it to be a coherent revelation of God and statement of authoritative apostolic doctrine. Furthermore, this approach may be an excuse for not doing the hard work of exegeting individual texts in their context and striving to discern how they fit together.

Secondly, some have argued that there is a discontinuity between Paul's theological commitment and his pastoral leadership, between his theory and his practice. Elizabeth Schüssler Fiorenza advocates this saying, 'On the one hand, he affirms Christian equality and freedom . . . On the other hand, he subordinates women's behaviour in marriage and in the worship assembly . . . '[43] The pragmatic realities of mission in the Roman world meant that the early vision of equality was forced to compromise with the forces of a patriarchal culture; the vision was lost and women were increasingly restricted in the way they could serve in the church.[44] One problem with this is that some of the apparently more restrictive Pauline texts occur in his earliest writings, such as in 1 Corinthians, and so do not justify an argument of increasing accommodation to reality. Moreover, as 1 Corinthians superbly demonstrates, Paul consistently shows himself to be an adroit pastor who takes the one revealed gospel and applies it sensitively to different situations.

A third approach is to argue that Paul became fearful of the way his gospel of liberty had been applied by some who unwisely sought to overthrow conventional social and gender roles within society and became social radicals and misfits.[45] Again, this does not fit the chronology. Some apparent restrictions come early in Paul's writings while Colossians, one of Paul's later writings, considered by some to reassert patriarchal order, has its own freedom charter in 3:11.[46] Furthermore there is no evidence to support the idea that the gospel caused such general social unrest.

More satisfactory is the fourth approach, which acknowledges that in his many writings Paul is addressing different real pastoral

[42] For a critique of this view see H. O. J. Brown, 'The New Testament against itself: 1 Timothy 2:9-15 and the "Breakthrough" of Galatians 3:28', in *Fresh Analysis*, p. 206.

[43] E. S. Fiorenza, *In Memory of Her: A Feminist Reconstruction of Christian Origins* (10th Anniversary Edn, New York: Crossroad, 1994), p. 236.

[44] Fiorenza, *In Memory*, pp. 251–279.

[45] J. E. Crouch, *The Origin and Intention of the Colossian Haustafel* (Gottenberg: Vandenhoeck, 1972), who applies it particularly to the question of slavery in Col. 3:22–25.

[46] As with Gal. 3:28 the emphasis here is on the creation of the new community in Christ rather than on an individual's standing before God.

situations and they require that different truths be highlighted and different applications made.[47] As a skilled pastor, Paul does not parrot slogans or repeat platitudes but constantly reapplies the same gospel to the different needs of the churches to which he is writing.[48] Careful exegesis of each 'restrictive' text in their context will show that the apparent inconsistencies between them are not nearly as great as is often supposed.[49] The situation Paul was answering in Galatians with the challenges thrown up by the Judaizers was different from the one he was answering in Roman-influenced Corinthians (or Timothy). In Galatians women (and Gentiles and slaves) were being denied liberty in Christ. In Corinthians they were pushing 'their new-found liberty to extremes. Liberty could easily degenerate into license'.[50] Paul does not draw back from the gospel of liberty; he merely applies it sensitively as the occasion demanded. Adopting this approach means we do not need to choose between the various things Paul wrote on the subject but can do justice to them all and this, in turn, means we do not have to restrict Galatians 3:28 to a person's spiritual status and deny it any real social impact.

4. Concluding comments

In Galatians the doctrines of creation and redemption go hand in hand. Those who are justified by faith in Christ form a new humanity on the basis of God's redemption. That new humanity points both backward to the original creation and forward to the new creation still to come. In pointing backward they rediscover God's original creation intention in making male and female in his image. They refuse to succumb to the effects of the derailment that happened as a result of the fall and by the grace of Christ are put back on track to fulfil God's plan. In pointing forward they anticipate the final destination of the new creation in which the task of reconciliation will be complete.[51] En route, they will often struggle to live out the implications of their faith in the realities of their yet-to-be fully redeemed world.

As a showcase of the new humanity, however, they cannot restrict the charter of liberty in Christ to a person's spiritual standing alone. It does not do justice to the text in its context to say that it is only

---

[47] Fiorenza, In Memory, p. 220.

[48] See Derek Tidball, Ministry by the Book: New Testament Patterns for Pastoral Leadership (Nottingham: Apollos, 2008), pp. 126–142.

[49] See Part 4.

[50] W. W. Gasque, 'Response', in A. Mickelsen (ed.), Women, Authority and the Bible (Downers Grove: IVP, 1986), p. 191.

[51] Col. 1:20.

63

concerned 'about the basis of membership within the body of Christ' and not on relationships within that body.[52] No doubt, Paul did not have the contemporary equality agenda in mind as he wrote.[53] Yet, in its context, Galatians 3:28 cannot but have social and practical implications for the way the new humanity in Christ operates now. Other texts in the New Testament do nothing to undermine it.

Susie Stanley's quotation from the commentary of holiness advocate Adam Clarke sums it up well: 'Under the blessed spirit of Christianity, women have equal *rights*, equal *privileges*, and equal *blessings*, and let me add, they are equally *useful*.'[54]

---

[52] Hurley, *Man and Woman*, p. 127.

[53] R. Briggs, *Gender and the New Testament* (Grove: Cambridge, 2001), pp. 10–12; E. A. Judge, 'The Impact of Paul's Gospel on Ancient Society', in P. Bolt and M. Thompson (eds.), *The Gospel to the Nations: Perspectives on Paul's Ministry* (Downers Grove: IVP and Leicester: Apollos, 2000), pp. 297–308.

[54] Cited by S. C. Stanley, 'Response', in Mickelsen (ed.), *Women*, p. 183.

Part Two
Women under the old covenant

Genesis 24:1–67; 25:19–34; 26:34 – 27:46
4. Family women

Beyond question, Israel's way of life was patriarchal and the woman's place was largely that of being a wife and mother. The fact that this was the way it was then does not necessarily bind us to practise patriarchy now, any more than we are bound by other aspects of ancient culture. A jigsaw is not composed of a single piece and neither should our understanding of God's role and intention for women be composed of a single element. Other pieces of the biblical jigsaw will need to be placed on the table before a complete and undistorted picture emerges. Nonetheless, given the importance of the woman's place within the family, as wife, child-bearer and mother, it is appropriate that we place this piece in the centre on the table first.

1. Eve: the mother of all

Eve's first calling, as we saw in chapter 1, was to be an equal partner in her marriage to Adam, serving as his companion and helper. Close upon the heels of that, however, and as an expression of their sexual intimacy, there was a second important role that Eve would play as the bearer of children, fulfilling her side of the creation command to 'be fruitful and increase in number'.[1] Her very name means 'life giver'. 'Adam named his wife Eve, because she would become the mother of all the living.'[2] God's judgment, imposed as a result of Adam and Eve's disobedience, meant that bearing children would from that time on be a severely painful experience.[3] And yet bearing

[1] Gen. 1:28.
[2] Gen. 3:20.
[3] Gen. 3:16.

children would still be an instinctive and irrepressible expression of what it meant to be human.

So, 'Adam made love to his wife Eve, and she became pregnant and gave birth to Cain. She said, "With the help of the LORD I have brought forth a man." Later she gave birth to his brother Abel.'[4] Eve's claim to have given birth 'with the help of the LORD' is ambiguous.[5] Read in the worst light, it could be that she is adopting a cynical tone and claiming to be equal with God. Read in the half-light, it could be that her faith 'is discoloured by a measure of pride'.[6] Yet seen in the best light, her words suggest she understands her dependence on God and understands that she is a partner, albeit a lesser one, with God in the process of creation. Procreation is thus elevated from a mechanical act to a sacramental act, a visible sign of God's grace at work in his world. This best-light interpretation may be supported by the recognition that at this early time in history giving birth was an extremely precarious experience in which neither the survival of the mother nor child was guaranteed unless God, the ultimate source of all life, was actively protecting them.

After the tragic murder of Abel we read, 'Adam made love to his wife again, and she gave birth to a son and named him Seth, saying', with a genuine note of humility and gratitude, '"God has granted me another child in place of Abel, since Cain killed him"'.[7]

Much of Genesis takes its cue from this early presentation of Eve as a child-bearer and concerns the significant role of mothers. The matriarchs, Sarah, Rebekah, Leah and Rachel follow in quick succession and play more than an incidental part in the story. Alongside them are numerous other wives or mothers, like Hagar, Milcah, Esau's wives, Zilpah, Bilhah, Dinah and so on, even though several of them are only briefly identified as mothers in a genealogical list without further details being given.[8] The very survival of the human race, as well as the prosperity of any particular family, depended on these women playing their very significant role. Reflecting on this, John Ortwell concluded: 'Motherhood thus was not only a biological and sociological function. It was a sacred act of great magnitude which only the woman could perform. The very high esteem in which the mother was held [is] reflected in similes of God's care for Israel and

---

[4] Gen. 4:1–2.

[5] For a discussion see, G. Wenham, *Genesis 1-15*, WBC (Waco: Word 1987), pp. 101–102.

[6] D. Atkinson, *The Message of Genesis 1-11*, BST (Leicester: IVP, 1990), p. 100.

[7] Gen. 4:25.

[8] For a full exposition see T. J. Schneider, *Mothers of Promise: Women in the Book of Genesis* (Grand Rapids: Baker, 2008).

of God's judgment upon Israel.'[9] Otwell adds, 'no higher status could be given anyone than was given the mother in ancient Israel'.[10] To be called 'a mother in Israel' was a badge of honour.[11]

2. The life of mothers in early Israel

Yet, truth to tell, the Bible tells us little about how mothers performed their role. Marriages were overwhelmingly arranged marriages. We glimpse the wives engaging in a range of domestic chores. While the men went hunting, ploughed the fields and tended the crops, constructed buildings and dug wells, the women undertook the more 'domestic tasks'. Using that phrase, however, can be misleading for the domestic task then was a productive one involving heavy labour, of a somewhat different kind than domestic work today. It involved not only looking after small children but also producing textiles from scratch and transforming the raw materials of food into edible meals. The wool would have needed carding, spinning and weaving before sewing. The grain would require milling and grinding before the flour could be mixed into dough for baking. Fuel would need to be gathered for the fire and water drawn for washing and drinking. Heavy water pots would be carried on head or shoulders some distance from the well or spring to the dwelling place. It was arduous and extensive work that, in comparative situations to those found in ancient Israel, has been estimated to have required 'upward of ten hours per day' to complete the 'indoor, outdoor and courtyard chores'.[12] Working in close family units where the separation between home and work, characteristic of later industrialized societies, had not yet taken place, men and women were highly dependent on each other to sustain life. Their work was complementary to each other, different but equal in demand and significance. It was in the course of doing this work that mothers would be playing a significant role in socializing and educating their sons and their daughters.

Caring for children was an important part of a mother's responsibility, especially in their early years, and yet, curiously, it is never explored. 'The mothers of Genesis are rarely evaluated by what they

[9] J. H. Otwell, *And Sarah Laughed: The Status of Woman in the Old Testament* (Philadelphia, Westminster Press, 1977), p. 66.

[10] Otwell, *Sarah Laughed*, p. 66.

[11] Deborah applies the title to herself in Judg. 5:7.

[12] L. G. Perdue, J. Blenkinsopp, J. J. Collins and C. Meyers, *Families in Ancient Israel* (Louisville: Westminster Press, 1997), p. 25, see further pp. 22–28. Also C. Meyers, *Discovering Eve: Ancient Israelite Women in Context* (New York and Oxford: Oxford University Press, 1988), pp. 139–157.

do for their children, since for most there are no depictions of the woman acting as a mother.'[13] It is not until much later, in the book of Proverbs, we are given any real insight into their life and then it is in the form of an idealized portrait.[14] Moreover, in line with much of the teaching of the law, Proverbs indicates the father's role in child rearing is at least as important as the mother, especially as far as the education of the son is concerned.[15] Mostly it presents their roles as complementary to each other, father and mother both playing a role.[16] Child-rearing practices are not the Bible's central concern but the picture given is clearly one in which 'husbands and wives shared responsibility for the rearing of children'.[17] The early law treats father and mother as a couple, both equally responsible and both equally deserving of respect, without distinguishing between their roles.[18] Detailed child-rearing practices may have changed over time and it is certainly unwise to assume that there is one model of Old Testament family or one pattern of the roles and relationships that existed within it. Family life and structure then, as now, to some extent changed according to the circumstances of the time.[19]

The early stories of the family are essentially the story of God and how his will is accomplished in the messiness and failure of human relationships, rather than a human story which sets out a model of marriage and child-rearing practices. That is illustrated by the most extensive account we have of a wife and a mother in the early books of the Bible, that of the story of Rebekah.

3. Rebekah: the mother of Jacob (Genesis 24:1–67; 25:19–34; 26:34 – 27:46)

a. Rebekah as a chosen wife (24:1–67)

After Sarah's death, in Abraham's late old age, he took the initiative in finding a wife for Isaac, the son of the promise. He entrusts the responsibility for arranging the marriage to a servant who proves himself to be ideal, both fully alert to God's providence and anxious to seek God's blessing at every stage of his journey.[20] He offers, as Walter Brueggemann puts it, 'a worldview in which no parts of

---

[13] Schneider, *Mothers of Promise*, p. 218.
[14] Prov. 31 is explored in ch. 10.
[15] Prov. 1:1 – 9:18.
[16] Prov. 1.8; 6:20.
[17] Otwell, *Sarah Laughed*, p. 61.
[18] Exod. 20:12; 21:15, 17.
[19] See further Perdue *et al*, *Families in Ancient Israel*, pp. 22–28.
[20] 24:12–15, 21, 26–27, 31, 35, 40, 42, 45, 56.

experience lie beyond the purposes of God' and in which God works not in the 'spectacular' or miraculous but through the steady process of discernment.[21] Abraham's stipulations were that the servant should not find a wife among the Canaanites but from among his extended family back in Mesopotamia and that he should bring the woman back to Isaac not take Isaac to her.[22]

On reaching Nahor, on the caravan route in Abraham's ancestral territory, the servant made his way to the well outside the town so that his camels could be given water. It was evening, *the time the women go out to draw water* (11), so the servant prayed for God's leading and *before he had finished praying Rebekah came out with her jar on her shoulder* (15). Rebekah's attentiveness to his needs immediately revealed her qualities. Having provided the servant with a drink she offers to water the camels as well. Superficially this does not seem a great act – she was after all there with her water jar – but it is evident that she willingly volunteers more than the servant had a right to expect: 'the young woman's performance surpasses even the most optimistic expectations'.[23] She is revealing herself to be a woman of energy and initiative. All this time the servant is evaluating the woman. Is she a suitable partner for his master's son? Is she the one God has chosen for Isaac? She passes with flying colours on three scores: she is beautiful, she is a virgin and, as mentioned, she displays positive and active qualities. Beauty is a quality mentioned in reference to both Sarah[24] and Rachel.[25] It is obviously not insignificant. If the precise vocabulary chosen to describe Rebekah is different than that used of Sarah and Rachel they mean the same. Rebekah is said to be 'good in appearance'.[26] It all seems very promising, but what of her family?

Having rewarded her lavishly for her kindness, the servant asks who she is. Her reply signals that she comes from the right family line and when she continues to demonstrate her generosity in offering him hospitality and further supplies[27] the servant offers praise to God because he knows that *the LORD has led me on the journey to the house of my master's relatives* (27). As the servant rehearses his story in a long speech to Bethuel, her father, and Laban, her brother,

[21] W. Brueggemann, *Genesis*, Int (Atlanta: John Knox Press, 1982), p. 201.

[22] This is the reverse of the thrust of Gen. 2:24, which indicates it is the husband who leaves home and the wife who stays, thus having some continuing measure of protection, if necessary, from her blood family.

[23] Sternberg, *The Poetics of Biblical Narrative* (Bloomington: Indiana, 1985), cited by G. Wenham, *Genesis 16–50*, WBC (Dallas: Word, 1994), p. 144.

[24] Gen. 12:11, 14.

[25] Gen. 29:17.

[26] Cf. Schneider, *Mothers of Promise*, p. 44.

[27] Gen. 24:22–33.

carefully crafted to achieve his mission, they immediately agree in principle to the match, declaring, *This is from the LORD; we can say nothing to you one way or the other* (50). Laborious financial negotiations follow. Laban had already revealed his hand when, in verse 30, his actions in providing the servant with hospitality have been shown to be more to do with greed than the open-handed generosity that characterized his sister. The *costly gifts* which the servant gave to Laban and his mother (53) were probably the payment of the bride price since 'betrothal was customarily affected in the ancient Near East by large capital transfers from the bridegroom's family to the bride's family'.[28] Resisting any attempt at delay, the servant and Rebekah set off on the return journey the next day (55–61).

When they reached their destination, Rebekah, typically alert, caught sight of Isaac, her new husband, in the distance and once the servant had identified him *she took her veil and covered herself* (65). The wearing of a veil was not common in the Old Testament, and at least in Tamar's case sent out the signal that she was a prostitute.[29] Here it is a simple sign of modesty, anticipating her wedding day when brides were veiled.[30] The match indeed seems to have been 'made in heaven' for Isaac not only takes her as his wife (about which he might have had little choice) but *loved her and . . . was comforted* by her after the loss of his mother (67).

b. Rebekah as a flawed mother (25:19–28)

The marriage may have been made in heaven but that did not mean everything would be perfect on earth. God's providence did not exempt Isaac and Rebekah from experiencing the hardships and heartache which many other couples experience. The next time we read of Rebekah we read that Isaac *prayed to the LORD on behalf of his wife, because she was childless* (21). Rebekah shared with Sarah[31] and Rachel,[32] the positive blessing of beauty but also the heavy burden of infertility, a burden she also bore with later women like Hannah.[33] Each story testifies to the humiliation the childless woman suffered because of their inability to produce an heir, especially a male heir. It was a burden which, given the comment about Isaac's age when their

[28] Wenham, *Genesis 16–50*, p. 149. On the basis of Deut. 22:29, Wenham states the bride price was limited to fifty shekels, but that was the equivalent of several years' wages.
[29] Gen. 38:14, 15, 19.
[30] Wenham, *Genesis 16–50*, p. 152. Cf. Schneider, *Mothers of Promise*, pp. 53–55.
[31] Gen. 16:1–2.
[32] Gen. 29:31.
[33] 1 Sam. 1:1 – 2:11.

boys were eventually born (26), Isaac and Rebekah bore for many years. But there were no short cuts. Neither Rebekah's excellent lineage, nor her very positive qualities of character, nor her bustling activism, all very evident in chapter 24, could ensure the future.

The future of the chosen family, from a human viewpoint, was anything but secure. Rebekah's infertility was part of a God-given pattern. 'The matriarchs,' Schneider explains, 'are not a fertile group, highlighting how important the role of the Deity is to them to ensure they have children to carry on the promise.'[34] Just as Isaac was himself 'a child of promise' so the children of Isaac and Rebekah must also unmistakably be gifts of God, not accidents of biology. Like Eve at the beginning of time, giving birth required the help of the Lord. The role of the father and the mother, given that Isaac prays *on behalf of his wife*, is simply to pray. 'Barrenness cannot be overcome by the shrewdness of the parents. It can be dealt with only by the LORD of life.'[35]

When Rebekah falls pregnant and her hormones are playing havoc with her body, she receives an early signal from God that the twins to whom she gives birth will not have the easiest of relationship but they, and the families and nations to which they would give birth in turn, would find themselves in a conflicted relationship (23). One might have expected that the children who were born in the answer to such fervent prayer, and so evidently a gift of God's grace, would live in harmony with each other, the younger knowing his place and being subordinate to the older. But God has a deeper plan in mind and the children a different destiny than the one custom would have chosen, one in which against all odds *the elder will serve the younger* (23).

From the moment the birth occurs, the prophecy Rachel had received while pregnant is seen to be working itself out. When the younger brother, Jacob, *came out* he did so *with his hand grasping Esau's heel* (26). His challenge to Esau's supremacy is immediately apparent. 'The symbolism is everything,' writes Gordon Wenham. 'Here the second twin is seen trying desperately to catch up with the first. The struggle in the womb is obviously going to continue outside. The pattern for the rest of the story is set.'[36]

As often with siblings, these non-identical twin brothers were very different in appearance, interest and character, giving rise to very different ways of life. Esau was amply covered in red hair and Jacob had a smooth body; Esau became a hunter of game and Jacob was the home-bird who cooked the game; Esau was passive and had a

[34] Schneider, *Mothers of Promise*, p. 48.
[35] Brueggemann, *Genesis*, p. 214.
[36] Wenham, *Genesis 16–50*, p. 177.

'couldn't-care-less' attitude, given to satisfying immediate desires, and Jacob was restless, manipulative and always scheming for the long-term. The difference in character drew out different loyalties from their parents, with Isaac favouring Esau while Rebekah favoured Jacob. Although the subsequent story illustrates the destructive influence of favouritism in a family, this is not the narrator's primary concern, nor are we given any other information about Rebekah's childcare techniques. The storyteller does not use the apparently disastrous outcome to wag the finger and instruct his readers in the folly of preferring one child to another. Rather his interest lies elsewhere. In the subsequent story, neither Rebekah nor Isaac come out with credit but the account never deviates from its central purpose by providing lessons in child education or instructing us in the ancient art of motherhood. Any such lessons are implicit. The explicit reason soon becomes apparent.

c. Rebekah as a divine instrument (25:29–34; 26:34 – 27:46)

The love which Isaac and Rebekah once knew (24:67) had long since died and, as often happens when parents have become strangers to each other in a loveless marriage, they used their children as the means of communicating their true feelings for each other.

The twin peaks of the story of the rivalry between the sons fittingly enough involve food, both peaks revealing the real purpose of the story. The first peak occurs when Jacob manipulates Esau into selling his birthright as the older son in exchange for a good square meal (25:29–34). The agreement was 'no boyish prank that parental authority could reverse, for the transaction was sealed with an oath and oaths were binding'.[37]

The second peak occurred some time later when Isaac, now virtually blind, sought to do his duty and formally pass on his blessing (and so his rights) to Esau, his oldest son. Esau had obviously been a disappointment to his parents because he married not one but two Hittite women (26:34–35). Even so, regardless of his merits the unquestioned expectation was that according to the law of primogeniture, Esau would inherit his father's place and property. The transfer of blessing would occur once Esau had prepared his father a gourmet meal of wild game.

Eavesdropping on Isaac's conversation with Esau, Rebekah demonstrated that she had lost nothing of her earlier abilities to seize the initiative. So she got Jacob to rush ahead of Esau, kill and cook two young goats and prepare *some tasty food to eat* (27:7). There was

---

[37] J. Baldwin, *The Message of Genesis 12-50*, BST (Leicester: IVP, 1986), p. 106.

one fly in Rebekah and Jacob's ointment. Being blind, Isaac would identify his son not through his sight but through his touch, and Esau and Jacob had unmistakably differently textured skin. No matter, Rebekah is equal to the challenge and arranges a disguise which ensures Jacob would trick his father into thinking he was Esau when his stew was served before his brother's. The plot was successful and Jacob receives the birthright that conventionally belonged to Esau. Having solemnly blessed Jacob there was nothing Isaac could do to rescind the blessing.

Jacob was of course holding Esau to his word, even if in an underhanded way. What of Rebekah? Rebekah's role in Jacob obtaining Isaac's blessing bears out the truth of Tammi Schneider's observation that, 'The women [in Genesis] serve as more than just people who bear – who the mother is controls the destiny of the children.'[38]

At this stage Rebekah has become an unattractive person; she becomes a trickster who only cares about her favourite son and abuses her husband's frailty. Joyce Baldwin describes Rebekah's scheme as hare-brained and says it 'ran considerable risk of discovery, but she had thought it all out with care, and was prepared to take the consequences if it misfired'.[39] Her actions cannot be mitigated on the basis that she knew what she was doing and acted to bring about God's plan for Jacob. 'There are no hints in the entire narrative that she knows what she is doing.'[40] Her actions were plainly duplicitous and lacked integrity by any standard. Although it is perhaps unjust to put all the blame on her for what transpired. Gordon Wenham comments how, 'her energy complemented her husband's retiring nature'. Adding, 'but just as his love of the quiet life led him to neglect of his parental duties and indifference to ancient propriety, so her nature led her to overstep the bounds of moral behaviour'.[41]

Rebekah's manipulative action was used by God to bring about the fulfilment of his plan and the outworking of the prophecy she had received when pregnant. It does not justify her behaviour. God would have brought about his will for the elder to serve the younger in some other way if she had not acted as she did. The end does not justify the means. Even so, the story points to the way in which God's will triumphs not just when people are perfect, circumstances are ideal and actions above reproach. God's plan is achieved through less than perfect people, behaving in less than holy ways. An energetic and smart woman proves to be a fallible and biased mother, and yet

[38] Schneider, *Mothers of Promise*, p. 217.
[39] Baldwin, *Message of Genesis*, p. 115.
[40] Brueggemann, *Genesis*, p. 235.
[41] Wenham, *Genesis 16-50*, p. 215.

is chosen by God to bear a child who will inherit the promise, against all the conventional wisdom of the time. The future of God's chosen people belongs to Jacob and his heirs, thanks, humanly speaking, to his mother who behaved badly. Manipulative she was, but equally she was a conduit of God's grace.

The Bible's portrait of Rebekah is an honest one of a woman of great qualities but whose qualities are tarnished over time. In a marriage that began well she comes to experience the pain of disappointment and the dimming of the flame of love. She has the joy of being a mother of twins but one child disappoints and she becomes unhelpfully prejudiced in favour of the other. In a family which in some respects, although not all, appears typical, we are not presented with a subservient stay-at-home wife who was content to do the cooking and the sewing but who was devoid of her own opinion. In their earlier more ideal days, the partnership between father and mother seems equal, until the father's passivity brings the mother's activity to the fore. And God uses this flawed family to fulfil his purposes and the flawed relationships of the family to ensure that Jacob, not Esau, becomes the child of promise and the father of the great nation of Israel.

4. Women in contemporary society

Throughout the twentieth century, women in the Western world experienced progressive liberation. Some of the freedoms, as with the Suffragettes and their campaign for the right to vote, were hard fought. Others, like women in the employment market, were largely irreversible once women had played their part in the factories and the fields during the Second World War while the men were away. Opportunities in education and developments in contraceptive methods accelerated the movement towards equality and liberation.[42] Some people have been keen to blame the ills of the post-1960s society on the fact that women were no longer captive wives,[43] confined to their homes. So, the cry has gone up in some quarters, 'The woman's place is in the home!' Those who use the slogan often claim it is a biblical principle and departure from this Bible teaching lies at the root of our loss of a more stable and 'innocent' society.

---

[42] For details, see S. Bruley, *Women in Britain since 1900*, Social History in Perspective (London: Palgrave MacMillan, 1999) and I. Zweiniger-Bargielow, *Women in Twentieth Century Britain: Social, Cultural and Political Change* (London: Longman, 2001).

[43] The phrase 'captive wives' recalls a seminal book in the area by Hannah Gavron, entitled *The Captive Wife* (Harmonsdsworth: Penguin Books, 1968).

The reality is somewhat more complicated. Neither the explanation of changes in contemporary society,[44] nor the picture of 'the woman's place' is quite as straightforward.

Several factors need to be taken into account if we are to avoid applying the Bible's teaching superficially with the result that we are in danger of distorting it.

First, as we have seen, the Bible's emphasis on the upbringing of children is that it is the joint responsibility of the parents, not primarily the responsibility of the mother. Fathers, if anything, were considered to be more responsible. The Bible does not put forward a particular pattern or structure of child-rearing, even if there are principles to be observed.

Secondly, the separation of the home from work, which became so institutionalized through the Industrial Revolution and which is characteristic of our modern societies, was not characteristic of the cultures of the Bible. Men's work, although it may have been different from the woman's role, was not usually very distant from the home. The fields would have been adjacent to the home and the hunting not taken them away too far or for long. Some occupations, like that of shepherd, may have taken people away from home periodically but that was not the norm. Even in the later period of the Roman world, where role difference between men and women had developed and where men occupied the public spaces and women were more confined to the private space of the home, we should not think in terms of the contemporary separation of home and work. The public space men occupied in doing their work was usually the front part of the house, or a workshop immediately below an upstairs living place. There was a degree of family togetherness throughout the biblical cultures that is still largely absent today, although technological change once again is returning some work to the home and will have implications for the shape of family life to come.

Thirdly, the home was a place where the women, as we have seen, engaged in aspects of economic production. In biblical times, the woman's role involved the production and processing of food and materials, not simply the cooking or the mending. In larger households, as we shall see in chapter 10 and in reference to women who led house churches in the New Testament, the role of the wife in a

---

[44] For a wider view of the changes see F. Fukuyama, *The Great Disruption* (New York: The Free Press, 1999); R. Putnam, *Bowling Alone: The Collapse and Revival of American Community* (New York: A Touchstone Book, 2000). One significant change was that women no longer passed on religious knowledge and practice to their children. See C. G. Brown *The Death of Christian Britain* (London and New York: Routledge, 2001) and the challenges to Brown's argument in H. McLeod, *The Religious Crisis of the 1960s* (Oxford: Oxford University Press, 2007).

large household was a skilled and complex managerial task. Children would have shared with their parents in these economic tasks from an early age, much education being provided on the job. Wives, then, were not child-focused in the way some contemporary Christians imply, nor just about doing the housework chores or cooking the meal for their husbands after a day at the office.

Fourthly, while the formal situation has an undeniable bias towards patriarchy, the informal outworking of that within marriage may have been somewhat different and in practice there may have been a greater equality than the term patriarchy suggests. Undoubtedly it is Isaac, as the father, who has the legal right to transmit divine blessing to the next generation. But Rebekah subverts this right and ensures the blessing goes unexpectedly to Jacob, the younger son. Isaac and Rebekah's marriage seems to be one in which Rebekah plays a very active role in managing affairs and Isaac passively colludes with this. While it might be argued that Isaac and Rebekah's marriage may have been unusual in this regard, the picture is far from unique.

Faith and Roger Forster have pointed out the curious fact that, contrary to popular belief, the only time when someone is told to obey their marriage partner in the Bible is when Abraham is instructed to obey his wife Sarah, not vice versa.[45] This is usually disguised by our English translations, as when the NIV typically translates Genesis 21:12 as God saying to Abraham 'Listen to whatever Sarah tells you'. The word translated 'listen' in this verse is correctly translated in Genesis 22:18 as 'obey'. Gordon Wenham explains that 'it was Abraham's right to decide family policy, not Sarah's. [But] now he must submit to her, for her demands fit in with God's plans'.[46] Truth to tell, 1 Peter 3:6 puts Sarah forward as an example for wives to follow because she 'obeyed Abraham and called him her lord'.[47] But the apparent tension is resolved when Wenham's explanation, which goes to the heart of the matter, is taken as the determining factor. Blind submission by either party is never

[45] F. Forster and R. Forster, *Women and the Kingdom* (London: Push Publishing and Ichthus Christian Fellowship, 2010), p. 13. This has implications for those who argue for the retention of the word 'obey' in the marriage service. Eph. 5:22 instructs wives to 'submit yourselves to your husbands' which is a different concept than that of obeying and is an instruction given in the context of a discussion about mutual submission in marriage (see Eph. 5:21).

[46] Wenham, *Genesis 16–50*, p. 83.

[47] Faith and Roger Forster comment on this that 'the only occasion where Sarah humorously refers to Abraham as her "lord" was in regard to them having intercourse together in order to conceive the promised child. In other words it expressed her sexual submission to her husband even though she was 90 years old (cf. 1 Corinthians 7:4)!', *Women and Kingdom*, p. 13.

encouraged. The dominant biblical strain of teaching is one of voluntary and mutual submission within marriage[48] and even more one where both parties submit themselves to the will of the Lord. When this is done, concepts of hierarchy and questions of who's in charge become irrelevant.

5. Concluding comment

The Old Testament presents the role of women as mothers and homemakers as an honourable one, not to be considered in any way of secondary importance to the work of men. Women were never *only* or *mere* wives and mothers.[49] Even in a patriarchal context, their role was much more complex than these titles suggest to a contemporary reader. They were far from being chattels of their husband but are presented as persons able to think and act for themselves. They serve with their husbands in the education and upbringing of their children and in the economically productive tasks of the household. They are shown respect and have freedom to use their gifts and abilities. The Old Testament is far from matriarchal, but it is 'seemingly less patriarchal than is often assumed'.[50]

Given this, we should not draw a straight line from the Old Testament picture to the contemporary world and argue simplistically that contemporary women should not work but be confined to the role of homemaker. The contemporary role of homemaker does not neatly equate with that of the patriarchal world where there was no separation of the home from the work place. The honourable role of wife and mother may be fulfilled in a number of ways but its significance is never to be underestimated. What the many stories of wives and mothers in Scripture teach us is that God's will does triumph through the different patterns that men and women may adopt for family life and in all the less-than-perfect rough and tumble of their ordinary, not textbook, lives.

[48] See 1 Cor. 7:1–7; Eph. 5:21.
[49] Meyers, *Discovering Eve*, p. 139.
[50] Forster and Forster, *Women and Kingdom*, p. 12.

Judges 19:1–30
5. Victimized women

The Bible is nothing if not realistic. It presents the world as it is, both in the splendour of human relationships and in their savage awfulness. Its stories frequently bear witnesses to how far relationships have degenerated since Adam and Eve's original disobedience and how far short of God's creation intention men and women have fallen. This is never more so than when it reports a number of frightening incidents that involve women, which Phyllis Trible has appropriately named *Texts of Terror*.[1]

1. Reading Scripture

The horrifying experiences of some women are recorded matter-of-factly, usually without interpretation and often even without emotion. Telling a story can never be an entirely neutral act. The act of story-telling necessarily involves the narrator adopting a particular perspective, selecting some aspects as more significant than others and giving more attention to some people than others. Even so, the primary narrative approach of the Bible, in line with all good story-telling, is to let the story speak for itself. So, the stories where women are victims are told without interpretation, without moral lessons being appended and usually without blame being apportioned. We are left to make up our own mind as to what was right and wrong, good or bad. Sometimes the verdict is clear, or the context drives us to a particular, inescapable conclusion. But often this is not so.

As readers, of course, we need to be aware that we cannot help but bring our own perspectives to our reading of the stories. And since the vast majority of teachers and preachers have traditionally been

[1] P. Trible, *Texts of Terror: Literary-Feminist Readings of Biblical Narratives* (London: SCM, 1984).

men, the stories are often seen from a male perspective – even the texts of obvious female terror – which results in minimizing the blame men shoulder for the acts of cruelty and even shifting the blame onto the women, or explaining the horror of the male behaviour away.[2] The passage that will be examined in more detail below has often been explained in terms of an abuse of hospitality. And so it is. But the woman who is the one who suffers most in the story can sometimes be seen almost as if she is a non-person in the story.

2. Women as victims

Several prominent women are victims in the Old Testament. Among them is Hagar, the victim of Abraham's impatience and Sarah's displeasure.[3] Dinah, Jacob and Leah's daughter, is another victim. She was raped by Shechem with fatal consequences for him and his fellow citizens.[4] Tamar is also victim to her family's indifference and then the almost-victim of male justice until she exposes its hypocrisy.[5] Later, there is another Tamar who was raped by the royal prince Amnon and avenged by her brother Absalom two years later.[6] But the most shocking of all is the woman with no name who fell victim to a Levite's lust, a city's violent abuse and her master's callous indifference. Her tragic story is recorded in Judges 19.

3. The woman with no name

a. In those days . . . (1)

The setting of this episode is significant. *In those days Israel had no king* (1) signals much more than this incident happened in the time before there was a monarchy. The phrase occurs four times at the end of Judges[7] and captures the increasing lawlessness, violence and immorality of Israelite life, which it attributes particularly to the absence of godly leadership. Early judges had exercised some restraint on people's sins, but later judges had been progressively less effective in doing so, not least because their own personal godliness was in rapid decline. The path on which Israel was set inexorably led to the despairing picture that is painted in the final

---

[2] Still today, a considerable number of people believe that women who are rape victims have themselves to blame for it in some way or another. See below, pp. 88–89.

[3] Gen. 16:1–16; 21:9–21.

[4] Gen. 34:1–31.

[5] Gen. 38:1–26.

[6] 2 Sam. 13:1–38.

[7] 17:6; 18:1; 19:1; 21:25.

chapters of Judges of a society that had rejected God, where anarchy reigned and people were dehumanized. On this path women increasingly become the victims.

Women play a prominent role in the book of Judges. To start with, heroines like Deborah or Jael[8] save the nation at a time of crisis, as well as, in Deborah's case, serve it well as a leader in less troubled days. But as law disintegrates and godliness declines they are more and more presented as the victims of men's foolish behaviour. Jephthah's daughter pays for such folly with her life, even if Jephthah's vow was well-intentioned.[9] Even Samson's unnamed mother must have wept as her longed-for son came to behave with spiritual recklessness.[10] The finale, in every sense the climax of the message of Judges, is an account of the rape of the women of Benjamin.[11] What immediately leads to that scenario is the story of one unnamed woman who suffered extreme terror at the hands of men.

Dennis Olson rightly captures the significance of the role of women in Judges:

> the changing power relationship, independence and treatment of the many women characters in the book function as benchmarks for the health and faithfulness of God's people . . . The general decline from women as the subject of independent action to woman as the object of man's actions and desires in the book of Judges coincides with the gradual decline of Israel's social and religious life during the Judges era. The decline culminates with the atrocity of rape and murder committed against the Levite's concubine in Judges 19, certainly one of the most brutal and violent scenes in all of Scripture.[12]

The treatment of women, then, serves as a thermometer, measuring Israel's spiritual temperature.

b. Now a Levite . . . took a concubine (1–2b)

The subject of the story is a Levite, a man of person and rank. In other words, this is a story about him. The man lives in remote

---

[8] Judg. 4:1–23.
[9] Judg. 11:29–40.
[10] Judg. 13:1 – 14:4, after which she disappears from the scene. We should note the more ambiguous role of other women in Samson's life who are both victims and villains in the role they play as temptresses (14:1 – 16:22).
[11] Judg. 21:1–25.
[12] D. T. Olson, 'The Book of Judges', NIB, vol. 2 (Nashville: Abingdon, 1998), p. 872.

Ephraim but *took a concubine from Bethlehem*, which would have been much more populous and where women would have been more accessible to him than in his own community. At this stage, there is nothing on the surface of the story to alarm us even if the bells begin to ring when we dig a little deeper. It could be that he used his position as a Levite to his own advantage but taking a concubine would then have been considered acceptable practice and would not have been viewed as questionable sexual behaviour. Trent Butler points out that Gideon had done this and the concubine's role might be better understood if she was seen as a 'secondary wife'.[13] Acceptable or not, one is struck by the fact that the concubine is presented as the silent, passive object in the story. She is not even given her name. She is the property of the men in her life, for them to dispose of her according to their wishes.

Before long she runs away from the Levite and returns to her father. The NIV's *she was unfaithful to him* (2) implies she was responsible for the fracture in their relationship. The key Hebrew word may mean she was 'angry' with him, rather than 'unfaithful'.[14] It could well be that his behaviour had provoked her into leaving and she did what everyone else was doing, namely, what was right in her own eyes.[15]

c. Four months later (2c–10)

After four months the Levite went after her. This simple statement raises several questions to which there are no answers. Why did he wait *four months* (2)? Does it show indifference or was he seeking to put himself in the right frame of mind before setting off? Was he waiting for her true character to show itself, if indeed she had committed adultery? Why did he go after her? Was it because he loved her or was he seeking cold justice, desiring to get his 'property' back? If he was seeking genuine reconciliation, why in his subsequent behaviour does he frequently ignore her? Why did the father greet him so warmly (3)? Was it that he was 'lonely and looking for a drinking partner'?[16] The questions flow but the answers are unyielding.

Whatever his motive, the Levite is welcomed by the concubine's father and seems to bond with him immediately. For a few days the

---

[13] T. Butler, *Judges*, WBC (Nashville: Nelson, 2009), p. 417. The result of Gideon's taking of a concubine suggests it was not a wise or right action on his part. The word *pîlegeš* seems to suggest an ambiguous status which is akin to marriage in some respects but not in others.

[14] NRSV and ESV mg.

[15] Judg. 17:6; 21:25.

[16] Butler, *Judges*, p. 420.

Levite enjoys her parents' hospitality. The wine flows, the food keeps coming and the company is convivial. Nothing is said of the concubine. The focus is on the men. They remain the subject, the lead actors; she is a mere bit part.

After a few days, the bonhomie begins to wear thin and the Levite is anxious to depart for his own home, concubine safely in tow. The father presses his hospitality on his increasingly impatient guest until the Levite would have no more of it. Their bonding, as Trible comments, unravels and is replaced by rivalry and a power struggle in which the daughter/concubine is a silent pawn who 'suffers through neglect'.[17] *Unwilling to stay another night, the man left and went towards Jebus (that is, Jerusalem)* (10). Is the writer being deliberately ironic when he adds, *with his two saddled donkeys and his concubine?* Is she of no more worth to him than they are?

d. We will go on to Gibeah (11–21)

If the decision to leave Bethlehem in the evening was foolish, the decision to bypass Jerusalem and press on to Gibeah was disastrous. The arrangements to head for Gibeah are made not with the concubine but with the man's *servant* (11–12). She is apparently not consulted and her wishes not considered. The reason given is that Jebus would not have been a safe haven for them, as Israelites were not resident there. So they made for Gibeah and reached it as *the sun set* (14). Modern anxieties about arriving late at night without pre-arranged hospitality would not have been a concern for them. The obligation to provide hospitality to strangers ran deep in Israelite veins and they were confident that if they made for the *city square* they would soon be invited into someone's home. So that is what they did but, alas, for some time without success.

Eventually a man who was not a local, *an old man from the hill country of Ephraim* (16) and so from the same home territory as the Levite, who had been working late, came to the rescue and offered them hospitality. Accepting the invitation, the Levite seems ingratiating, referring to himself and his companions as *your servants* and saying that they have enough provisions with them so they would be no trouble: '*We don't need anything*' (19). When he refers to the concubine, however, he is condescending, speaking of her as a 'maidservant' (NIV simply translates the word he uses as 'woman'), which is a 'negative and demeaning term'.[18] So a quiet evening of refreshment begins, or so they think.

---

[17] Trible, *Texts of Terror*, p. 69.
[18] V. Matthews cited by Butler, *Judges*, p. 423.

e. Bring out the man . . . (22–26)

What followed was terrifying for all concerned, but most of all for the concubine. Their enjoyable and relaxed evening was brought to an abrupt halt as a mob of 'downright boorish'[19] local men pounded on the door and demanded the male visitor be sent out so they could make him the object of their sexual sport (22). By any standards it was a perverted violation of the rules of hospitality. The tragic irony was that 'having eschewed the hospitality of foreigners and entrusted himself to Israelites he finds himself in a virtual Sodom'.[20] The host appears courageous as he goes out to negotiate with the mob and refuses to surrender his male guest. But any sense that he is a decent man doing the right thing quickly evaporates when he immediately uses his own daughter and his guest's concubine as a bargaining chip: two women in the place of one man. Acting in accordance with the values and customs of his time, the host stood his ground. To abuse a man was unacceptable. Homosexual rape would grossly violate the hospitality code, which was heavily biased in favour of men. To violate a woman or two, on the other hand, did not seem to have the same implications or carry the same weight.

The most troubling aspect of this episode of this story is the ease with which men are willing to hand over women to become play-things of the mob. They are told *'Do to them whatever you wish'.* Literally translated, the host ominously says, 'Do to them what is right in your own eyes'. The women are powerless pawns to be moved about the board at the will of the men who wield the power in a totally unequal relationship. Men are to be protected. Women are to be dispensed with, whenever it suits. The woman becomes a victim of the cowardly male host, the indifferent Ephraimite Levite and the baying men of Gibeah, who are all complicit in the evil that follows.

The crowd seem to be left outside the door while the men discuss what to do inside. The host's daughter drops out of view. But when the mob become more restive, the Levite does not hesitate but volunteers his concubine to be their prey. He opens the doors and pushes her outside where she is subjected to prolonged, gang rape (25). As Tammi Schneider points out, 'The text does not attempt to minimize or sanitize what happened to her,'[21] but neither does it glory in it. It briefly reports what happened without any encouragement

[19] B. G. Webb, *The Book of Judges: An Integrated Reading*, JSOT Sup (Sheffield: JSOT Press, 1987), p. 189.

[20] Webb, *Judges*, p. 189. Cf. Gen. 19.

[21] T. J. Schneider, *Judges*, Berit Olam: Studies in Hebrew Narrative and Poetry (Collegeville: Liturgical Press, 2000), p. 262.

to voyeurism. After hours of torture, when the men had finished with her they dumped her body on the doorstep, as if she were a mouse who has been the plaything of a cat. Like the mouse, having served their purpose, she is now discarded and just as lifeless.

Her master has apparently slept comfortably and securely inside, untroubled by a guilty conscience, and shows no concern for her. He was not up early, ready to care for her the moment she returned, still less did he go searching for her. So she is left lying there, abandoned *until daylight* (26). When the Levite eventually stirred, it reads as if he was quite prepared to go back home without her if she had not returned by the time he was ready to depart.[22] He finds her on the doorstep but could get no response from her. In fact, she has never once spoken in the entire story. She has been a voiceless one, a silent object to whom things are done, throughout. Now the experience has either deeply traumatized her and left her unconscious, or, more likely, killed her. The abuse, rape and violence had culminated in murder. So the Levite picks up her battered body as if she was 'a sack of wheat'[23] or a carpet for sale in a market, and *put her on his donkey and set out for home* (28). Nothing in the story gives us any indication of his feelings. He does not mourn her. The silence seems calculated to present him as an uncaring, cold and heartless man.

f. He took a knife and cut up his concubine . . . (27–30)

The horror of the treatment the concubine received at the hands of the men of Gibeah is compounded by the horror of the treatment she then receives in death from the hands of her husband. When he gets home *he took a knife and cut up his concubine* (29). Years before, Abraham had taken a knife in order to slice up his son as a sacrifice, but the difference is that in Genesis 22, God steps in and stops the heinous act. 'In Judges the acts were initiated by men against women and carried through to completion.'[24] The Levite callously dissects her corpse *into twelve parts and sent them into all areas of Israel* (29). In an 'unnecessarily brutal' act,[25] he shows no respect for her, does not treat her body with any tender affection, and pitilessly carves her up just as if she were an animal carcass to be displayed for sale in a butcher's shop window. Yet, instead of displaying her dismembered body in a shop, he distributes its segments all over Israel. One can imagine the Levite justifying his action. He did it as a

[22] Trible, *Texts of Terror*, p. 78.
[23] J. C. McCann, *Judges,* Int (Louisville: John Knox Press, 2002), p. 131.
[24] Trible, *Texts of Terror*, p. 80.
[25] McCann, *Judges*, p. 133.

warning sign to Israel. It was to teach them a lesson. The gruesome nature of his parcel would get the people to sit up and take notice of the depths to which they had sunk. Shock tactics were needed. Nothing less would suffice. What he did was 'a morbid and twisted adaptation of the customary means of calling up an emergency military force in the ancient Near East'.[26] It was akin to what Saul would do later when he cut a pair of oxen in pieces and distributed them to the tribes of Israel to summon them (successfully) to battle.[27] On the surface, the Levite's action seems to have paid off. The people's reaction is one of horror. *'Such a thing has never been seen or done, not since the days the Israelites came up out of Egypt. Just imagine! We must do something! So speak up!'* (30).

Yet, however much he may rationalize his action, the truth is that in degrading her body he confirms that he is no better than any of the other men in the story. He treats her as his property, an object to be used and abused as he pleases and disposed of in a manner that suits him. His speech that rallies the crowd to the cause confirms he is self-absorbed. He tells them how the mob 'came after me and surrounded the house, intending to kill me' (20:5), before mentioning that his concubine was raped and killed. His words seem intent on playing down any responsibility he has for the tragedy.[28] Olsen's verdict on the man seems hard to refute: 'although subtly construed' he may be 'the most sinister character' in the story.[29]

Furthermore, on closer examination the people's reaction is more ambiguous than it might seem. 'Something must be done', they cry. But what? Thinking the best, we hope they mean they should repent of their lawlessness and reform their lives with a view to creating a more wholesome, less violent, society. But what follows suggests they have other forms of response in mind. What the people have in mind is civil war. The Levite's action only serves to unleash further violence, not to stem it, as the whole of Israel gathers at Mizpah for a war council and agree to give Benjamin 'what they deserve for their outrageous act done in Israel'.[30] The outcome is that 25,000 Benjaminite soldiers die in battle and their towns are set on fire.[31] It is a form of justice, but chiefly one in which they have taken the law into their own hands and one in which they only consult God rather belatedly rather than consulting him to start with.[32]

---

[26] Olson, 'Judges', p. 878.
[27] 1 Sam. 11:7.
[28] Webb, *Judges*, p. 191.
[29] Olson, 'Judges', p. 877.
[30] Judg. 20:1–12.
[31] Judg. 20:35–37.
[32] Judg. 20:18, 26–28.

The slaughter of 25,000 of their brothers and the sacking of their towns did not satisfy the tribes' appetite for vengeance, so further violence is unleashed. In the second phase it is the women who become the focus of suffering again. Many women are killed, along with men who remain alive, and four hundred virgins are raped. Later still, a further two hundred young women are abducted from a festival in Shiloh and forced into marriage with the surviving Benjaminites to ensure the continuance of the tribe.[33] The rape and death of one woman has escalated into the rape, abduction and murder of many. The women are the ones who pay the most costly price for the social and sexual anarchy of the men of Gibeah.

Chapters 17 – 21 are a carefully crafted section of Judges that brings its message to a climax. The story does not just happen to end there. These stories are not incidental but deliberately chosen because they epitomize what happens when God's laws are set aside. Society becomes rotten and individualism runs riot. Everyone does as they see fit, without reference to anyone other than themselves. And when that happens, the least powerful, who are the most vulnerable, become the victims. Repeatedly through history women are found among the vulnerable. They become not so much the sinners as the sinned against.[34]

4. The contemporary picture

The story of the concubine with no name is all too contemporary. Newspapers continue to report women who are abused and raped by soldiers on the battlefield, drunks in the town centre and relatives behind closed doors. Securing justice for the victims of rape is often difficult and men still excuse their behaviour and find reasons to blame women for the suffering inflicted upon them.

One survey of recent statistics, which is consistent with other research in the field, reports as follows:

In Britain:
- 45% of women have experienced some form of domestic violence, sexual assault or stalking.
- Around 21% of girls experience some form of child sexual abuse.
- At least 80,000 women suffer rape every year.

---

[33] Judg. 20:12, 20–23. The figure is inferred by the reference, in 20:47, to 600 Benjaminite men.
[34] Trible, *Texts of Terror*, p. 81, says of the Levite's concubine that 'this woman is the most sinned against'.

- In a survey for Amnesty International, over 1 in 4 respondents thought a woman was partially or totally responsible for being raped if she was wearing sexy or revealing clothing, and more than 1 in 5 held the same view if a woman had had many sexual partners.
- On average, two women a week in England and Wales are killed by a violent partner or ex-partner. This constitutes nearly 40% of all female homicide victims.
- 70% of incidents of domestic violence result in injury. [35]

Domestic violence is estimated to cost victims, services and the state a total of around £23 billion a year.

Around the world:

- At least one in three women is beaten, coerced into sex or otherwise abused by an intimate partner in the course of her lifetime.
- Women aged 15–44 are more at risk from rape and domestic violence than from cancer, motor accidents, war and malaria, according to World Bank data.

In addition there is the scandal of human trafficking:

The United Nations estimates that 700,000 to 4 million women and children are trafficked around the world for purposes of forced prostitution, labor and other forms of exploitation every year. Trafficking is estimated to be a $7 billion dollar annual business.

50,000 women and children are trafficked into the United States from no less than 49 countries every year. As many as 750,000 women and children have been trafficked into the United States over the last decade. [36]

5. Conclusion

Contemporary Western culture has become a culture of victimhood, often trivializing it, with the result that we fail to identify genuine victims and are blind to the real injustice that has made them so. Nothing should be allowed to trivialize the indisputable tragedies of the women victims of the Old Testament or of their contemporary successors.

[35] <http://www.whiteribboncampaign.co.uk/node/218>.
[36] <http://humanrightsteam.org/educational-information/human-trafficking-facts-figures/>.

In words that could apply exactly to the Levite's concubine, Jonathan Sacks writes:

> The politics of victimhood is bad politics. The psychology of victimhood is bad psychology. A victim is by definition an object not a subject, passive rather than active, a done-to rather than a doer. If you see yourself as a victim, then you locate the cause of your condition in something outside of yourself. This means you cannot change your situation.[37]

He continues, quoting Martin Seligman, that victimhood is 'learned helplessness'. That is often true but it is not the whole story. Genuine victims suffer not so much from *learned* helplessness as *enforced* helplessness. Some victims may be able to do something to overcome their lot, but there are some real victims who cannot do so. The Levite's concubine was one such.

The day of the Judges is not past and its sobering message is still needed. Yet Judges is but one voice, albeit a painful and not-to-be ignored voice, in the biblical conversation about women. Phyllis Trible points out that in the Greek Old Testament Judges is followed by Ruth and the arrangement is no accident. In Ruth, which is also set in the time of the judges, there is no 'misogyny, violence or vengeance'. The women are not passive victims or objects; they are clearly active subjects. Ruth speaks with a different voice, one that brings a 'healing word in the days of the Judges'; a message which speaks of the possibility of redemption even in a patriarchal society.[38] Judges' voice must be heard loud and clear, but so too must that of Ruth.

---

[37] J. Sacks, *The Home We Build Together* (London and New York: Continuum, 2007), p. 62.
[38] Trible, *Texts of Terror*, p. 85.

Judges 4:1 – 5:31
6. Leading women

We have grown accustomed to women occupying high positions of power and authority in our contemporary world. Several women have served as the presidents or prime ministers of their countries since Mrs Sirimavo Bandaranaike became the first women head of government as Prime Minister of Sri Lanka in 1960. In education, industry, medicine, law, welfare services and civil administration, women have occupied the highest offices. While they may still be under-represented,[1] the glass ceiling of yesteryear has been irreparably damaged.

Some hold strongly that the Bible teaches leadership should be male,[2] but is this truly the picture it presents? The issue needs defining more carefully. Are we asking about what the Bible describes or what it prescribes, what it reports or what it teaches? Are we asking about what is or what ought to be? Are we asking about the nation of Israel or the New Testament church? Are we talking about leadership in any sphere or leadership within a defined sphere, such as the church?

The Bible encompasses a rich variety of situations, times and cultures and, unlike a contemporary book of systematic theology, there is no single chapter or passage that contains the comprehensive answer to the variety of questions we may wish to raise. In approaching an answer we need to examine carefully the several relevant passages in their own right, with all the tensions and differences between them, and then build a cumulative picture before coming to a coherent biblical answer, assuming there is one. Once we have done that, we are still left with the question of how this coherent

---

[1] At the time of writing 18 women are CEOs of Fortune 500 companies in the USA and less than 14% of FTSE-100 companies in the UK had women on their boards.

[2] E.g., D. Pawson, *Leadership is Male* (Crowborough: Highland Books, 1988).

biblical picture relates to our contemporary world.[3] R. T. France somewhat starkly phrased the problem of application when discussing the legitimacy of women in ministry like this:

> To put it simply, even if one concludes that Paul forbade women in Ephesus and Corinth to hold positions of authority in the church, does this mean that they may not do so in our churches today? Indeed, had Paul been writing to twentieth-century Manchester, would he have said the same as he said to first-century Ephesus?[4]

Here we begin the task of composing a cumulative picture of women in leadership by examining one part of the picture. Other chapters, particularly in Part 4, will focus on other aspects that are necessary if a cumulative picture is to be achieved.

Several women occupy specific leadership roles in the Old Testament. Micah 6:4 speaks of Miriam as a leader alongside Moses. Less happily, Jezebel exercises huge political influence as Ahab's queen[5] and Athaliah usurps the throne and reigns as sole sovereign for six years.[6] Positively, Esther courageously used her position as Xerxes' queen at a crucial time[7] and her interventions led to the threatened genocide of the Jews being abandoned. James Hurley, himself a complementarian, rightly comments that 'the Old Testament does not offer many examples of women holding civil office. When it does, however, it shows no prejudice against them on account of their sex'.[8] He subsequently adds, 'Women were not usually in the public eye; they were, however, mightily used of God in the deliverance of his people and, whenever they do appear in public roles, are readily accepted in them'.[9]

The most outstanding example of a woman leader is Deborah. Women play a vital role throughout the book of Judges either as

---

[3] See further R. Hays, *The Moral Vision of the New Testament: A Contemporary Introduction to New Testament Ethics* (London and New York: T & T Clark, 1996). Hays helpfully sets out four steps to take in the process of coming to contemporary ethical decisions based on scripture. Step 1: descriptive, reading each text carefully. Step 2: synthetic, placing each text in its canonical context. Step 3: hermeneutical, relating the text to our contemporary culture. Does the text have the status of law, principle, paradigm or metaphor? Step 4: pragmatic, working out how to live the text in today's world.

[4] R. T. France, *Women in the Church's Ministry: A Test Case for Biblical Hermeneutics*, The Didsbury Lectures 1995 (Carlisle: Paternoster, 1995), p. 23.

[5] 1 Kgs 16:29 – 21:26; 2 Kgs 9:30–37.

[6] 2 Kgs 11:1–21; 2 Chr. 22:2, 10 – 23:21.

[7] Esth. 4:14.

[8] J. B. Hurley, *Man and Woman in Biblical Perspective* (Leicester: IVP, 1981), p. 48.

[9] Hurley, *Man and Woman*, pp. 48, 50.

courageous heroines or tragic victims. Among the most prominent characters in the book are Achsah, Jael, Jephthah's daughter, Samson's mother and his several lovers, the Levite's concubine and wives for the Benjaminites.[10] But this list is far from complete.[11] Given the patriarchal context of Judges, the numerous references to women are surprising, although patriarchy was to develop more under the later monarchy than at this earlier stage. The role of women in Judges, it has been suggested, is often to shed light on male arrogance. And so it does, even if that is not the only explanation for their role. No woman in the book plays a more vital part than Deborah, who is named as one of Israel's major judges.

1. Deborah: the female judge (4:4–5)

The precise meaning of the role of the judges is debated but all are bringers of justice in one way or another. Deborah achieves this both in her judicial role and as an outstanding spiritual and inspiring military leader. The writer takes enormous care in introducing Deborah. Trent Butler comments that in introducing her, as a 'woman',[12] 'prophetess' and 'wife', 'the writer does everything the Hebrew language allows to emphasize this is a female not a male'.[13] Perhaps the order in which she is introduced, as a woman first, prophet second and only then as a wife also indicates the writer's view of what is significant about her.

To say that she was the wife of Lappidoth does not mean that she would have spent her time doing domestic chores. It is evident that in her role as judge she would have had little time for such concerns.[14] Nor does the reference to her as a wife reduce her status, as if she only has significance by being identified through her husband. It is a natural as well as traditional way of speaking. Sirimavo Bandaranaike was introduced at the beginning of the chapter as *Mrs* Bandaranaike. She was Prime Minister of Sri Lanka as a widow on three occasions for a total of over eighteen years[15] in her own right and the reference to her married status does not carry any implication that she was in

[10] 1:12–15; 4:18–23; 11:29–40; 13:1–25; 14:1 – 16:22; 19:1–30; 21:1–25.

[11] There is also mention of Sisera's mother and her wise ladies (5:28–30), Gideon's concubine who is Abimelech's mother (8:31 – 9:3), an unnamed woman (9:53), Jephthah's mother and stepmother (11:1–2), friends of Jephthah's daughter (11:37–38) and young women who remember her (11:40), Micah's mother (17:1–6), the virgin daughter in Gibeah (19:24) and the young women of Shiloh (21:21).

[12] The word 'woman' is curiously omitted from the NIV and NRSV.

[13] T. Butler, *Judges*, WBC (Nashville: Thomas Nelson, 2009), p. 90.

[14] Hurley, *Man and Woman*, p. 48.

[15] Mrs Bandaranaike was Prime Minster of Sri Lanka 1960–65, 70–77 and 94–2000. Her husband had been Prime Minister of Ceylon but was assassinated in 1959.

some way governing under the authority of her husband. Indeed, given that Lappidoth is not otherwise known as a name and 'he' is not described as 'the son of . . . ' some hold that the Hebrew is a mistranslation and does not refer to Deborah's husband so much as describing her as 'a woman of fire'[16] or 'torch lady'.[17] This suggestion is probably ill-founded and there is no persuasive reason to deny the phrase is intended to identify Deborah as Lappidoth's wife. Nonetheless, the comment may be intended as ironic, especially as Judges is full of irony.[18] This 'mere wife' of Lappidoth turns out to be a powerful judge and military leader, while Lappidoth himself is unknown, 'scarcely more than a footnote' in the account of a 'formidable lady'![19]

Some have made much of the absence of any reference to her being raised up by the Lord and the absence of the formula that 'the Spirit of the LORD came upon her' which we read in reference to others.[20] Indeed, Deborah does stand out as different from other judges and not simply because of her gender. However, the significant differences do not relate to the absence of any particular formula of words and what marks her out as exceptional provides evidence that she was indeed called by God and filled with the Spirit of the Lord. She is the only major judge 'the narrator casts in an unequivocally positive light'.[21] She 'is the only character-judge who does something besides killing enemies' and alone is qualified and respected as a judge before any military crisis erupts.[22] She speaks unequivocally the word of the Lord (6) and her credibility in doing so is unquestioned. Furthermore, her work has an impact on more tribes than that of any other judge.[23]

In her judicial role *she held court under the Palm of Deborah between Ramah and Bethel in the hill country of Ephraim, and the Israelites went up to her to have their disputes decided* (5). This simple, factual statement is a rich commendation of her character and work. It tells us she had established a public reputation for the exercise not only of great wisdom and judicial knowledge but, given

---

[16] W. C. Gafney, *Daughters of Miriam: Women Prophets in Ancient Israel* (Minneapolis: Fortress Press, 2008), p. 90.

[17] J. C. McCann, *Judges*, Int (Louisville: John Knox Press, 2002), pp. 51–52.

[18] Butler, *Judges*, p. 92.

[19] M. Wilcock, *The Message of the Judges*, BST (Leicester: IVP, 1992), p. 61.

[20] T. R. Schreiner, 'The Valuable Ministries of Women in the Context of Male Leadership', *RBMW*, p. 216. The formula 'the Spirit of the LORD came upon him' (or equivalent) is found in 3:10 (Othniel); 6:34 (Gideon); 11:29 (Jephthah); 14:6, 19 and 15:14 (Samson) but is not used of every male judge.

[21] D. I. Block, cited by Gafney, *Daughters of Miriam*, p. 93.

[22] M. Bal, cited by Butler, *Judges*, p. 93.

[23] Butler, *Judges*, p. 91.

the context, of spiritual insight too. There is no basis for suggesting that she exercised a more restricted ministry than her male prophetic colleagues because her prophetic role 'seems to be limited to private and individual instruction' rather than being exercised in a public forum.[24] Such a claim is mystifying and only justified on the basis of an ideological reading of the text. The point of verse 5 is surely rather the reverse. It enhances her reputation by pointing to the public (and typical) location of her ministry.

2. Deborah: the military motivator (4:6–23)

Once Judges has established her standing and the nature of her existing ministry, it turns its attention to her role in the defeat of King Jabin's Canaanite army who were the latest in a series of tribal neighbours to trouble Israel. Characteristic of any leader, Deborah acts while others passively watch and do nothing.[25] She need not have troubled herself. The various geographic notes in the chapter tell us that she lived in the south of the country and the troubles were focused in the north. She could have excused herself as busy with other things and argued that the northern tribes should have taken the initiative in sorting out their own problems. What could she do about it, living so far away? But what makes a leader is their determination to act to make a difference, and Deborah certainly does that.

When she takes action it is first to call for Barak and to pass on the Lord's instruction to him: he was to go into battle against General Sisera's troops at the River Kishon. Her ear was tuned to God's wavelength while others were deaf to his voice. The position she adopted was not only that of a natural leader but one who was spiritually sensitive, full of faith and attuned to God. Secondly, she assured Barak that God had granted him victory, which, true to her prophecy, came about in a surprising way. Thirdly, at his request and whatever his motivation, she agrees to accompany Barak as he summons all the tribes of Israel to arms and goes into battle. We are told three times (9 twice, 10) that she went with him, which seems 'to rule out the conclusion that commentators have sometimes reached – namely, that Deborah needed a man to do the fighting'.[26] Fourthly, she prophesies that because of Barak's hesitancy, in spite of victory, *the honour will not be yours for the LORD will deliver Sisera into the hands of a woman* (9), which happens when Sisera,

[24] This position is argued by Schreiner, 'Ministries of Women', p. 216.
[25] Examples of such passive non-involvement are cited in the Song of Deborah, on which, see below p. 98.
[26] McCann, *Judges*, p. 52.

fleeing exhausted from the scene of battle, is assassinated by Jael, another robust woman (16–24). The timorous man Barak[27] is thus sandwiched between two women who prove the real heroes of the story.

However much Judges unabashedly records her leadership, some have sought to qualify it and we must now consider the basis on which they do so. It has often been argued that Deborah was only trusted with leadership because the men were too cowardly to step up to their responsibilities. Piper and Grudem, for example, write that she 'was a living indictment of the weakness of Barak and other men in Israel who should have been more courageous leaders (Judges 4:9)'.[28] But such an explanation is not present in the narrative and, as James Hurley comments, while it is sometimes suggested that 'Deborah's calling as judge and prophetess constituted a shaming of Israel, the evidence for such a view is simply lacking in the text'. No shame is implied in Barak receiving orders from a woman.[29]

There is even less basis for arguing that Deborah acts merely in a supportive role, and for claiming that because, unlike the male judges, she does not immediately lead Israel into battle herself but instructs Barak to do so, she 'is not asserting leadership for herself; she gives priority to a man' and is thus acting consistently with a concept of male headship.[30] To seek to draw significance for a doctrine of male headship from the claim that, 'she handed over the leadership, contrary to the pattern of all other judges, to a man'[31] is skating on very thin ice. She may not have led on the field of battle, although she was clearly at Barak's right hand, but she was still the leader who, under God, prophesied the outcome and strengthened the resolve of others to fight. She remained the leader. Female military leaders on the actual field of battle have been extremely rare in history, almost certainly because of basic physical and psychological gender differences rather than because of any notion of male headship! The argument that women are equal in status but subordinate in function finds no encouragement in the story of Deborah.[32]

By definition, leaders inspire and unite others to achieve a common task. Deborah proves to be a true leader who is able to motivate and

[27] I recognize that it is possible to see Barak's request as recognizing his need to have God's representative alongside him in battle but this seems less persuasive than believing it to stem from his diffidence, especially in view of Deborah's response about the honour of the victory not going to him.

[28] J. Piper and W. Grudem, 'An Overview of Central Concerns', *RBMW*, p. 72.

[29] Hurley, *Man and Woman*, p. 47.

[30] Schreiner, 'Ministries of Women', p. 216.

[31] Ibid.

[32] See comment in G. G. Hull, *Equal to Serve: Women and Men in the Church and Home* (London: Scripture Union, 1989), p. 121.

unite Israel in the task of defeating its enemies. Judges records this with no sense of apology or need to explain why a woman should prove equal to the hour when apparently the men were not. As Ailish Eves concludes: 'The text takes Deborah's status and responsibilities for granted. She is not introduced as an emergency substitute for the men who have failed to come forward.'[33]

3. Deborah the national mother (5:1–31)

Deborah disappears from the text in 4:14 while the battle is successfully concluded by Barak and followed through by Jael. In the following chapter Deborah reappears and celebrates, with Barak, Israel's victory, attributing the success to God: *When you, LORD, went out from Seir, when you marched from the land of Edom, the earth shook, the heavens poured . . .* (4). Without detracting from God's determinative role in the battle, however, the song also reflects on Deborah's strategic role in achieving victory. Divine theophany and human action go hand in hand.

In describing her part, Deborah calls herself *a mother in Israel* (7). The richness of this evocative and 'endearing title'[34] is capable of many interpretations but is best understood through the words that surround it. Mothers are fierce protectors of their children and as a *mother*, Deborah was unable to let her children continue to suffer as they had been doing from the days of Shamgar and Jael (6). Enemy oppression meant it was no longer safe for the Israelites to use the main roads and had to resort to the back and circuitous paths. Since the main roads were the ones the commercial caravans used, Israel's trade suffered. The unwalled villages offered them no protection from marauding bands of Canaanites who raided their crops. The population began to hide and take refuge at home rather than go about in the open fields.[35] The people became dispirited. But like a mother who will not let her child be bullied in the school playground and who intervenes to champion his or her cause, so Deborah *arose, a mother in Israel.*

As a mother, Deborah was concerned about the future of her children and so under God *chose new leaders when war came to the*

---

[33] A. Eves, 'Judges', in C. C. Kroeger and M. J. Evans (eds.), *IVP Women's Bible Commentary* (Downers Grove: IVP, 2002), p. 133.

[34] D. T. Olsen, 'The Book of Judges', *NIB*, vol. 2 (Nashville: Abingdon, 1998), p. 787: 'the phrase is probably more than just an endearing title. [It] may represent the place of a wise woman prophet who delivers divine oracles to resolve disputes . . .'

[35] The first line of v. 7 is better translated 'The peasant population disappeared in Israel' than NIV's *Villagers in Israel would not fight* although both translations relate to Israel being fearful in avoiding rather than engaging the enemy. See Butler, *Judges*, pp. 117, 138.

city gates (8).[36] She rouses others to action, to join the cause and appoint the next generations of leaders in Israel. She did this even though they had nothing to fight for and their resources were non-existent. She proved an inspiration to those who were so de-motivated that they could hardly keep going.

And, as a mother, she felt matters deeply. Her brave actions were motivated by deep emotions, not by rational, cold, task-oriented calculation. She had empathy for the people's suffering and bore their sorrow with them. But she equally expressed the opposite emotion when things began to change and the future began to be full of promise again. *My heart is with Israel's princes, with the willing volunteers among the people. Praise the LORD!* (9). She was a leader who knew how to weep and how to sing, as any mother does.

Part of the purpose in using the phrase must be to draw attention to the way in which Deborah's family was the whole of Israel rather than just her immediate family circle. Another part of the purpose is to communicate the surprise involved in the fact that Israel's new situation stemmed from a *mother in Israel* rather than a father, as most might expect. She *arose.* 'She stood on her feet, meaning that when all looked hopeless and no masculine leaders stepped forward, this woman – known as prophetess, wife, and judge – took a stand . . . '[37] Deborah's initiative stands in marked contrast to others who might have taken a stand against the Canaanites but also in marked contrast to a number of whole tribes who failed to mobilize once the call to arms was issued. Reuben was too diffident to act (15–16); Gilead, too comfortable at home (17a); Dan, too busy in fishing (17b); and Asher, too fearful, so stayed hidden in the coastal coves (17c). But this woman woke up, arose, inspired *the willing volunteers among the people* (9) from all over the land, and then with them engaged the enemy in battle.

Although the spotlight has been focused on Deborah in verses 6–9, she does not stay in the spotlight in the rest of the victory song. While she expresses with undisguised bewilderment the indifference of some and even curses Meroz *because they did not come to help the LORD, to help the LORD against the mighty* (23), the dominant note celebrates the bravery of others and the risks they were prepared to take (18). She also gives more space to another woman than to any other person or group who played a part in victory. Jael is called *most blessed of women* (24) and her deeds are recalled in some detail

---

[36] The translation of v. 8 is disputed and may mean 'they chose new gods', which could refer to Israel turning to other gods for help in desperation, but the NIV's translation makes more sense in the context.

[37] Butler, *Judges*, p. 139.

in verses 24–27. Like any good leader she puts others centre stage when handling out the praise.

A third woman is also mentioned in the song, only this time it is a woman who is on the side of the defeated army. Sisera's mother is pictured peering through the window waiting for her son's return (28), not realizing that he was never going to do so. The mention of Sisera's mother may display something of the empathy Deborah herself might feel as a mother. Her mention, as a mother in Canaan, also provides a neat literary balance to Deborah as a mother in Israel. Yet, whatever the tide of emotions might be at this point, they are not permitted to overwhelm the strong flow of justice. Deborah may have some natural human sympathy for a bereaved mother, but her greater commitment is to the honour of the Lord and his people. Hence she concludes with the prayer: *May all your enemies perish, O Lord! But may all who love you be like the sun when it rises in its strength* (31).

4. Concluding comment

Deborah is the outstanding example of a woman who serves in a true leadership capacity among God's chosen people, equal in standing and ability to any man.[38] Although she is outstanding she is not unique and is one of several who exercise national and public leadership. While women leaders are rare, their gender is never a matter of adverse comment. A number of indicators suggest Judges emphasizes the surprise of Deborah's success because she was a woman, but it never does so to undermine or question her achievements but rather to enhance and celebrate them. The fact that other women occupy leadership positions seems to be taken for granted and not even be deemed worthy of special comment.

---

[38] It is sometimes pointed out that Barak, rather than Deborah, is mentioned in the list of heroes of the faith in Heb. 11:32. But it is difficult to attribute any significance for the gender issue from this since Hebrews is clearly selective in its illustrations and rhetorical in its style rather than seeking to provide a definitive theology of leadership. Only four judges are mentioned, not in chronological order, all of whom were leaders in battle. Commentators suggest the author's list may reflect 1 Sam. 12:11 (LXX) rather than anything else.

Ruth 1:1 – 4:22
7. Resolute women

1. Resolute women in the genealogy of Jesus

Four women make their appearance in Matthew's version of the family tree of Jesus. The appearance of any woman in the genealogy is astonishing enough, since contemporary culture put such a premium on the male line. When, however, one looks at who the women are the astonishment level rises. All of them would be an embarrassment, for different reasons, in any decent society.

The first woman Matthew mentions is Tamar, the hard-done-by widow of Er, Judah's oldest son, who, when Judah's family failed to meet their obligations to her, acted like a prostitute and tricked her self-righteous father-in-law into sleeping with her in order to secure an heir.[1] Rahab is legendary for her courage and commended in Hebrews 11:31 as an example of faith.[2] Yet the very verse that commends her calls her 'the prostitute', to which might be added that she was also a deceiver and was not an Israelite by birth. Ruth[3] seems the sweetest of the women listed but, as we will explore more fully below, she was an outsider from Moab, whose enmity with Israel was long-standing, and who broke with convention. The last woman Matthew mentions is not given her own name but introduced as Uriah's wife,[4] probably to ensure that the responsibility for the illicit sexual act of which she was a victim lies squarely with King

---

[1] Matt. 1:3; Gen. 38:1–30.
[2] Matt. 1:5. See Josh. 2:1–24. Rahab is the only woman mentioned by name in Heb.11 where even Deborah is supplanted by Barak (Heb. 11:32), though women are mentioned generally in their capacity as wives and mothers (Heb. 11:35).
[3] Matt. 1:5.
[4] Matt. 1:6.

David.[5] The very choice of words draws attention to one of David's most shameful episodes in his reign. These women are clearly not selected because they are unblemished paragons of virtue, or because they had an easy path in life.

What binds these women together? What was it about them that qualified them as entrants in Matthew's genealogy of Christ? Several reasons have been put forward. In reviewing them, Richard Bauckham finds the most convincing explanation is that they were all Gentiles,[6] 'outsiders', who found a place among the people of God. While this is undoubtedly true and justified by Matthew's universalistic vision,[7] it is not the whole story.

These women have at least two other things in common. First, for each there is 'evidence to suggest that there were "irregular circumstances" in their union with their male partners, through which God nevertheless acted to further his purpose'.[8] This goes hand-in-hand with the second feature they had in common. They were resolute women who did not passively accept their unfortunate lot in life but actively took initiatives to transform their circumstances. For different reasons, each of them had the odds stacked against them and all of them at some stage demonstrated more verve than the male actors in their story. They took risks and held their nerve, demonstrating initiative and resolution. They were not afraid to act in an unconventional, irregular manner and to contravene the accepted practices of their day. Yet in doing so, they were neither behaving arrogantly, nor displaying indifference to God's law. Rather they were becoming active partners with God in the fulfilment of his plans and purposes. Ultimately their actions led to the birth of the Messiah.[9]

2. Resolute women in the Old Testament

The four women Matthew mentions are select examples drawn from a much wider group. The list of resolute women in the Old Testament is a long and varied one and the women display courage in the face

[5] R. Bauckham, *Gospel Women: Studies in the Named Women in the Gospels* (London: T & T Clark, 2002), p. 24. David's adultery with Bathsheba and its aftermath is recorded in 2 Sam. 11:1 – 12:25.

[6] This assumes, quite reasonably, given her marriage to Uriah, that Bathsheba was a Hittite.

[7] Matthew's particularism (e.g., 10:6 and 15:24) should not eclipse his equal concern for the gospel to be good news to the Gentiles (e.g., 2:1–12; 4:12–17; 24:14; 28:19–20). The particularism is a step towards the universalism.

[8] Bauckham, *Gospel Women*, p. 25, drawing on R. E. Brown, *The Birth of the Messiah* (Garden City: Doubleday, ²1993), p. 25.

[9] Bauckham, *Gospel Women*, pp. 26–27.

of a wide range of adverse circumstances.[10] Miriam displays initiative in cunningly saving her baby brother Moses from Pharaoh's attempt at ethnic cleansing.[11] The daughters of Zelophehad courageously question the justice of the inheritance laws of their day.[12] Deborah[13] and Esther[14] show initiative and formidable leadership skills in the face of national enemies. Jael shows remarkably acute resolution in assassinating Sisera.[15] The unnamed woman living in Thebez who executed God's judgment by dropping a millstone on Abimelek's head showed some nerve.[16] Hannah shows determination in passionately pleading with God for the gift of a son, which resulted in the birth of Samuel; she then showed even greater strength of character by dedicating him to service in the tabernacle.[17] Others, such as the lover in Song of Songs who appears to be the real suitor, or the excellent wife of Proverbs 31, demonstrate it in the ordinariness of human life and experience: falling in love and managing a home. Their characters are marked by a creative energy that does not appear to need stirring into action by anything in particular. It is not that they could show strength when necessary, it is rather that they were constitutionally strong.

Resolute women form a spectrum from good to evil in the Old Testament. Some are recorded as using their strength for good purposes, like the woman from Tekoa who, at Joab's request, took her life in her hands to challenge David's treatment of Absalom.[18] Some are more ambiguous. Abigail, for all her wisdom in paying respect to David and averting a potential conflict, proves a less-than-straightforward character in undermining her husband, Nabal, and eventually marrying David.[19] Other women clearly use their determined characters for less wholesome ends. Rebekah forwards her own selfish plans in her favouritism of Jacob,[20] even though in this case God's sovereign purposes were achieved through it. Some work for even more explicitly evil ends: as Delilah did when she played on her feminine emotions to entrap Samson,[21] as Jezebel did in

[10] There are, of course, plenty of resolute men in the Old Testament but they are often highlighted while the resolute women are often neglected and this is a 'balancing' book.
[11] Exod. 2:1–10.
[12] Num. 36:1–12.
[13] Judg. 4:1 – 5:31.
[14] Esth. 1:1 – 10:3.
[15] Judg. 4:17–22.
[16] Judg. 9:50–57.
[17] 1 Sam. 1:1–28.
[18] 2 Sam. 14:1–23.
[19] 1 Sam. 25:1–40.
[20] Gen. 27:1–45.
[21] Judg. 16: 4–21.

putting steel into Ahab's crumbling backbone when he sought illegally to take possession of Naboth's vineyard,[22] or as Athaliah did when she sought, but ultimately failed, to liquidate the royal house of Judah and seize the throne for herself.[23] In this respect women are no different from men. It is not their gender that makes them automatically good. They have the potential to channel their strength, as men do, either for good or ill. They can be a blessing or a disgrace.

That these strong women surface so frequently in the Old Testament story is surprising, given the overwhelmingly patriarchal context of that era. On several occasions there seems to be a conscious attempt to portray them in a good light in contrast to listless and feeble men who are at a loss as to know what to do.

3. Ruth: a model of a resolute woman

Several women, such as Esther,[24] would serve as an example of a resolute woman worthy of close study. But Ruth has been chosen partly because of the distorted and sentimental way in which she is often portrayed. She is often presented as a good example of sacrificial loyalty in her commitment to Naomi, or of dogged but fairly passive submission in the face of life's trials, knowing that God would sort it out in the end. Given that she came from Moab, the story is sometimes legitimately presented as a corrective to the nationalistic emphasis of other books like Ezra or Nehemiah with their stands against inter-marriage.[25] But it is equally a corrective, along with Esther and Song of Songs, to the predominant androcentric view presented by much of the Old Testament.[26] 'The value of Ruth,' writes Richard Bauckham, 'as women's literature is precisely that it renders visible what is usually invisible. Naomi and Ruth, as women of independence and initiative, respected as such by men, are not exceptions to the Israelite rule, but examples of the rule that only a women's perspective of the book allows us to recognize.'[27] How does it do that?

---

[22] 1 Kgs 21:1–26.

[23] 2 Kgs 11:1–3.

[24] For an exposition of Esther see Dianne Tidball, *Esther: A True First Lady. A Post-Feminist Icon in a Secular World* (Fearn: Christian Focus Publications, 2001) and D. G. Firth, *The Message of Esther*, BST (Nottingham: IVP, 2010).

[25] Ezra 9:1 – 10:44; Neh. 13:23–27.

[26] Bauckham, *Gospel Women*, pp. 14–15. See his whole chapter 'The Book of Ruth as a key to the Gynocentric Reading of Scripture', pp. 1–16.

[27] Bauckham, *Gospel Women*, p. 10.

a. Act 1: 'Call me Mara' (1:1–22)

Set in the time of the Judges, Ruth tells the story of the collapse of Naomi's world and its rebuilding. At every stage, Naomi is conscious of God's hand on her life and never doubts that he is the God of *ḥesed*, of covenant loyalty, kindness, love and faithfulness, and yet in the opening scene everything she experienced gave her reason to call God's *ḥesed* into question. The story starts, as she herself put it, with Naomi enjoying life, with her family, to the *full* (21). Her very name means 'pleasant', 'lovely'. But drop by drop the fullness is drained away until, back among her own people, she whispers in anguish *Call me Mara, because the Almighty has made my life very bitter. I went away full, but the LORD has brought me back empty. Why call me Naomi? The LORD has afflicted me; the Almighty has brought misfortune upon me* (20–21). How was the fullness of life sucked from her? What misfortune befell her? Why had she cause for bitterness?

Bethlehem was the bread basket of Israel but during one particularly difficult time when famine took its toll, Elimelek, whose name testified to God being king, and his wife Naomi, left their home to travel in search of food, as the Patriarchs had done before them.[28] They made their way to Moab where they had heard the food supply had not run out. Desperate circumstances call for desperate measures and perhaps that is why Elimelek and Naomi, who were by all indications an old-established, aristocratic Israelite family, made their way to a people who had been enemies of Israel for generations.[29] They took their sons Mahlon and Kilion with them, although their names, which meant something like 'sickness' or 'sterility' and 'pining' or 'alienation' respectively, perhaps hinted at worse trouble ahead.

Living in Moab was a roller-coaster experience for Naomi. The first dip came when Elimelek died, leaving her with the responsibility of two sons to bring up far away from her family and friends in a foreign land. Some time later – the timescale is not given and the story is told in an economy of words – Naomi began to climb again as the two sons, now presumably old enough to earn a living and provide support for the family, married, even if they married local girls rather than women from their own kith and kin. But Naomi's life soon careered sharply down again when both her sons died, leaving her wrecked at the bottom of the pile. With no husband and no sons she had lost her identity and security. The family of

[28] Gen. 12:10; 26:1; 42:1–2.
[29] R. L. Hubbard Jr, *The Book of Ruth*, NICOT (Grand Rapids: Eerdmans, 1988), p. 91. Leon Morris, *Judges, Ruth*, TOTC (London: Tyndale Press, 1968), p. 249.

four that had set out from Bethlehem was reduced to one. True, she had her daughters-in-law, who were presumably young and fit, but they too had lost any meaningful status when their husbands died and, in any case, they came from another culture and owed allegiance to the foreign god Chemosh. Naomi's lot was catastrophic. 'There were', as Carolyn Custis James, puts it, 'no heroic rescue workers charging in to carry her to safety, no grim-faced news anchors choking back the tears as they reported a relentless sequence of disasters that sent her into shock, no half-mast flags or weeping nation to grieve.'[30] She was alone, left to battle through her Job-like circumstances as an unsupported, voiceless and 'invisible' widow, for that is how society perceived widows then, and often now. Society did not share the high view of widows that God has.[31]

Naomi's heart was set on returning to her native land, where she learned the famine had come to an end. To Naomi, home was Bethlehem in Judah; to Orpah and Ruth, home was Moab. Sensibly, then, she set out to return, taking her daughters-in law with her just to start with, but fully expecting to separate from them before long. When the point where she expected to part company was reached, Naomi instructed them to return, curiously to their *mother's home* (8), not their father's home as might be expected. The choice of words appropriately draws a contrast between going on with their mother-in-law or going back to mother, and the significance of *mother's house* may be no more than that.[32] But it may be more significant than this, not because Naomi is making a feminist statement but because the mother's home, or more specifically part of the home, is associated with the arrangement of marriage and Naomi longs for them to remarry and have children and so a future.[33]

When Naomi sought to dismiss them she prayed more than a conventional 'God bless you' over their lives. For all the suffering she believed God had brought into her life – and she does believe God is responsible as seeps out when she says *the LORD's hand has turned against me!* (13) – her 'bitter complaint cloaked firm faith'.[34] She genuinely asks God to bring blessing on her daughters-in law: *May the LORD show you kindness (ḥesed) . . . May the LORD grant that each of you will find rest in the home of another husband* (8–9). They both protested and said they would go back with her to Judah.

[30] C. C. James, *The Gospel of Ruth: Loving God Enough to Break the Rules* (Grand Rapids: Zondervan, 2008), p. 37.
[31] Pss. 68:5–6; 146:9; Isa. 1:17, 23; Jer. 7:6; 22:3; Zech. 7:10.
[32] F. Bush, *Ruth, Esther*, WBC (Dallas: Word, 1996), p. 75.
[33] Hubbard, *Ruth*, p. 103, building on Gen. 24:28.
[34] Hubbard, *Ruth*, p. 113.

But when she pressed the point Oprah changed her mind and returned to her home in Moab.

We should not look down on Orpah's decision as if it were a betrayal of Naomi. It was an entirely rational, logical decision, which she was free to make and which evidently she did not reach lightly. She stands in contrast to Ruth, 'not because [she] is selfish or wicked, but because she is sensible'.[35] Ruth, however, refuses to return home and takes the much riskier decision to continue with Naomi and settle in Judah with her. It was risky because she had never lived there, had no ready-made means of support there, and did not know how the locals would react to this strange incomer. It seemed a non-sensical choice to make. Why travel with an older, dependent woman rather than search for a new beginning with a young husband among your own people? It was an act of self-denial, of losing one's own life without the certainty of finding it again. The journey in itself would be risky enough. Two unescorted women would soon find the world a 'hostile and unsafe' place, especially when 'the combined forces of widowhood and childlessness' had robbed them of 'the security of husband and home'.[36]

Ruth's commitment to Naomi was movingly expressed and could not have been more comprehensive or more profound: *Where you go, I will go, and where you stay I will stay. Your people will be my people and your God my God. Where you will die I will die, and there I will be buried* (16–17). Neither geography nor ethnicity, neither culture nor faith, neither life nor death, would be permitted to drive a wedge between Ruth and Naomi from that day on. Ruth's decision signals a determination that would be put to good use in the future. From then on, these two vulnerable women move centre stage and become the showcase of God's grace, not as the passive victims they might have been, but as the active and audacious participants in the unfolding of God's plan.

Safely back in Bethlehem, the women evoke sympathy for the tragedies that had befallen them. The sympathy comes from the women. Men do not figure in the story of homecoming, perhaps because they were away in the fields or because this is typical of the different way we might expect men and women to react. They receive sympathy, but apparently no practical help. We do not read of anyone stepping in to assist. They are left to make their own way and the only hint given that the future might hold better things for them is that they arrived *in Bethlehem as the barley harvest was beginning* (22).

[35] James, *Gospel of Ruth*, p. 47.
[36] James, *Gospel of Ruth*, p. 78.

b. Act 2: 'Let me go to the fields . . . ' (2:1–23)

(i) Ruth takes the initiative (1–3)

Since the barley harvest had already started, it cannot have been long after they returned to Bethlehem before Ruth announced to Naomi that she would go *to the fields and pick up leftover grain behind anyone in whose eyes I find favour* (2). It was a bold decision that Naomi doesn't object to even though she would have had good grounds for doing so.

More than once in what follows we read hints of the danger which Ruth faced in taking this step. First she was a foreigner and might be subject to racial prejudice as the several references (6, 10, 21) to her being from Moab hint. Secondly, she was an unprotected woman, without a husband, and would be easy sport among the laddish culture of the male harvesters. She was likely to be subjected to abuse and being molested. Thirdly, she was to be a gleaner, that is the lowest rung of the agricultural ladder, who was permitted to pick up the scraps after the more important people, the employers and regular employees, first male, then female, had had their pick. The law required landowners to leave some pickings for the poor to collect in order for them to survive.[37] It was Israel's ancient welfare system. But we should disabuse ourselves of any romantic notions of what this meant. The gleanings were never plentiful and, whatever the law stipulated, there were plenty of unscrupulous landowners who 'obstructed the efforts of gleaners by ridicule, tricks and in some cases outright expulsion'.[38] Even other hungry gleaners could be less than welcoming to those who invaded their patch. Did Ruth really appreciate what her announcement entailed?

'Passivity,' Carolyn James adjudges, 'is not one of Ruth's strengths. To the contrary, she is decisive and proactive.'[39] To the human eye she chooses this course of action as a free agent, but there is another eye overseeing her steps. With tremendous irony, the writer tells us: *As it turned out, she was working in a field belonging to Boaz, who was from the clan of Elimelek* (3). Coincidence indeed! The story-teller has already said enough, in verse 1, to alert us to the significance of this. We know little of Boaz yet, but we do know he was a relative of Naomi's by marriage and *a man of standing*. We know, but Ruth did not. What seems to her ordinary human action is, all unseen, being guided by the God of *ḥesed*. A 'divine intentionality' directs her.[40]

---

[37] Lev. 19:9–10; 23:22; Deut. 24:19–22.
[38] Hubbard, *Ruth*, p. 136.
[39] James, *Gospel of Ruth*, p. 92.
[40] P. Trible, *God and the Rhetoric of Sexuality* (London: SCM, 1978), p. 176.

(ii) Ruth stands her ground (4–6)
Ruth's determined character soon surfaces again. Rather than meekly taking the customary and lowly place normally allotted to gleaners, Ruth asks the head reaper if she might *glean and gather among the sheaves behind the harvesters* (7). Although the Hebrew text is problematic and there is no certainty as to its precise meaning, it seems she is not content merely to go through the stalks once the harvesters had finished their work but wanted a closer involvement than that, which would give her a much greater harvest. The request exceeds the authority of the man in charge and so he parries the question until Boaz comes later in the day to check up on his workers. Ruth, undeterred by the delay, patiently waits until she can gain the answer she wants.[41] When quizzed by Boaz, the foreman remarks: 'She has practically taken up residence here'.[42]

When Boaz arrives he easily recognizes her as a stranger and asks his foreman, '*Who does that young woman belong to?*', reflecting the typically patriarchal perspective of his day, as if she has no identity or legitimacy in her own right.[43] What follows, however, reveals Boaz to be a tender and virtuous man, a man not only of superior social standing but also of outstanding character.

(iii) Ruth reaps her reward (8–16)
Whatever the attitude other landowners might betray, Boaz shows himself to be a godly man who more than exceeds what the relevant laws might require. He encourages Ruth to stay in his fields rather than risk going elsewhere (8). He instructs her to follow the group of women reapers but not to be one of them. This would provide her with protection from the males and place her in a different position than other gleaners, while doing justice to the fact that she was not a member of his staff (8b–9a, 13). He sends out warning signals to his men not to take advantage of her and to let her glean unhindered (9b, 15). He generously encourages her to take refreshment from the scorching sun, whenever she needs to *from the water jars the men have filled* (9c). This is not an insignificant step since, as Hubbard comments, 'a foreign woman who customarily would draw water *for* Israelites was welcome to drink water drawn *by* Israelites'.[44]

Responding to such generosity, Ruth bows low before him, a gesture that recognizes their difference in social standing, and expresses

---

[41] Again the Hebrew is problematic and it is unclear whether she had already begun to glean, as v. 3 implies, or simply waited in the hope of being granted the greater privilege she sought. Either way, she did not give up!

[42] Hubbard, *Ruth*, p. 151.

[43] Trible, *God and*, p. 176.

[44] Hubbard, *Ruth*, p. 160.

her gratitude and wonder at his generosity (10). But Boaz, who now reveals he knows of her story (it was probably common knowledge in the community), prays that *the God of Israel, under whose wings you have come to take refuge* (12) may reward her for her extraordinary faithfulness to Naomi. Moreover, Boaz has not exhausted his own generosity yet. At the meal break she is included among the party and fed more than sufficiently by Boaz himself (14). She is treated as belonging, even though, as yet, she does not. When the time comes for the workers to resume their labours, he instructs them not only to give her free rein but to assist her by deliberately pulling out some stalks from their bundles and dropping them for her to pick them up. She would return home with a good harvest (15–16).

Ruth was no shirker and *gleaned in the field until evening* (17) before turning to the onerous task of threshing *the barley she had gathered* (17). When she had finished she took home an astonishing ephah of flour. Estimates vary as to what an ephah would mean in contemporary terms, but it was clearly no small quantity. The word ephah had its origin in a vessel large enough to hold a person and Ruth, in this single day, had collected 'the equivalent of at least half a month's wages'.[45]

(iv) Ruth reports to Naomi (19–23)

Imagine Naomi's astonishment when she saw how much Ruth had gathered. They were secure for many weeks to come. In the excited chatter, Ruth talks through the day and eventually reveals that the man who had enabled this to happen was Boaz (19). Naomi cannot hold herself back and exclaims a benediction over him for his faithfulness (*ḥesed*) before disclosing to Ruth that he is *a close relative; he is one of our guardian-redeemers* (20). Given Naomi's knowledge of Boaz, why hasn't she approached him to help? Was she still deep in grief, depressed, or fearful of further disappointment?[46] Whatever might have prevented her acting up to now, this day's happenings helps Naomi turn a corner and she understandably encourages Ruth to continue working under Boaz' protection.

Naomi's mind might already be contemplating a possible marriage between Ruth and Boaz.[47] But, if so, the story-teller hints that it is not going to happen smoothly. Chapter 1 ended with a cliff-hanger, so too does chapter 2. *Ruth stayed close to the women of Boaz to glean until the barley and wheat harvests were finished. And she lived with her mother-in-law* (23). The statement is a bit of a let-down. No budding romance, no sound of wedding bells, no visit

[45] Hubbard, *Ruth*, p. 179.
[46] Trible, *God and*, p. 179.
[47] Some find a parallel in Gen. 24:27.

to the printer to issue the wedding invitations! Boaz has been generous but takes the matter no further. If he knows of his obligations as a *guardian-redeemer* he does not act on them, and apparently takes no steps to ensure others in the family do either. Perhaps he thinks he has done more than enough. Or perhaps, the story is preparing us to see Ruth, again, true to character, initiating the unconventional steps that will restore the fullness of life to her and her mother-in-law.

c. Act 3: 'Spread the corner of your garment over me . . . ' (3:1–18)

(i) Naomi directs (1–4)

Buoyed by the generous welcome Ruth has received from Boaz, Naomi seems to have recovered something of her old self and at some stage – we do not know how much later since the text only tells us *one day* – stirred herself into action to ensure Ruth has a secure future, which, in effect, meant marriage. She instructs Ruth to return to Boaz, giving her step-by-step directions as to what to do. After bathing, perfuming and clothing herself in her *best clothes*, she was to make a carefully timed visit to Boaz *and uncover his feet and lie down* (4). The timing combined discretion with opportunism. Ruth was to visit at night when Boaz, exhausted from his labours and replete from his feasting, was well asleep, and when others would have left for their homes.

As Hubbard points out, Naomi is beginning 'to answer her own prayer!'[48] She had prayed (1:9) that the Lord would grant Ruth (and Orpah) *rest in the home of another husband.* Now she takes the initiative and exploits the opportunity God had provided. God is acting through Naomi; the divine and human actors together overcoming emptiness in Ruth's life. Naomi no longer passively accepts the misfortunes of their lives but seizes the opportunities given to rebuild them.

(ii) Ruth proposes (5–9)

Ruth obeys Naomi, at least to begin with. She prepares herself, makes her way to Boaz and silently lies down at his feet. When he stirs *in the middle of the night,* which is probably just a very natural reaction in his sleep rather than needing a more fanciful explanation, he is understandably *startled* by having a woman at his feet and immediately wakes and asks her who she was.

Ruth's action was in itself provocative enough. To lie at his feet like this was a sexually suggestive act. We do not know her inner

[48] Hubbard, *Ruth,* p. 199.

motives for taking this course of action but perhaps they were less than pure and she was being explicitly flirtatious. We do know that Boaz was a man of integrity and so Ruth was risking embarrassment, rejection and expulsion at the very least at his hands. What follows was even more daring. Ruth goes beyond Naomi's instructions and asks outright for Boaz to marry her: *Spread the corner of your garment over me, since you are a guardian-redeemer of our family* (9). The request for Boaz to *spread the corner of your garment over me* was not Ruth asking Boaz to 'lend me your coat because I'm cold' as a contemporary young lady might ask of her boyfriend. It's expressive metaphorical language for marriage.[49] The Boaz who had prayed that Ruth would be *richly rewarded* by God *under whose wings you have come to take refuge* (2:12) is now being asked to be the means of answering his own prayer as she asks to take refuge under the wings of his garment in marriage.

Ruth immediately backs up her proposal of marriage by giving Boaz a fairly powerful reason for agreeing to it: *since you are a guardian-redeemer (gō'ēl) of our family* (9). The role of the guardian-redeemer is less definite than some have assumed and raises particular questions here.

Several factors coalesce in the idea of the *gō'ēl*, all of which witnesses to the high premium placed on the family in the laws of Israel. One is economic, relating to inheritance, based on Leviticus 25:25–28, where the next of kin was obliged to buy back property which was about to go out of the family because one of them had fallen into poverty. Another, based on Leviticus 25:47–50, is social and required a close relative to purchase the freedom of a family member who for financial reasons had fallen into slavery. A third aspect related to blood vengeance (Num. 35:9–28). A fourth custom was that of Leverite marriage, mentioned in Deuteronomy 25:5–10, in which a man was instructed to marry his brother's childless widow in order to provide her with an offspring and to perpetuate the family line. Genesis 38 gives us an example of the expectations of Leverite marriages. But the term *gō'ēl* is not used in reference to Leverite marriage.[50]

Ruth, like Naomi before her in 2:20, seems to be using the term in a general sense rather than in a specific legal way, but however much the lawyers may have considered her request vague, it was

[49] Ezek. 16:8. Morris, *Ruth*, p. 289, comments, 'The spreading of the skirt over a widow as a way of claiming her as a wife is attested among Arabs of early days . . . and still exists among some modern Arabs'.

[50] On the meaning of *gō'ēl* and Leverite marriage see Bush, *Ruth*, pp. 165–167 and Hubbard, *Ruth*, pp. 48–63. Also D. Atkinson, *The Message of Ruth* (Leicester: IVP, 1983), pp. 86–98; K. D. Sakenfeld, *Ruth*, Int (Louisville: John Knox, 1999), pp. 59–61.

111

clear to Boaz, as his reply indicates. Boaz focuses on the marriage dimension of the *gōʾēl*, although the property and inheritance dimensions come to the fore in the next chapter.

(iii) Boaz agrees (10–15)

How would Boaz respond? Would he be angry with Ruth, ridicule her, be dismissive, haughty, or what? Boaz' response gives ample evidence that Naomi had read his character correctly and his reputation as a man of moral worth was justified. He immediately accepts Ruth's proposal: *I will do for you all you ask* (11), expressing only surprise that she has proposed to him, an older man who was presumably Naomi's age, rather than a younger man (10). She had sacrificed herself again, for the sake of the family, rather than pursuing her own interests. He compliments her, explaining that she has established herself as *a woman of noble character* (11), which must have made his answer easier.

There is, however, one complication. There is a *guardian-redeemer* in the family who is more closely related than he (12) – Boaz has only been introduced as *a close relative* and *one of our guardian-redeemers* – and his rights need to be addressed before any marriage can proceed. It would seem from this that the primary *gōʾēl* was not obliged to marry the childless widow, even if encouraged to do so, which may explain why neither this closer *guardian-redeemer*, nor Boaz, had acted before.

Boaz' sensitivity is displayed further as he encourages Ruth to lie down and keep warm until morning. Doubtless it was an anxious night but as she leaves early the next morning, Boaz fills her apron with an extraordinary quantity of barley to provide a ready answer to gossips who questioned where she might have been all night.

(iv) Naomi and Ruth wait (16–18)

Naomi and Ruth, who have both shown themselves to be activists, have done what they can. The next and final step is out of their hands. However resolute they are, they remain women, subject to a patriarchal culture and the men have to have their say. Even so, the fact that Ruth did not return home *empty-handed* was a powerful sign that their lives would soon be filled again.[51]

d. Act 4: 'I have bought . . . I have also acquired . . . ' (4:1–22)

Finally the voices of the women fall silent and Boaz, at last, takes the initiative. The scene shifts to the man's world, the world of business,

---

[51] Cf. 1:21.

property and formal transactions, and seems out of step with the preceding chapters.[52] But in a patriarchal world, such a conclusion was necessary if Naomi and Ruth were to experience fullness in life again.

The chapter is full of surprises. Gathering where business was done and justice dispensed, at *the town gate,* Boaz discussed the matter with the one whose rights as *guardian-redeemer* took precedence over his, in the presence of the town's elders. Boaz' introduction contains a surprise. There is obviously some property of Elimelek, Kilion and Mahlon which has not been mentioned before, perhaps because the property belonged to the men, rather than the women. He invites the unnamed *guardian-redeemer* to exercise his rights and purchase it, which he is just about to do (4) until Boaz mentions a catch. Redeeming the property would also mean he would *acquire Ruth the Moabite* (5). *Acquire* suggests that Ruth is being depersonalized and is no more than part and parcel with the property. The nameless man demurs at this, saying that he cannot afford to go that far because in doing so *I might endanger my own estate* (6). He might, in other words, just about be able to afford to buy the property but if Ruth was later to have a child who would then become the legal heir to it he would lose out on his investment.[53] He couldn't take that risk. Ruth and Boaz have shown *ḥesed,* but he fails to do so. They have taken risks and gambled with their lives for the sake of others, but he plays safe. To prove faithful to Naomi, Ruth has acted in unconventional and creative ways, but this unnamed *guardian-redeemer* acts entirely on the right side of custom and convention.

In this way, the path is cleared for Boaz to purchase the property and in the process also acquire *Ruth the Moabite, Mahlon's widow, as my wife, in order to maintain the name of the dead with his property, so that his name will not disappear from among his family or from his home town* (10). So the transaction purchasing property and wife is done and sealed in the customary way by the primary guardian-redeemer taking off his sandal and giving it to Boaz.[54]

The men may be restrained in their attitudes: business has been done. By contrast, later, the women who had earlier welcomed Naomi back to Bethlehem re-enter the scene, this time full of joy. After Boaz *made love to* Ruth, *the Lord enabled her to conceive, and she gave birth to a son* (13). Emptiness has been replaced by plenty; curse transformed into blessing; affliction has given way to happiness; and

---

[52] Trible, *God and*, pp. 188, 193.

[53] Hubbard, *Ruth*, p. 245.

[54] Deut. 25:5–10. The meaning of the act seems obscure but may refer to the idea that 'in the OT "feet" and "shoes" symbolized power, possession and domination (Josh. 10:24; Ps 8:7; 60:10, 108:10)', Hubbard, *Ruth*, p. 251.

despair is supplanted by hope. The Lord has proved himself to be full of kindness – a covenant God indeed! All this and more was from the Lord, using the human participants in the story to achieve his purpose. The 'more' comes in the story's final note of joy: the child born to Ruth the Moabite turns out to be the grandfather of King David. True the text only traces his lineage through Boaz (ch. 4 is, after all, a male preserve!). But Matthew corrects the omission of her name. He traces Jesus' lineage through 'Boaz the father of Obed, *whose mother was Ruth*, Obed the father of Jesse, and Jesse the father of King David'.[55]

4. Conclusion

Ruth was one of the outstanding resolute women of the Old Testament. But she was representative of many others, not unique. Even in the narrow confines of her own story Naomi is shown to be her companion in arms, working out in harmony with God, their 'salvation in fear and trembling'.[56] Ruth is the story of women in a man's world who are subject to their culture, yet stand against it, and in doing so transform it to bring about life and hope in the face of death and despair.[57]

[55] Matt. 1:6.
[56] Phil. 2:12.
[57] This paragraph owes much to Trible, *God and*, p. 196.

2 Kings 22:11–20
8. Prophetic women

On the day of Pentecost, Peter explained that what the people were witnessing was nothing less than the fulfilment of Joel's prophecy:

> 'In the last days, . . .
>> I will pour out my Spirit on all people.
>> Your sons and daughters will prophesy . . .
>> Even on my servants, both men and women,
>>> I will pour out my Spirit in those days
>>> and they will prophesy.'[1]

Those who advocate the right of women to speak for God as men's equals in the church often quote Peter's words in support and point to the recognition given to women as prophets in the apostolic church.[2] Sometimes, however, this leads to a false impression, as if women prophets are only to be found after the day of Pentecost. Whatever the differences between prophecy in the Old and New Testaments,[3] it is important not to overstress the discontinuity between them. The female prophets of the New Testament are inheritors of a rich tradition which occasionally breaks through the patriarchal surface of the Old Testament.

---

[1] Acts 2:17–18; Joel 2:28–29.

[2] Acts 21:9; 1 Cor. 11:5.

[3] W. Grudem, *The Gift of Prophecy* (Eastbourne: Kinsgway 1998), pp. 26–27, 144–146. Grudem argues that the apostles were the true successors of Old Testament prophets and that New Testament prophets did not have an authoritative role in determining doctrine or interpreting apostolic teaching. For a critique of Grudem which recognizes an important issue here but finds Grudem's distinction somewhat simplistic, see M. Turner, *The Holy Spirit and Spiritual Gifts: Then and Now* (Carlisle: Paternoster, 1996), pp. 185–217.

1. The women prophets of the Old Testament

Israel's priesthood was restricted to the sons of Aaron who were free from any physical defect.[4] Consequently women, along with the vast majority of men, including even some of Aaron's own descendents, were ineligible to serve as priests.[5] But several women are called to be prophets and are given due recognition and honour for the work, even if their contribution seems quite varied. The word prophet is used in 'a fluid manner' and given 'a variety of meanings' in the Old Testament.[6] It is neither restricted to Moses' understanding of a prophet as one who receives visions and dreams from God,[7] nor limited to the later ethical writing prophets whose works have been included in inspired Scripture. The title is given to those who are 'vessels of divine communication' whether it be through interpreting dreams, receiving visions, making oracles, interceding passionately, working wonders or interpreting the words of earlier prophets.[8] Women prophets, no less than their male colleagues, demonstrate this variety as they conveyed 'the word of the Lord'.

a. Miriam

Miriam is the first woman to be named a prophet when she led Israel in the musical celebration of victory after their release from Egypt and escape from Egypt's army at the Red Sea. Her prophetic gift took the form of an exuberant song and the playing of musical instruments, and her example inspired other women to join her.[9] However, her ministry was far from limited to leading the people in worship. In spite of her complaining against Moses – a foolish step, but one she shared with Aaron, for which God punished both of them[10] – Micah later acknowledged the significance of her leadership when, without making any distinction between them, he wrote, 'I sent

---

[4] Lev. 21:16–23.

[5] The Levitical priesthood was a temporary institution and has been superseded by the priesthood of all believers in the New Testament church, so it cannot be said to have implications for the role of women in the contemporary church. See R. Groothius, 'Equal in Being, Unequal in Role', *DBE*, pp. 326–329.

[6] W. C. Gafney, *Daughters of Miriam: Women Prophets in Ancient Israel* (Minneapolis: Fortress Press, 2008), p. 17.

[7] Num. 12:6.

[8] Gafney, *Daughters of Miriam*, p. 24.

[9] Exod. 15:20. Music is sometimes associated with prophecy (1 Sam. 10:5; 2 Kgs 3:15) while women are often mentioned in connection with singing (1 Sam. 18:6; 2 Sam. 19:35; 2 Chr. 35:25; Ezra 2:65; Neh. 7:67).

[10] Num. 12:1–16.

Moses to lead you, also Aaron and Miriam'.[11] It is remarkable that her role is spoken of in this way in such a patriarchal climate.

b. Deborah

Although presented primarily as a judge and leader of Israel, when Deborah is first introduced she is called 'a prophet'.[12] We have already explored Deborah as one of the leading women of Israel in chapter 6, so here we confine ourselves to a few addition remarks specifically in relation to Deborah's prophetic ministry, with the reminder that the way she is introduced emphasizes that she is 'a female not a male'.[13]

Deborah's prophetic gift appears to be much wider than that of Miriam. She operates on a number of different levels to bring the word of the Lord to people. Sitting under her palm tree between Ramah and Bethel she would pronounce judgment on the various personal disputes people brought to her. It would seem that her she was widely respected in that role and people would come from all over Israel to seek her ruling. No information is given about the process by which she discerned what decision to reach. It may be that she used a blend of her study of the law, wise experience, feminine intuition and divine revelation to come to a judgment. While there is no specific mention of her receiving visions or hearing the divine voice, it is probably that she did so and that this, in part, led to her recognition as a prophet.

Beyond the personal level, Deborah also functioned on a national level in commanding Barak to fight the Canaanites, in summoning the tribes of Israel to arms, and then in leading the people in celebrating their victory. Despite the attempt of some to say she only operated in a private way and, unlike her male prophetic counterparts, she did not function in a public capacity and so was not a prophet on a level with them, her prophetic gifts seem to have been pretty public, not to say national, in their delivery and impact. Having sent for Barak she instructs him using the words 'The LORD, the God of Israel, commands you . . . '.[14] Whatever else this might mean, it indicates that Deborah displayed the true prophetic quality of listening to the word of the Lord and then passing it on to those to whom it was addressed. Here is the heart of prophecy and Deborah is every inch a prophet.

In directing individuals in the routine affairs of their ordinary lives or the nation in a time of military crisis, Deborah proves an unerring

[11] Mic. 6:4.
[12] Judg. 4:4.
[13] T. Butler, *Judges*, WBC (Nashville: Thomas Nelson, 2009), p. 90.
[14] Judg. 4:6.

channel for God's voice whose prophecies are authenticated by the outworking of events.

c. Other women prophets

The unselfconscious way in which a couple of other women are introduced suggests that the gift of prophecy was more widely exercised by women than we are specifically told. Isaiah's wife was said to be a prophet.[15] Less happily, Ezekiel, in condemning false prophets, speaks of 'the daughters of your people who prophesy out of their own imagination',[16] using all sorts of questionable techniques to receive and convey their messages. For our purposes, however, the significant point seems to be that women were accepted in Israel alongside men as prophets. Nehemiah, equally less happily, mentions a co-conspirator of Tobiah and Sanballat, 'the prophet Noadiah and how she and the rest of the prophets have been trying to intimidate me'.[17]

2. The prophet Huldah (22:11–20)[18]

The most remarkable, and in some respects classical, female prophet in Israel is Huldah. The most important episode in her ministry occurs late in Israel's monarchy, giving the lie to the argument of some that a position like that held by Deborah could only have occurred before the monarchy developed and imposed more central-ized control.[19]

a. Huldah's background

Israel had been set for some generations on a reckless course of covenant breaking that could only end in exile. Late in the day, King Josiah (641-609 BC) was presented with the Book of the Law[20] that had been rediscovered while the temple was being renovated, and having been reacquainted with its message, he was at a loss to know how to respond to it. After tearing his robes, a clear sign of 'con-trition and distress',[21] the king demanded that his advisers *go and*

---

[15] Isa. 8:1.

[16] Ezek. 13:17.

[17] Neh. 6:14.

[18] The parallel is found in 2 Chr. 34:14–33.

[19] For the debate see Butler, *Judges*, p. 91.

[20] Whatever the exact nature and extent of the scroll almost all see it as at least part of the Book of Deuteronomy.

[21] G. H. Jones, *I and 2 Kings*, NCB, vol. 2 (Grand Rapids: Eerdmans and London: Marshall, Morgan and Scott, 1984), p. 611.

enquire of the LORD for me and for the people and for all Judah about what is written in this book that has been found (13). Without hesitation, his advisers make their way not perhaps to a prophet as one might have expected but to a prophetess, Huldah.

From the information given, Huldah seems to have married into a family who served in the temple or the palace. She lived in the *New Quarter,* which was the area north of the temple where such employees and officials lived and this probably gave her easy access to the royal court, making her perhaps a familiar figure in establishment circles. But, truth to tell, we can say little about her family or situation with any confidence. However, it is obvious that she was well known as a prophetess and must have already proved a reliable guide in the past to be trusted with such a responsibility as speaking for God at such a pivotal time in Israel's history. It has been suggested[22] she had been used to tutor Josiah when he was a boy, but that is conjecture and we cannot be sure how she came to the king's attention. Whatever her hidden past, she was chosen as God's visible spokesperson at a very crucial moment in Israel's history.

b. Huldah's prophecy

Huldah's role would be remarkable enough if we took the report at a superficial level but it is even more remarkable once deeper consideration is given to it. Several factors heighten its significance.

First, the king's close advisers choose to consult Huldah, in spite of their being two better known (to us) prophets who were active at the time. Jeremiah had begun his ministry just five years earlier[23] and Zephaniah was in his prime.[24] Possibly Nahum or Habakkuk could have been consulted. But they did not turn to any of these men and chose to consult Huldah in preference to them. Various explanations are offered to explain why this should be so, including the idea that Jeremiah was away at the time or that, as a woman, she might have been chosen as they thought she would be gentler in her response to Josiah than a man. But such responses are unconvincing attempts to avoid the unembarrassed statement that they chose to hear God's voice through a woman.

Secondly, one cannot but be impressed by the high-level nature of the 'carefully composed'[25] delegation who make their way to consult Huldah. Since they were the powerful men in the land one might have expected them to summon her. It would have been

---

[22] E.g., Gafney, *Daughters of Miriam*, p. 98.
[23] Jer. 1:2.
[24] Zeph. 1:1.
[25] Gafney, *Daughters of Miriam*, p. 99.

impressive enough if any one of them had gone to visit her on behalf of the others, but it is even more impressive that they all went together in person, seeking to enquire carefully about any direction she might have from the Lord. The official delegation consisted of Hilkiah, the high priest, Ahikam, a member of an important Jerusalem family and father of Gedaliah who was known to aid Jeremiah,[26] Akbor (or Achbor) the son of a prophet, Shaphan, the 'Secretary of State', and Asaiah, the king's personal officer. The composition of the delegation witnesses both to the importance of the occasion and the respect in which Huldah was held.

Thirdly, there is the nature of Huldah's response. She immediately responds to their request with the words *'This is what the LORD, the God of Israel, says . . . '* (15). She speaks as confidently, authoritatively and unambiguously as any of her classic male prophetic colleagues, using the typical formula for introducing a prophetic utterance. Her voice is the voice of one who has received a sure revelation from God. Consequently she predicts the future accurately and conveys a clear command of God for the present.

Fourthly, there is the content of Huldah's response. Huldah's prophecy is, like that of all the great classic prophets, a fine balance of judgment and grace. Verses 16–17 prophesy that God will invoke the negative terms of the covenant; that God will indeed shortly unleash the curses stipulated in Deuteronomy 27 – 28 for those who break the covenant. Far from being a softer option than a male prophet might have been, Huldah speaks an uncompromising word from God which spells disaster for Israel. She proves utterly faithful to the revelation of God both as it is recorded in Deuteronomy and as she has received it for her own day. Yet, her stern words about Israel's national future are coupled with tender words about Josiah's personal future. Because *your heart was responsive and you humbled yourself before the LORD . . . and because you tore your robes and wept in my presence . . . I will gather you to your ancestors, and you will be buried in peace* (19–20). God's justice was such that he would not condemn a repentant king to witness, still less endure, his nation's destruction but rather will permit him to die peacefully.

Fifthly, it should be noted that her prophecy, which is given under the inspiration of the living Spirit, endorses the words of the written scroll. She might be said to be the first to affirm the authoritative nature of the scroll and the continuing relevance of the ancient text as a contemporary word from God. What God said to his people in times gone by is what he still says to them centuries later. His word

---

[26] Jer. 26:24.

is neither redundant nor outmoded. Here is one of the many examples we find in Scripture of Spirit and word working together, the former endorsing and applying the latter but never correcting it or making it superfluous. Huldah's approach is a warning against those who would drive too great a wedge between the role of the prophet and that of the teacher. Their respective callings may be distinguished, their emphasis different, and even their tone dissimilar, but there must nonetheless be total consistency between them. Paul's use of the body metaphor in 1 Corinthians 12 tells us they need each other.

Finally, we should note the effect of Huldah's pronouncement. Huldah's prophecy strengthened the king in his resolve to reform Israel's worship and lead it in a spiritual revival. The revival is detailed in 2 Kings 23, and offered a significant opportunity for Israel to get right with her God, even if it was sadly to prove a brief and fairly shallow experience. Huldah was the God-appointed means by which the king was encouraged to fulfil his responsibilities as the spiritual leader of the nation. A prophet and a king complemented each other, as an ideal team, to stimulate a revival. Humanly speaking, since Josiah was already swimming strongly against the popular currents of unfaithfulness, without Huldah he might have lacked the determination needed, or have simply been left floundering, unaware of the action to take.

c. Huldah's significance

Later Jewish tradition regarded Huldah with great respect. Two sets of gates at the south-eastern entrance to the temple mount were named in her memory at the time of the second temple.[27] They became the most frequently used access to the temple. But more than this, in her capacity as an Old Testament prophet Huldah also proves to be a very significant person for our understanding of the way in which God speaks through women.

Wayne Gruden, as mentioned, has argued that there is 'a clear distinction' between the prophets in the Old and the New Testament and the difference is that 'the authority' of the earlier prophets 'was not limited to the general content of just the main ideas of their messages. Rather they claimed repeatedly that *their very words* were words which God had given them to deliver'.[28] As such, they have 'absolute divine authority' and to 'disbelieve or disobey a prophet's words is to disbelieve or disobey God'; their words, assuming them to be true prophets, were 'beyond challenge or question'.[29] Huldah

[27] *The Mishna,* Tractate of Midot 1:3.
[28] Grudem, *Gift of Prophecy,* p. 18, italics his.
[29] Grudem, *Gift of Prophecy,* p. 20.

certainly endorses this understanding by the language she uses: '*This is what the* LORD, *the God of Israel says . . .* ' She certainly seems the equal of an Isaiah, Amos or Jeremiah as an authoritative channel of the voice of God.

By contrast, Grudem, and others, argue that prophets in the early church were exercising a rather weaker gift which lacked such authoritative status. They were passing on insights or revelation which had been 'potentially fallibly received and interpreted by the one who prophesies', and not speaking the very words of God.[30] On this basis, many complementarians permit women to exercise the 'weaker' gift of prophecy in the contemporary church, and find no problem with women as prophets in this sense, but restrict them from adopting the 'stronger' gift of teaching which involves the authoritative interpretation of God's revealed word.

Huldah proves somewhat of an obstacle to this argument. As a prophet in the Old Testament era, she, a woman, does speak *the very words of God* and is in a position of unquestionable authority as she instructs the king and leaders of Israel and explains to them the implications of the word of God (the Book of the Law) they have found. If God uses a woman in the Old Testament, in a role which, it is argued, is equivalent to that of the apostles in the New, then how can women be prohibited from exercising a similarly strong gift in the post-Pentecost church? Surely God may continue to use women as authoritative teachers and public preachers who communicate his word, not just as prophets who function in the weaker sense, in the church that since the day of Pentecost has experienced the greater, not lesser, liberty prophesied by Joel?

One way complementarians overcome this obstacle is to say that Huldah is not of equal status to her male prophetic colleagues because she 'evidently exercised her prophetic gift not in public preaching ministry but by means of private consultation'.[31] However, this is unconvincing. We do not know the full extent of Huldah's prophetic experience but, just as some of the classic male prophets sometimes brought a private word from God to individuals, so it is more than likely that on other occasions Huldah exercised a public ministry. But such an argument is really unnecessary since, even if the message she passed on from God was passed on privately, it was spoken to the most public of delegations and directed to the least private of persons, the king, and its repercussions could not have

---

[30] This is Turner's helpful and concise summary of Grudem's position in his Cambridge PhD on the subject and of his more popular *Gift of Prophecy*, in *Spiritual Gifts Then and Now*, p. 187.

[31] J. Piper and W. Grudem, 'An overview of Central Concerns', in *RBMW*, p. 72.

been more public in the nation if she had erected a platform outside the temple or shouted it from the rooftops.

The accumulated weight of the portrait of Huldah is that she was an authoritative prophet who proved to be a genuine voice of God in that her predictions came to fulfilment. Although she is not as well known to us because she was not among the writing prophets whose numerous messages have come down to us, she is as worthy a prophet as any whose words we continue to treasure and study.

3. Conclusion

Women exercised a significant role as prophets during every phase of the Old Testament story. Miriam ministered during the wilderness period, Deborah during the period of the Judges, Huldah during the monarchy, Ezekiel condemns them during the exilic period, and Nodaliah prophesies for good or ill after the restoration from exile.[32] Like the men, they exercised their calling in a variety of ways and with a variety of emphases. Like their male counterparts there are true women prophets and false ones. No prophet is automatically infallible because they claim the title, but every prophecy, whether from the voice of a man or a woman, needs to be tested. Some are named but many, not surprisingly given the patriarchal context, lurk unnamed in the background. But never is the right of a woman to be a vehicle for a message from God questioned. In comparison with the later ethical prophets of Israel, few of their words were recorded. But it is abundantly clear that at the time they were active their prophecies had profound and nation-shaping consequences. We may not only say 'men spoke from God' but also 'woman spoke from God' as well.

---

[32] Gafney, *Daughters of Miriam*, p. 115.

Song of Songs 1:1 – 8:14
9. Passionate women

The Song of Songs speaks of relationships in the most breathtaking, mystifying and indefinable of ways. Although scholars disagree over how many there might be, it is a series of poems that give an insight into the relationship between a young woman and her betrothed as she progresses towards marriage and the consummation of their relationship. At one level it is an overt account of the young couple exploring their delight in each other and exploring love in its sensuous depth. At another level it provides insight into a believer's relationship with God. The most committed of relationships between a husband and wife is seen in the New Testament as an analogy of the profound relationship between God and his people.[1] If human love with all its fragility and flaws can be so powerful and profound, how much more can the relationship of God's people be with their God, who is love?[2]

1. Interpreting the Song of Songs

The interpretative history of Song of Songs[3] tracks the varying theological understandings of women down the years. Understanding this text as a simple portrayal of human love is a relatively recent phenomenon and would have astonished most readers prior to the twentieth century. It would have been almost unheard of to acknowledge that the Song describes a growing physical relationship; that it affirms the woman is valued for her deep feelings, yearnings and desires; that it demonstrates that she is not required to temper her authentic self-expression; and that it gives full expression to her

[1] Eph. 5:25.
[2] 1 John 4:8.
[3] For a full but concise history of interpretation see T. Longman III, *Song of Songs*, NICOT (Grand Rapids: Eerdmans, 2011), pp. 20–47.

strength of character and to her parity in the relationship as the poems progress.

Origen, in the third century, and Jerome, in the fourth, popularized the allegorical interpretation of the Song of Songs. Jerome personally struggled with his sexual feelings and condemned lust and desire, advocating some fairly drastic measures to avoid temptation. Temper Longman comments of him, 'Nothing expresses his attitude toward sexuality and the Song of Songs better than a letter he wrote to his disciple Paula concerning the course of biblical study that he suggests for her daughter' Paulina. He advised her: 'Let her treasures be not silk or gems but manuscripts of the holy scriptures'. He instructs her to read all the other Bible books first and only then says, 'When she has done all these she may safely read the Song of Songs but not before: for were she to read it at the beginning she would fail to perceive that though it is written in fleshly words, it is a marriage song of a spiritual bridal. And not understanding this she would suffer from it.'[4]

Bernard of Clairvaux (1090–1153) was known for his 'contempt for the flesh and for females'[5] and unsurprisingly approached the Song allegorically. Since he viewed the physical body negatively he could not conceive or permit a literal understanding of the Song. The whole course of the allegorical interpretation of the Song is evidence of an inability to appreciate and understand sexuality as a gift of God and appears to arise from a hostility towards female sexuality in particular. From Jerome and Bernard down the centuries, many leaders and traditions have denied that sexual expression is a gift from God and this has led inevitably to a repression of female sexuality.

Unusually Theodore of Mopsuestia (c. 350–428) viewed the Song not as allegory but as a passionate love poem between Solomon and an Egyptian princess. This resulted in him concluding that the book was unworthy of inclusion in the canon of Scripture.[6] His student Theodoret (c. 393–458) remained faithful to the allegorical interpretation of the Song and 'judged his teacher's literal interpretation as "not fitting the mouth of a crazy woman"', which is a revealing comment that not only dismisses a perfectly reasonable and helpful explanation of the Song but also reveals a disrespect for women.[7]

The Reformers generally saw the Song as a political or historical allegory but did not interpret it as speaking of human love. Indeed,

[4] Longman, *Song*, p. 31.

[5] W. E. Phipps, 'The Plight of the Song of Songs', *JAAR* 42 (1974), cited in Longman, *Song*, pp. 32–33.

[6] Longman, *Song*, pp. 38–40.

[7] Quoted by Longman, *Song*, p. 39.

the *Westminster Confession of Faith* 'condemned those who read it as "a hot carnal pamphlet formed by some loose Apollo or Cupid"'.[8] Nor could John Wesley in the eighteenth century accept a literal understanding of the Song, writing:

> the description of this bridegroom and bride is such as could not with decency be used or meant concerning Solomon and Pharaoh's daughter; that many expressions and descriptions, if applied to them, would be absurd and monstrous; and that it therefore follows that this book is to be understood allegorically concerning that spiritual love and marriage which is between Christ and the church.[9]

Since the Enlightenment, the allegorical approach to the Song has largely fallen out of fashion. The human body with its physical attributes has been re-evaluated, by Christians as well as others, and enjoys a greater favour and more positive understanding than in any previous era. People, both women and men, are seen as whole beings and integrated units of body, mind and soul. The senses are understood to feed the soul in ways that previous generations would not have readily perceived, except negatively. Perhaps this means there is a hope of recognizing the value of and of affirming a female's body, thinking and emotions today in a way that has traditionally been denied them by the church.

David Clines, ironically, suggested that the Song could not have been written by a woman, and so cannot be taken at face value, since it represents the ideal woman of a man's dreams.[10] Yet, while there is some disagreement over the identity of who is always speaking, it is agreed that over fifty per cent of the Song gives expression to the female voice while the male voice occupies a mere thirty-four per cent.[11] Put another way, as Weems notes, 'The Song of Songs is the only Biblical book in which a female voice predominates . . . more than fifty-six verses are ascribed to a female speaker (compared to the man's thirty-six)'.[12] Furthermore, the voice of the woman is

---

[8] R. M. Davidson, 'Theology of Sexuality in the Song of Songs: Return to Eden', *AUSS* 27 (1989), p. 3, quoted in Longman, *Song*, p. 34.

[9] J. Wesley, *Explanatory Notes Upon the Old Testament* (Bristol, 1765), quoted in Longman, *Song*, p. 34.

[10] D. J. A. Clines, 'Why is there a Song of Songs and What Does It Do to You if You Read it?', *Jin Dao* 1 (1994), p. 6.

[11] T. Gledhill, *The Message of the Song of Songs*, BST (Leicester: IVP, 1994), p. 93, based on A. Brenner, *The Israelite Woman: Social Role and Literary Type in Biblical Narrative* (Sheffield, JSOT Press, 1985), pp. 46–50. The rest is composed of the voice of the chorus (6%) and heading or unresolved cases (7%).

[12] R. J. Weems, 'The Song of Songs', *NIB*, vol. 5 (Nashville: Abingdon, 1997), p. 364. NIV identifies sixty-six verses.

recorded directly, rather than reported through the voice of a narrator. Add to this, the interjections of the Daughters of Jerusalem[13] and the references to the 'mother's house', as opposed to the more customary 'father's house', and this makes the Song a female book through and through.[14] Not for nothing does it, contrary to much theological interpretation over many centuries, portray a young women with vivid colour and great vitality at every level of her being without criticizing or stifling her as she lives out her ebullient life. The Song of Songs gives women their own voice.[15]

2. Women and emotions: a biblical validation

The woman in the Song of Songs is one of several passionate women portrayed positively in Scripture as expressing their emotions, women like Naomi, Hannah, Mary, Elizabeth and Martha, yet they have often been dismissed as being 'too emotional'. Some claim they do not have the emotional stability or resilience needed for challenging and demanding roles. The evidence for this is usually anecdotal and relies on interpreting women's behaviour pejoratively, with men's emotions being viewed positively while women's are adjudged negatively. But the Song unequivocally affirms the legitimacy and richness of a wide range of female emotions.

In the opening chapter the woman is portrayed as both warm and expressive: *let him kiss me with the kisses of his mouth* (1:2) and *take me away with you – let us hurry* (1:4). She can be assertive. In 1:6 she is robust, energetically resisting people's stares and managing her siblings' anger. In 2:3–13 we read of the woman's deep emotional pleasure in the company of the beloved; she expresses her joy and delight and sees everything through the lens of love. In 3:1–3 the sense of yearning and desire for the one she loves is present. She is not afraid to express her needs. These particular emotions are smothered in expressions of intimacy, deep relationships, sexuality, imagination and sensual delight which are found throughout. Later she conveys the emotion of loss and disappointment: *My heart sank at his departure. I looked for him but did not find him. I called for him but he did not answer* (5:6).

For a woman to be emotional means she is sensitive to the nuances of relationships and the rhythms of life and feels them deeply. This can be both helpfully positive and at times negative and disadvantageous. However, there is never a sense that the young

---

[13] Or, 'friends': 1:4b, 8; 5:1, 9; 6:1, 10, 13; 8:5, 8–9.

[14] Weems, 'Song of Songs', p. 364. 'Mother's house' is referred to in 3:4 and 8:2.

[15] NIV justifiably identifies the woman's voice as found in: 1:2–4a, 4c–7, 12–14, 16; 2:1, 3–13; 2:16 – 3:10; 4:16; 5:2–8, 10–16; 6:2–3; 7:9a – 8:4; 8:5a–7, 10–12, 14.

woman of the Song is censured for her emotions. She is not required to rein them in or control them. Rather, the Song, with its acknowledgment and affirmation of the full range of our emotional expression, leaves the strong impression that life is intended to be lived passionately.

3. Women and romance: a positive affirmation

The social changes which have occurred in Western culture over the past fifty years have impacted both women and men, but perhaps women have especially seen their roles and opportunities revolutionized. With the changes in lifestyle in terms of careers, sexuality, marriage and family, the Song may be thought to sound something of a traditional note. It affirms the teaching of the creation story, which spoke of Adam needing a suitable helper, since he was not fulfilled on his own.[16] For a man and a woman to come together in committed love and to take delight in each other is God's original plan and creation purpose. Within that relationship there should be total intimacy, trust, openness and pleasure without any shame in their nakedness as they are united as one.

The pursuit of a romantic path to union is commended, not disparaged, by the Song. The young couple's star-crossed view of each other and their exuberant expression of love as they approach marriage and finally consummate their relationship is not criticized. The voice of the woman's friends encourages their relationship and does not censure it.[17] Romance is a gift of God to be enjoyed and experienced to the full within the bounds of appropriateness. In it all, the woman is never portrayed as the quarry, the helpless, weaker partner in the chase for love and intimacy. She is as much the proactive partner as the man. She plays her part as fully and confidently as he. Yet the Song not only emphasizes the pleasure of romance, its anticipation, its longing and its adventure in learning about the other person, but is also realistic about the difficulties, struggles and anxieties which will be encountered in such an intense relationship.[18] The romance celebrated is not the idealized romance of the helpless female being saved by the knight in shining armour as in so much contemporary romantic fiction. The woman energetically leads as much as the man and shares equal influence and responsibility in all the ups-and-downs of the relationship.

[16] Gen 2:20–25.
[17] With the exception of the question in 5:9 (which is not necessarily negative) and the reference to her physical immaturity in 8:8–9, their comments all spur the couple on.
[18] 3:1–2; 5:6–8.

How different is much contemporary romantic fiction. Many contemporary novels unhelpfully create stereotypical images of male and female roles that are far removed from the reality of ordinary lives. Equally many magazines depict a fantasy world. For all that, romantic fiction remains hugely popular, with some women, according to a survey in the USA, reading a romantic novel every two days.[19] The popularity of such fiction suggests not only escapism but a craving for relationships which recognize the importance and joy of committed intimacy that a one-night stand in a serial-relationship culture has lost. In presenting an idealized view of relationships, however, such publications add to people's problems. Psychologists have expressed concern about the 'huge number of the issues that we see in our clinics and therapy rooms [which] are influenced by romantic fiction'.[20] Yet none of this is a reason to dismiss the celebration of courtship and the eager anticipation of marriage which the Song of Songs heartily endorses. Rather, given its realistic and authentic portrayal of romance, the Song proves even more relevant and necessary in our culture than before.

4. Women and other women: an illuminating insight

When the issue of a woman's role and function is being debated it is often women who prove the most critical of other women. Many women support the campaign to prevent women from being ordained or accepted in other forms of church leadership and women also alternatively criticise mothers for working or being unemployed. Furthermore, it is often said that women dress not to please men but to impress other women.

In a passing verse the Song of Songs recognizes the tensions that result from the social pressure that some women experience from their own gender. *Dark am I, yet lovely, daughters of Jerusalem . . . do not stare at me because I am dark, because I am darkened by the sun* (1:6). The young woman is aware of the condescending glances of other women in the city. Unlike her, they were not required to work in the heat of the sun and so their skin was fair. In their appearance and behaviour, they represented the sophisticated culture of the city. She, on the other hand, was probably 'a labourer or lower-class woman',[21] working in the fields, and she felt the demeaning nature of their glances. At first she was intimidated and disheartened by the comparisons as she saw her skin darkened by the sun, and her dress and her upbringing as falling short before the beauty and elegant

[19] Source: Business of Consumer Book Publishing 2010.
[20] A. Flood, *Guardian*, 7 July 2011.
[21] Longman, *Song*, p. 96.

style of others. Yet she recovers quickly: *Dark am I yet lovely*. She may be dark because she works as an agricultural labourer, perhaps as a result of the bullying attitude of her brothers, but she knows she is 'black and beautiful'. Moreover, the commitment of her lover adds to her security, giving her the confidence not to be cowed by the apparent disdain of others. She is at ease with her appearance, finds strength in knowing her true self and in the affirmation she receives from the one that matters to her.

The tone of Western culture is one that constantly intimidates and disheartens women and, absurdly, it is often women themselves who are behind the oppressive messages it communicates. With its addiction to image in all its myriad expressions, the average women is often measured by comparison with the exceptional models which are seen in the press and on film and television. A 'normal' woman cannot hope to compete with the touched up photographs, the designer clothes, the alleged competence and the vaunted attributes of 'superwomen' that are presented day in and day out in the media. However the Song teaches us that women need not lack confidence and should find security and strength in knowing they are loved and beautiful in ways that the media would never even want to understand.

Women may look down on other women. They may set demands that are impossible to achieve, but the woman who knows God's love knows also that she is affirmed and beautiful to him. As a consequence of that relationship, hopefully she also finds the loving affirmation of a Christian community who sees her as gifted and valued whatever her style, image, physical attributes or relationship status. When intimidated by other women's comments, by the public representation of women in general, or by how the secular world grades her image, a woman needs to be reminded that regardless of her age, social standing, experience, achievements, in God's family she is *a rose of Sharon, a lily of the valleys* (2:1).

5. Women and discrimination: a painful truth

Throughout history and throughout the world women have faced discrimination on many fronts. They have been declared weak, overly emotional, unstable, of less value than men, worthy of less pay, and unable to take responsibility and leadership as men can. The Song picks up on the discrimination to which women are often subject. In addition to the bullying of her brothers, one of the later poems, in 5:7, reports that she was harassed and abused by the night watchmen. She was on the streets after dark for a good reason, since she was trying to find her lover who had been knocking on her door but had gone before she answered it. Whatever her reason, as a woman out 'after hours' she was most likely considered 'fair game'. The freedom men enjoyed to be out in the public sphere at any time, was not a privilege accorded to her and is still not accorded to women in many cultures today. The man is not subject to harassment when out at night. He is considered strong, powerful, safe and secure by comparison. But one major message of the Song is that as a woman she is of equal value to a man. She too can be assertive and capable. She is a full human being in her own right with feelings, emotions, senses, sexuality and character, and so is worthy of being treated with dignity. The discrimination she received was unjust and the abuse immoral.

The Song mirrors the reality that women are more vulnerable to discrimination than men. Like the main character of the Song, many still find themselves readily mistreated and misunderstood, made to suffer and subject to verbal or physical abuse. If they are clever, capable, assertive and sensual they are a threat and a danger; if they are gentle, submissive, intuitive and warm they are weak and inadequate. The social context for women across the world echoes the 'no win' situation of the woman in this Song, and they too are bound to suffer unless they, like her, find an inner security and strength which enables them to distance themselves from the expectations and demands of others, and relax in the love of God and the affirmation he offers.

Women are discriminated against. For many it is a fact of life. The main character in Song of Songs knows that only too well.

6. Women and sensuality: a generous gift

The rich and colourful poetry of the Song of Songs would make us blush if we lingered over all its allusions and imagery. It focuses, among other things, on the sensual nature of our beings as women and men. The continuous reference to physical beauty, and even erotic experiences, and to a life rich with texture and attractiveness in all its varying shades, is a reminder of God's generosity in creating a world of such radiance and with such potential for joy.

The woman enjoys her physical being and even more so the physical being of her lover. She delights in his handsomeness, strength, caress and scent.[22] Her senses are something to be celebrated as rightly pleasurable. This is in stark contrast to the way the church has traditionally handled sensuality, which is usually driven by a fear that it will lead somewhere unhelpful. Consequently the church has

[22] 1:16; 2:8–13; 3:6–10; 5:10–16; 8:14.

usually been restrictive towards the senses and the delight they can bring. By contrast, in the Song of Songs women and men are encouraged not to stifle the senses but take pleasure in the stimulation they can bring and the happiness they can evoke. There is no hint of repression here, although there are wise cautions to be found as well. So, in 2:7, 3:5 and 8:4, the woman herself repeatedly cautions the Daughters of Jerusalem, *Do not arouse or waken love until it so desires.* The woman is telling her friends not to force the pace of their love but wait for it to blossom in an unhurried not premature way until it can achieve the fullest expression in marriage.[23] These words, as Geldhill puts it, 'act as a brake on the proceedings as if the lovers are being doused with some cold water to cool down the ardour of their passion which is being perhaps aroused at an inopportune time'.[24] But the more dominant theme is the permission it gives to live as a whole woman and experience, as any man might be expected to do, the whole range of sensual experience.

For many centuries the church seemed to have delighted in all that subdued the senses. Dark colours, grave music, sober design, rigid bodily control were advocated and anything which might create colour, noise and beauty, frowned on, particularly if it was a Sunday. (Perhaps I exaggerate to make the point!) Spurgeon in preaching on this poetry made the following comment:

> I like to see a cheerful countenance and to hear of eagerness in the heart of those who are God's saints. There are people who seem to think that faith and gloom are married, and must never be divorced. Pull down the blinds on Sunday and darken the rooms; if you have a garden, or a rose in flower try to forget there are such beauties: are you not to serve God as sombrely as you can? Put your book under your arm and crawl to your place of worship in as mournful a manner as if you were being marched to the whipping post. Act thus if you will but give me faith which cheers my heart, fires my soul and fills me with enthusiasm and delight – for that is likely to be faith of heaven and it agrees with the experience of the Inspired Song.[25]

This 'Inspired Song' portrays a woman enjoying her senses in a liberating way and serves as a model of permission for others to give full expression to them in ways that otherwise would not be heard. Love enables her to satisfy not only her eyes, but her

[23] Longman, *Song*, p. 115.
[24] Gledhill, *Message of the Song*, p. 128.
[25] C. H. Spurgeon, *Till He come: A Collection of Communion Addresses* (Fearn: Christian Focus Publications, 2011), p. 30.

touch,[26] hearing,[27] taste[28] and smell[29] as well. When women have a meaningful relationship with God through Christ then they can expect their senses to be heightened and to recognize the glory of the created world in new ways. Their sensual experience is not to be belittled or feared but to be heightened, as a glorious part of God's new vision of life in him and of having life in all its fullness.[30] It was encapsulated in the traditional hymn:

> Heaven above is softer blue,
> Earth around is sweeter green;
> Something lives in every hue
> Christless eyes have never seen:
> Birds with gladder songs o'erflow,
> Flowers with deeper beauties shine,
> Since I know, as now I know,
> I am His and He is mine.[31]

The Song of Songs is assigned to be read at Passover, during the four days of celebration which recalls God's deliverance of Israel from slavery. For all the strengths of this annual ceremony, 'the repetition of the celebration', as Eugene Peterson observes, 'carried with it a danger, the danger that salvation itself should be ritualized and institutionalized'.[32] The Song, with its emotion, passion, joy and tone of intimacy, serves as the ideal complement to the ritual and prevents it from becoming the cold celebration of a mere historical event. All who celebrated the Passover with its reminders of the trials and struggles of slavery and of the wilderness journey to the Promised Land were also reminded that God gives gifts that make life joyful and pleasurable, not least in the relationships forged by love.

In considering the authorship of the Song of Songs, LaCocque suggested 'the author of the Song was a female poet who intended to "cock a snook at all Puritans"'.[33] There were Puritans in the eighth century BC long before the name was given to Puritans in the seventeenth century AD. Down the ages there have always been those who would seek to repress all expression of sensual pleasure in case

---

[26] 7:6–9.
[27] 2:8, 14; 5:16.
[28] 2:3; 4:11; 5:1.
[29] 1:12–14; 4:16.
[30] John 10:10.
[31] 'Loved with everlasting love', George Wade Robinson (1838–77).
[32] E. H. Peterson, *Five Smooth Stones for Pastoral Work* (Grand Rapids: Eerdmans, 1980), p. 29.
[33] A. LaCocque, *Romance She Wrote: A Hermeneutical Essay on the Song of Songs* (Harrisburg: Trinity, 1988), p. 11.

it gets out of hand or leads to sin, but the Song of Songs upsets their unhelpful restraints.

7. Women and sexual expression: a divine gift

Feminist writings have recorded the existence throughout history of disparaging views of women's sexuality. Compared with men, it has often been popularly thought that a woman's sexual drive was second rate (as measured by men, of course!) and that a good woman would accept sexual relationships as a necessary part of marriage and procreation but was expected to endure rather than enjoy her sexual nature: a faint whisper, perhaps, of the curse of Eden. Continuing contemporary practices of genital mutilation indicate that there still is a view that women are not intended to enjoy sex, that they are to be kept in ignorance so that they might be innocent and available only to fulfil men's wishes. In some quarters there is the converse fear that women who are not controlled or constrained will become rampant sexual predators. So women are considered either godly and virtuous if they had little sexual inclination within marriage and no sexual relationships outside if it, or they are seen as loose women or worse.

The Song of Songs teaches a significantly different perspective. Women, like men, are given the gift of sexuality by God so that they can enjoy and experience love, fully and deeply. They are not confined to a passive role and they too can discover through wise and legitimate sexual encounters a profound fulfilment of their total beings.

What is meant to be a positive celebration of sexuality perhaps understandably causes some concern for those who are single, since Christian teaching rightly asserts that sexual intercourse is appropriate only within a committed, heterosexual, monogamous relationship. But sexuality is a gift for all people, including the single person, and involves a range of expression and different levels of companionship. It is wrong to define it simply in terms of intercourse. The lives of those who are single can be enriched by the enjoyment of the kind of physical and emotional relationships and sensual experiences in which the Song is drenched, while they remain alert, as the woman in the Song is and as partners in marriage need to be, to the need for wise boundaries.

8. Concluding comments

The Song of Songs celebrates love and intimacy in all its intensity and anxieties. Life is richer for it. The Song encourages us, and especially women, not to be dismissive of emotions and feelings; to explore relationships fully and adventurously; to use all the senses God has given; and, to persevere through times when relationships seem less certain and cause confusion.

While primarily about human love, it cannot but be read as an analogy of our love and relationship with God. The same enjoyment of his love, the same quest for intimacy, the same urgent intensity, the same fulfilment and security, the same on-going commitment, the same sense of adventure, and the same need to persist in the seeking after God all apply.[34] So too does one of the most memorable verses in the Song of Song which says, *love is as strong as death, its jealousy unyielding as the grave. It burns like a blazing fire, like a mighty flame* (8:6). Such is the love of God for us as seen in Christ and such should be our love, both as women and men, for God.

[34] Matt. 7:7.

Proverbs 31:10–31
10. Capable women

1. The role of women in Proverbs

From the seductive dress of the wanton temptress, through the stunning attire of Lady Wisdom, to the elegant wardrobe of the profoundly capable, Proverbs presents women in many and varied guises. The focal point in this chapter will be on the final verses of the book that are well known for their presentation of a capable woman or ideal wife, verses which have been used and abused in defining the role of women down the centuries.

The purpose of Proverbs is given in its introduction, 1:8–9. It provides instructions for a 'son', with the intention of guiding him and the young men he represents through the problems, pitfalls and possibilities they encounter as they are on the threshold of the adult world and marriage.[1] Consequently, Proverbs begins with the images of women that were prevalent in their society which focus, as so often they still do today, on physical attractiveness and sensual qualities by which young men could be seduced. So to begin with we encounter 'the negative female imagery of Proverbs 1–9'[2] which warns of the wayward woman with her seductive words (5:3–5) whose 'feet go down to death' (5:5), of 'the neighbour's wife' and the smooth-talking immoral woman (6:24), and 'another man's wife who preys on your very life' (6:26).[3] This negative picture culminates in 9:13–18, where such a woman is pictured as 'an unruly woman' sitting in a public place, calling out to passers-by in an

[1] R. Van Leeuwen, 'The Book of Proverbs', *NIB*, vol. 5 (Nashville: Abingdon Press, 1997), p. 31.
[2] C. V. Camp, *Wisdom and the Feminine in the Book of Proverbs* (Decatur: Almond Press, 1985), p. 115.
[3] See also Prov. 5:6–23; 7:1–27.

attempt to lure them into her trap. In portraying women in the guise of temptress, seductress, harlot and adulterer these verses seem unhelpful and harmful to women, blaming them for the young men's misdemeanours.

However, Proverbs also presents a very different picture about women. Roland Murphy correctly points out that, 'both at the beginning of the book as well as at the end, Wisdom and fear of the Lord [appear] as Woman'.[4] Wisdom is personified as a woman in 4:6–9, 7:1–5 and 9:1–6, with the fullest description of Lady Wisdom being found in chapter 8 where 'she' (8:4) is presented as 'a personification of God's wisdom'.[5] Listening to her as she offers counsel and teaching leads a person to life (9:6). Proverbs 31 fits comfortably with these passages in presenting a very positive view of womanhood.

This positive strand provides young men with an alternative insight about women. They may often appear as a risk or threat, but young men are mistaken in their understanding if women are seen as the threat simply because of their gender, since they are not. According to this strand, men should neither fear nor blame women but need to take responsibility for their own unbridled male passions.[6] To blame women for their own lust and sexual failings is unconvincing, at least if they bracket all women in the same category. 'Testosterone flooded men do have a problem,' admits R. C. Van Leeuwen, 'but it is not women. It is themselves.'[7]

Proverbs 31:10–31 completes the circle begun in the opening chapters of the book.[8] It provides a positive portrait of a woman who is unusually capable and who would make an ideal wife. The portrait is idealized and yet demonstrates what an outstanding contribution women can make not only to their husbands but also to their families and the wider community, if permitted to do so. If, because of all the negative things which might be said of them, men become afraid of women and unable to relate to them effectively, they would be denying themselves and their society the gifts and abilities God has given to women and intended for everyone's positive good.

Two of the most important clues to understanding this woman come respectively in the introduction and conclusion of the passage: she is *of noble character* (10), because she *fears the LORD* (30).

---

[4] R. E. Murphy, *Proverbs*, WBC (Nashville: Thomas Nelson, 1998), p. 249.

[5] T. Longman III, 'Woman Wisdom and Woman Folly', *DOTWPW*, p. 913.

[6] Prov. 6:25.

[7] Van Leeuwen, 'Proverbs', p. 264. Cf. Matt. 5:27–30.

[8] In addition to the concerns with women, note the resonance between 1:7 and 31:20.

This wise and capable woman balances the errant images of women which today, as much as in the ancient world, dominate the literature and thought of popular culture. The woman who fears God and lives in the light of his instructions will be of inestimable worth compared to the seductive and foolish woman who may offer an immediate attraction but who, in the long term, only serves to undermine society and bring destruction on it (30–31). 'In short, "charm" deceives because it promises a lifetime of happiness that it cannot deliver.'[9] 'Beauty is said to be deceitful because it passes away, and with it the hope of happiness based on it.'[10] But this woman demonstrates a depth of character which will neither deceive nor fail to satisfy.

2. The portrait of the woman in Proverbs 31:10–31

In style, Proverbs 31:10–31 is an acrostic poem. Each line begins with a letter from the Hebrew alphabet, which simplifies learning and aids recall. Therefore it needs to be read as poetry rather than as a clearly structured linear argument which is logical in its progression. It needs to be understood in the context of a book which addresses young men in search of a wife, rather than addressing young women themselves as its primary audience.[11] This is not, however, to say that it does not contain rich seams of meaning that will benefit all, whether young or old, male or female, in understanding what it means to be a woman in God's image. Quite the opposite, it gives enormous understanding of women in God's purpose and plan.

The poem does not intend to suggest that 'everywoman' will be like the woman of Proverbs 31, for this is 'a recognisable and credible portrait of a particular kind of woman'.[12] She is a married woman, the wife of a leading man of the city, with servants and her own resources which enable her to be entrepreneurial. 'The poem is rich with words of action'[13] and portrays a woman who is active, energetic and never idle. Presumably her ability to engage in commerce was made possible by education; her ability to read and write would have put her in a league beyond most women of her day. She was born with all the advantages of wealth and privilege, far above the average woman, but she did not allow the opportunities

---

[9] B. K. Waltke, *Proverbs 15-31*, NICOT (Grand Rapids: Eerdmans 2005), p. 535.

[10] Waltke, *Proverbs*, p. 548, quoting C. H. Toy, *The Book of Proverbs*, ICC (Edinburgh: T & T Clark, 1899).

[11] Camp, *Wisdom and the Feminine*, pp. 179–208, points out the close correspondence between this poem and chs. 1 – 9.

[12] W. McKane, *Proverbs: A New Approach*, OTL (London: SCM Press, 1970).

[13] Van Leeuwen, 'Proverbs', p. 260.

of wealth and privilege to make her idle, but rather uses those privileges for the benefit of others, especially of her family, although not in any exclusive way.

a. Highly valued (10–11)

She is a competent woman, described in verse 10 as *of noble character*. The word (*ḥayil*), which is variously interpreted as 'virtuous', 'strong', 'capable' or simply 'good' can also mean 'woman of worth'.[14] The word only appears on three occasions in the Bible. The other two occurrences are found in Proverbs 12:4 and Ruth 3:11, where it indicates the superior dignity of women of character and shows that they are to be honoured.[15] When the same word is used of men it is often 'translated "mighty man" and denotes persons at the height of their powers and capacities'.[16] The 'military' nuance of the term continues in verse 11, where it is said that *her husband . . . lacks nothing of value*. This choice of wording 'suggests the woman is like the warrior bringing home booty from her victories'.[17] So this woman is to be held in the highest esteem, and deserves the equivalent admiration that successful men would receive. These verses, then, serve as a necessary corrective to any cultural bias which devalues women, considering them 'too emotional, weak and vulnerable' to be comparable in value to men.

This woman is to be valued even though many of the usual attributes that men admire about women, such as physical beauty, youthfulness and sensuality, and which are so frequently in the limelight, have no place at all in this portrait. We know nothing of what she looks like. It is her character and inner qualities that make her significant; her spirit and temperament are what set her apart as being of value. Such teaching links readily to many other biblical passages which teach that 'The LORD does not look at things people look at. People look at the outward appearance, but the LORD looks at the heart'.[18]

The emphasis here is on the woman as a wife. She is of inestimable value to her husband, even though her value is not confined to him alone. It is her character, not her marital status, for which she is commended. Perhaps women should not be too sensitive to the way

[14] C. R. Fontaine, 'Proverbs', in C. A. Newsom and S. Ringe (eds.), *The Women's Bible Commentary* (London: SPCK and Louisville: Westminster/John Knox Press 1992), p. 151.
[15] Van Leeuwen, 'Proverbs', p. 260.
[16] Fontaine, 'Proverbs', p. 151.
[17] Van Leeuwen, 'Proverbs', p. 261.
[18] 1 Sam. 16:7.

this is phrased, as if she only has value because she is a wife, since even today a mother writing to her daughter might well say something similar and comment that a potential husband who is conscientious and of good character is worth far more than those who have £1 million in the bank.

b. Busy businesswoman (13–20, 24)

This woman excels in her activities and achievements as an entrepreneur. She is a buyer of raw materials (13, 16). The vocabulary chosen denotes her approach as one of careful enquiry and investigation, knowledge and understanding. Her purchase of *a field* demonstrates commercial acumen on her part, as does the way she exploits its creation potential by planting a vineyard in it *out of her* [own] *earnings* (16).

She engages in trade (14) and is a supplier of food and producer of goods (19). The goods she acquires from far away are used to good effect, both to clothe her children and servants and to earn respect for her husband and family (15), as well as to supply those outside the family who are in need (20). This is no small thing since in her area at the time 'a good woollen garment would cost over two months' wages and an inexpensive linen one half of a month's wage'.[19]

She is an investor (16). When she sees opportunities, she takes them. She is creative with her contacts and connections, seizing the initiative and proving resourceful and ingenious. Again, there is a military overtone to the words, since the way she buys a field suggests 'she puts together a plan or strategy to act on'.[20] Her enterprising impulse naturally arises from her desire to support and sustain her family.

She is also successful. Verse 18 reports that *her trading is profitable,* presumably because *she sets about her work industriously,* in a manner that has often been commended earlier in Proverbs.[21] Waltke notes that the idiom behind the wording in this verse is that of getting 'ready for some kind of heroic or difficult action'.[22] She is at work at all hours and *her lamp does not go out at night* (18). What she produces she then sells (24). Not only is she able to supply the clothing needs of her own family and household but she produces a surplus and has items available for others to buy.

---

[19] Waltke, *Proverbs*, p. 524, quoting B. Porten, *Archives from Elephantine: The Life of an Ancient Jewish Military Colony* (Berkeley: University of California, 1986), tables 2 and 75.
[20] Waltke, *Proverbs*, p. 525.
[21] E.g., Prov. 6:6–11; 12:27; 18:9; 20:13; 21:25; 24:30–34.
[22] Van Leeuwen, 'Proverbs', p. 261.

Yet, for all this busy and active trade and industry she is not a heartless profiteer. She has compassion and a heart for the poor and those who lack her advantages. Van Leeuwen[23] helpfully identifies verses 19–20 as pivotal: *In her hand she holds the distaff and grasps the spindle with her fingers. She opens her arms to the poor and extends her hands to the needy.* Here is the imagery, on the one hand, of grasping the tools of production and the making of a profit and then, on the other hand, of using its potential by opening her hands wide for those in need. Both the grasping and the opening are important symbols for women: there are times to grasp those things which women have been given and use them effectively, with energy and stamina, and times not to hold on to things too tightly or selfishly but to give freely and generously to others, especially to those in need.

c. Depth and strength of character (20–27)

This highly valued and busy businesswoman is presented as a woman of significantly good character. As mentioned, she is generous to the poor (20) and to her servants (15, 21) in the days when servants were not always cared for well. She is organized and thoughtful, anticipating future needs (21–22). She is not taken by surprise either by rough weather or unexpected events. She is a woman of dignity (25) who is strong and secure. She has an inner self-assurance that enables her to work competently and with determination.

According to Proverbs, the way a person speaks is often a gauge of their wisdom[24] and this woman continually speaks wise words (26). Her comments are far from superficial, merely intended to impress or please, but disciplined words that bring illumination, guidance, help and depth of insight to people and situations. She reflects all the qualities that Proverbs associates with wisdom, such as intelligence, good judgment, acumen, discernment and perception. She is also *faithful* in the *instruction* she gives (26), which in the original suggests 'her teaching is informed by her own loving-kindness',[25] rather than rigidly glued to the words of a textbook. There is about her too a loyalty to her family and her household and to God (27). Faithfulness carries the sense of being dependable, reliable and trustworthy. This woman is respected and admired not only for what she achieves but also for the way she achieves it, maintaining her personal integrity and never compromising on her admirable qualities in doing so.

[23] Ibid.
[24] E.g., 10:13; 12:18; 15:1, 2, 7, 28; 16:23–24; 23:15–16; 25:11; 26:4–5; 29:20.
[25] Waltke, *Proverbs*, p. 532.

Leeuwen concludes his 'Reflections' on these verses by saying that, 'the use of masculine images in praise of a woman (vv. 17, 25) must be considered in the light of the poem's masculine audience . . . The heroic terms of strength usually applied to men are here given to a woman so that her splendour and wisdom may be seen by all'.[26] The language of *do noble things*, in verse 29, is similarly used elsewhere mainly to refer to heroic warfare.[27] This corrective to false and disdainful views of women portrays her as anything but the weaker sex, as having the potential to be astonishingly successful and to be as forthright, strong and godly as any man in battle had ever been.

d. Recipient of acclaim (28–31)

As the portrait of the capable woman draws to an end, there is warm acclaim for her on many fronts. Her children and her husband have good reason to acknowledge that God looks on her with favour and so praise her. She is a woman of great accomplishment and an excellent model who surpasses others of her kind.

Verse 31 urges others to recognize her worth and the role she plays in the well-being of her family and more widely in the community. But people's praise must be based on the right criteria. Ancient and modern valuations of women, which have frequently been based on the grounds of their beauty and sex appeal, are implicitly condemned here. Proverbs discharges a healthy rebuke to this common error in reminding us it is not erotic appeal or superficial image by which a woman's worth should be measured but by her character and the contribution she makes to her family and community.

e. The secret of her strength

This portrait of the capable woman concludes with a theme that reverberates throughout Proverbs: that the secret of wisdom and of a fruitful and successful life is 'the fear of the Lord' (30). In essence, it is the 'fear of the Lord' that motivates this woman to fulfil her calling in the home and in marriage, in the vineyards and in the commercial markets. Her energy and stamina, her motivation and sense of purpose arise from her submission to God and his direction to use all gifts and talents for the benefit of those around her. It is 'the fear of the Lord' which gives meaning to her role and sustains her in the daily routines whether she faces discouragements or success, whether she is well in control or meets the unexpected.

[26] Van Leeuwen, 'Proverbs', p. 264.
[27] Waltke, *Proverbs*, p. 534.

It becomes clear that she would not have understood the sacred/ secular divide so common in our contemporary spirituality. Honouring God remains as much about how we relate in our families, approach our work and express our compassion to the needy, as it is about attending religious events or what we often see as more spiritual activities. The woman and man *who fears the LORD* (30) will demonstrate reverence for God in using all the opportunities that come to build up the community and not neglect those in need. Those who would seek to impose a domesticated role on women fail to see the wider scope of God's purposes and plans for women that are reflected here, and how serving him, whether as a male or a female, can result in undertaking significant responsibilities in many different fields.

For the father called to be a househusband, the motivating influence should be 'fear of the Lord'. For the woman chief executive of a global corporation, the compelling inspiration should be 'fear of the Lord'. God's calling to be all that he has gifted and equipped us to be is as relevant to the woman or man in the board room or on the factory floor as it is to the wife or daughter, the father or son in the household. The one calling above all others is to 'fear the Lord'. Fearing the Lord is the primary requirement for bringing wholeness and balance in life for both women and men, made equally in the image of God. It is the secret of living well for both men and women.

The capable woman of Proverbs 31 epitomizes the truth which Proverbs repeatedly sets out that 'the fear of the Lord' is the basis for well-being, prosperity and peace in life.[28] So the emphasis on her 'fearing God' (30) not only draws together all the strands which go to make up the capable woman but also serves as a fitting conclusion to the book of Proverbs as a whole. Jesus taught the same when he said: 'Seek first his kingdom and his righteousness, and all these things will be given to you as well.'[29]

3. The interpretation of this woman today

There is an enigmatic element to the woman of Proverbs 31 that gives rise to several ways of understanding her today. Does she maintain the traditional role of women within the domestic realm, essentially, perhaps almost exclusively, caring for and supporting her husband and family? Or, does she affirm a progressive role for women as independent and entrepreneurial people, with a role outside of the home? She is presented both as a woman in a supporting role to

[28] Prov. 1:7; 3:7–8; 9:10; 15:33.
[29] Matt. 6:33.

143

her husband and as a strong and assertive female role model in her own right.

a. Traditional understanding

Matthew Henry commented, 'she is very industrious to recommend herself to her husband's esteem and affection . . . A good woman, if she be brought into the marriage state, will be a good wife, and make it her business to *please her husband* . . . Though she is a woman of spirit herself, yet *her desire is to her husband*, to know his mind that she may accommodate herself to it and she is willing that *he should rule over her*.'[30] This construal of the text regards the woman as a competent extension of her husband, playing an effective part in the household economy and with character and qualities which make her the ideal wife, but little, if anything, more.

Many popular conservative writings on family life and a women's role reinforce this approach. Citing Proverbs 31:27, one recent publication argues that the woman's focus is to be 'directed inward to the family' while the husband's role is 'outward from the family in the work area'.[31] Perhaps we should be very careful not to dismiss the value and significance of a woman being effective as wife and mother.[32] Yet the portrait of the capable woman in Proverbs 31 hardly justifies the conclusion that her life is directed inwards towards the family. Such an argument in any case reads back into the Hebrew world the very modern separation between the home and the workplace which would have made little sense to them. Producing children and meals along with all the other household management issues, was work indeed, as essential to the economy and well-being of the family and community as other more market-place roles.[33]

b. Progressive understanding

Other writers understand the text differently. Some feminist interpreters object the woman is only seen as virtuous and competent when she acts in beneficial ways in relation to the men in her family.

---

[30] M. Henry, *Commentary on the Bible*, vol. 3 (London: Marshall, Morgan and Scott), 1953, p. 974. Italics original.

[31] G. Knight III, 'The Family and the Church: How should Biblical Manhood and Womanhood Work Out in Practice?' *RBMW*, p. 350. It is unclear how this argument can be sustained from the rest of Proverbs 31.

[32] See D. Patterson, 'The High Calling of Wife and Mother in Biblical Perspective', *RBMW*, pp. 364–377.

[33] See pp. 69–70, 146–147.

Thus, *The Women's Bible Commentary* claims, 'As always in male-centred scripture, the positive and negative roles of women are viewed primarily from the perspective of what they provide the men involved'.[34]

Other progressive interpreters see her as a positive role model, with her strength and energy, her intelligence and astute commercial engagement, her care in researching and gaining knowledge of the market and her ability to be successful in production, affirming the place of women in business and the public arena. Women, they argue, continue to need strong role models showing that it is 'normal' and 'appropriate' for women to have leadership strengths, business and production skills and to be effective in a number of non-domestic roles. Many women continue to face a male culture in the world of work that undermines their female confidence. In the church and the home, on the production line and in the boardroom women may derive affirmation about their competence and diligence from this passage. Their gender is not the issue, only their character, which is as relevant to men as to women.

Leigh Anne Tuohy, the woman behind the film *The Blind Side*, echoes some of the qualities of the capable woman of Proverbs 31. *The Blind Side* tells the story of how Michael Oher, who came from the wrong side of town, meets Mrs Tuohy, a privileged and wealthy homemaker. Her compassion for the disadvantaged and her willingness to use her sparkling talents and ingenuity to the full led, against all the odds, to Michael becoming part of her family and gaining education and achieving national fame as a sportsman. Mrs Tuohy's character and faith were central to her determination to do good and her achievements. She is a strong woman whose strength benefited not only Michael Oher and her own family but the wider community also.

c. Intimidating and unhelpful

There are others who have found the portrayal of the woman in Proverbs 31 unhelpful and intimidating. It certainly raises the question as to whether this poetry is meant to be descriptive of a special woman or prescriptive for all women.

In posing the question, *a woman of noble character who can find?* (10), the poem suggests from the start that such capable women are rare and not easily found. At first sight, this comment may not seem to be affirming women, nor have a gospel tone of God's love about it. However if we go back to the original purpose of Proverbs and

[34] Fontaine, 'Proverbs', p. 146.

realise this is a literary device for emphasizing to young men the need to give attention to the character of those they marry, and not just make the surface judgments, we can read it differently.

This is not a prescriptive account of how women ought to live but is descriptive of one woman in a particular, and gender-exclusive, socio-economic context. If it is read prescriptively then, like the models found in women's magazines, most women may be undermined and set up to fail before they have even started. She is so competent that those who seek to emulate her achievements and success are almost bound to fall short. She is an ideal type who shows how resourceful and effective a women can be, but she is not prescriptive of how all women must be. Most other women of her time lacked her opportunities, education and confidence and would have compared poorly to her. While this capable woman is a sound biblical portrait of a woman made in God's image, her superwoman image should not be a basis for expecting other women to measure up to her. Without servants and the other material advantages she had, she would not have enjoyed the success that she did.

4. Concluding comments

The portrayal of the capable woman supports the view that to restrict women to a narrow domestic role is not biblically justified. Those who have argued for a domestic/business divide, or a private/public divide, or a household/breadwinner divide for women and men have not fully come to terms with the teaching found here, nor with social structures which vary over time. In that regard, three important issues need to be taken into account. First, defined roles for female and male are not apparent in Proverbs 31. Secondly, the masculine imagery that is used in reference to the woman here indicates a broader participation in all aspects of social and economic life than some might think legitimate. And, thirdly, the home was the economic core, not just domestic centre, of the community, both then and for many generations to come.

However, those who take this heroic hymn of praise to this remarkable woman and hold it up as a pattern for all women also lack understanding and insight. At the time this poetry was produced the majority of women would have had no opportunity to follow such a path and even today most women around the globe are struggling to survive, rather than be successful businesswomen. And yet, even women struggling at the most basic level for freedom and power can take hope from the warrior tones of this portrait. The poetry of Maria Miguel, a Liberation theologian, resonates with the woman of Proverbs 31. 'One day the woman cried, "I am warrior!" And the echo of her voice resounded beyond the borders. I am woman: mother and warrior!'[35]

This woman is not the fictional housewife of a past era. She does not stay at home and do only the domestic chores, although she clearly cares deeply for her husband and children. She takes her place in the market square and in the wider community. She deals with traders from afar and neighbours from next door. It is a pleasure and honour to be connected to this woman, as not only her husband, children, and servants know but as the poor in her town know as well. Few can follow her example in all its detail, as she is exceptionally advantaged, but all can follow the values and principles by which she lives. She understands that her first priority is to pursue the focus of the book of Proverbs, which is wisdom. She knows wisdom begins with fearing God, acknowledging her dependence on him, offering gratitude for the skills and opportunities she has and then using those capabilities for the sake of all who are around her.

What she offers is the balance of serving and responsibility; of leadership and compassion; of enterprise and trust; and of freedom and commitment.

[35] A. M. Trepedino and M. L. R. Brandao, 'Women and the Theology of Liberation', in I. Ellacuria and J. Sobrino (eds.), *Mysterioum Liberationis: Fundamental Concepts of Liberation Theology* (Maryknoll: Orbis Books, 1993), p. 225.

Part Three
Women in the kingdom

Luke 1:26–56; Mark 3:20–35; John 2:1–12; 19:25–27
11. Women in the life of Jesus

Women are anything but invisible in the life and ministry of Jesus. They are prominent witnesses to the events of his life, faithful disciples to the end, recipients of his grace, subjects of his teaching and beneficiaries of his justice. Seventeen women are mentioned by name, but a host of others are unnamed although no less valued.[1] With the encouragement of Jesus they do not lurk on the margins, even if some initially shelter fearfully in the shadows because of the pressures of their culture, but become people whose presence is noted, whose voice is heard and whose lives are made whole. He treats them with an unprecedented dignity and worth and overturns the negative evaluation from which they mainly suffered in wider society.[2]

Several women play a part in the events of Christ's life. They are particularly evident at his birth and at his crucifixion and resurrection. The news of the incarnation is first announced to women; so, too, is the news of the resurrection. At both of these momentous moments men are relegated to play 'catch-up'. Elizabeth and Anna are significant in the stories of his birth, along with Mary his mother. Mary Magdalene, Joanna, Salome and Mary the mother of

---

[1] D. M. Scholer, 'Women', *DJG*, pp. 884–885. The named women, together with selective references, are: Anna (Luke 2:36–38), Elizabeth (Luke 1:5–45, 57), Herodias (Mark 6:17–29), Joanna (Luke 8:3), Martha (Luke 10:38–42; John 11 – 12:2), Mary Magdalene (Luke 8:2; 24:10; Matt. 20:1–18), Mary the mother of James and Joseph (Mark 15:40), Mary the mother of Jesus (Luke 1:26–56; 2:1–52), Mary the sister of Martha (Luke 10:38–42; John 11:1 – 12:8), Mary the wife of Clopas (John 19:25), the other Mary (Matt. 27:61; 28:1), Rahab (Matt. 1:5), Ruth (Matt. 1:5), Salome (Mark 15:40), Susanna (Luke 8:3), Tamar (Matt. 1:3), and the wife of Uriah (Matt. 1:6).

[2] B. Witherington III, *Women in the Ministry of Jesus*, SNTSMS 51 (Cambridge: Cambridge University Press, 1984), pp. 1–10.

James were the first unlikely but authentic witnesses to the resurrection.[3] In between women are involved in some of the most memorable episodes in his life and serve as exemplary role models of discipleship. There is, perhaps inevitably, one woman who assumes a role in the life of Jesus above all others, his mother Mary.

1. Mary: 'highly favoured' (Luke 1:26–38)

'But when the set time had fully come, God sent his Son, born of a woman . . . '[4] That woman was Mary, an as yet unwed girl from Nazareth who was a virgin and probably about twelve or thirteen years old, the age at which they would have usually married at the time.[5] From society's viewpoint she was insignificant, not only as a young unmarried woman but also as one who came from a lowly background. In the Magnificat she describes herself as being in a 'humble state' (1:48) which infers not only humility of spirit but that she was from a background of relative poverty. Mary and Joseph later offered 'a pair of doves or two young pigeons'[6] in the temple, which was the offering of poor people and confirms the picture. Mary's falling pregnant prior to her marriage would only have served to turn any ordinary lack of respect she suffered into contempt and disapproval. Yet, God esteemed her *highly favoured* (28).

No reason is given to explain why God chose her, although the subsequent story may give us hints as it testifies to her pious character. He chose her, apparently, for the same reason that he chose Israel according to Deuteronomy 7:7–8, not because of their intrinsic worth but because of his sovereign grace. Here is God typically overturning the world's conventional expectations. He had done it throughout history when, for example, he overturned the laws of primogeniture and chose barren women to be the bearers of significant leaders in Israel. Now, introducing a subject that will become one of the major themes of Luke's Gospel, Mary experiences a major reversal of her status.[7]

Mary reacts to the angel's appearance and message with a mixture of understandable apprehension and curiosity. She might have found *favour with God* and have been privileged to be the bearer

---

[3] See R. Bauckham, 'The Women and the Resurrection: The Credibility of their Stories', *Gospel Women: Studies of the Named Women in the Gospels* (London: T & T Clark, 2002), pp. 257–310.

[4] Gal. 4:4.

[5] J. Green, *The Gospel of Luke*, NICNT (Grand Rapids: Eerdmans, 1997), p. 86.

[6] Luke 2:24.

[7] Green, *Luke*, pp. 58–61.

of the Messiah, *the Son of the Most High*, but quite reasonably she asks *'How will this be . . . since I am a virgin?'* (34). Mary's status as a virgin is emphasized three times by Luke, twice in verse 27 and again in 34, as well as being confirmed in Matthew 1:22–23. The announcement stirs memories of Isaiah 7:14 but even if there the word might strictly mean 'young betrothed woman' with only the implication of virginity, here there can be no doubt. The NIV's *since I am a virgin* is, more literally, since 'I do not know a man'[8] which can only mean 'I do not have a husband with whom I have had sexual relations'.[9]

Mary's virginity is important theologically. The child she is to bear is to be God's appointed saviour ('Jesus')[10] and divine Son who will restore David's throne and inaugurate a *kingdom* that *will never end* (32–33). Even though Mary was to marry Joseph, who belonged to the family of David (27), she would not have been qualified to be the mother of such a royal person and his standing would always have been uncertain. But the angel explains that Mary would conceive this child because *'The Holy Spirit will come on you, and the power of the Most High will overshadow you'*. In this way the child's status as a saving king and unique Son is secured beyond doubt. Mary's role is crucial but 'the initiative and powerful work of God are much more so'.[11]

God's deliverance of Israel usually occurs through human agents. Sometimes women serve as the direct agents of deliverance as did Deborah, Jael and Esther. Like Jael and Judith, the mother of the Maccabean martyrs, Mary is called 'blessed'.[12] More often, though, women are noted as the indirect agents of deliverance by becoming mothers of sons who were to become strategic leaders in Israel. Several of these women were infertile, as was Mary's cousin Elizabeth, until God chose to miraculously grant them a child in a supernatural way. Mary belongs to this company, writes Richard Bauckham, 'not because she was barren but because she was a virgin and so could not have borne a child without God's miraculous intervention'.[13] Mary is blessed above all and outshines them all because the son whom she bears is in a class of his own, a universal Saviour and King without comparison.

---

[8] NRSV mg.

[9] I. Howard Marshall, *The Gospel of Luke*, NIGTC (Exeter: Paternoster, 1978), p. 69.

[10] Matt. 1:21.

[11] Green, *Luke*, p. 89.

[12] Judg. 5:24; Judith 13:18–20. See Bauckham, *Gospel Women*, p. 59.

[13] Bauckham, *Gospel Women*, p. 58.

2. Mary: radically vocal (Luke 1:46–56)

While visiting her cousin Elizabeth, whose own miraculous and unexpected child would play a significant role in announcing the arrival of the Messiah, Mary bursts into a song of praise. While many have debated whether such a young girl, who, unlike her male counterparts, would not have received the benefits of education in the Torah, was capable of such an exquisitely composed hymn, Luke's Gospel unashamedly attributes it to her.

The song is noteworthy for being soaked in the phrases of the Old Testament and patterned closely on Hannah's song as she rejoices in the gift of Samuel who was to prove such a strategic servant of the Lord.[14] It is however no mere copy and testifies to Mary's personal devotion to God and her deep absorption of Israel's faith. The song is also noteworthy for its radical teaching. The mindful God who remembers to be faithful to his covenant (54–55) and the merciful God (50, 54) who extends grace to the undeserving, is also the mighty God who fights against Israel's enemies and overthrows them in the name of justice. Like the Old Testament warrior God[15] he humbles the proud, scatters the powerful and denies the prosperous what they think they have earned. In doing so he exalts the humble, feeds the hungry and enriches the poor. The song has a radical intensity about it which is shocking, but totally consistent with the portrait of the God of righteousness who was at the heart of the covenant with Israel. The song has a spiritual intensity about it which is awesome, but one whose social and political implications cannot be sidestepped. This vulnerable teenage girl shows a depth of understanding about God and of faith in him that is astonishing.

There is at least one more aspect of this song which is noteworthy. Luke's attribution of the Magnificat to Mary and his inclusion of it in his Gospel meant it would be read widely in the church and used as the basis for Christian instruction. In identifying Mary as its author, as Kenneth Bailey has pointed out, 'he indirectly presents her as a teacher of theology, ethics, and social justice for all his readers'.[16] It has certainly been widely used as a significant element in Christian worship ever since and also been widely used for

---

[14] 1 Sam. 2:1–10. On the comparison between Mary and Hannah see Bauckham, *Gospel Women*, pp. 60–67.

[15] Ps. 24:8; Zeph 3:17.

[16] K. E. Bailey, 'Women in the New Testament: A Middle Eastern Cultural View', *Anvil* 11 (1994), p. 9. Bailey acknowledges the critical discussion that questions whether the song was originally Mary's but says 'irrespective of . . . sources or authorship, Luke *presents* Mary as the singer of this song and thus a teacher of the readers of his Gospel'.

teaching. As the Wesley brothers knew, many Christians learn their theology from what they sing, rather than from what they hear preached. The hymn or songwriter, therefore, has great significance as teacher in the church, which should cause us to exercise wise discernment over those we acknowledge as such. Ironically this means that even where churches forbid women a formal teaching role, many have performed that function, intentionally or otherwise, in the guise of being hymn writers. In this respect Mary may be said to be their pioneer. Complementarians see this as permissible because such teaching is '*occasional* and *periodic*'.[17] But this may well under-estimate the significance of how people learn their theology and assume too fine a distinction between the various forms teaching might take. Mary is to be honoured as a teacher of the church.

3: Mary: needlessly eager (John 2:1–12)

Every good mother rightly regards her son as special but none has ever had more cause to do so than Mary. She had been encouraged to think her child exceptional by a series of things that are associated with his birth, like the angelic messenger who announced his coming,[18] the appearance of angel choirs who celebrated his birth,[19] the homage offered to him by diverse people in his infancy[20] and the prophecies spoken about him when presented in the temple.[21] Even the opposition his birth provoked marked him out as no ordinary child.[22] Later, when he reached the age of Jewish adulthood and caused amazement by his understanding in the temple, Mary's grounds for believing her child would be like no other were strength-ened. It is, then, not surprising that when he emerged from his private family life and began to move about in a more public way that she should have been eager to advance his ministry.

Mary's opportunity came when they attended a family wedding at Cana and the embarrassing situation arose of the supply of wine running out. According to John's account, Mary did no more than remark to her son that *They have no more wine* (2), but the hint was barely concealed. It was an invitation for him to use his exceptional powers and come to the rescue, and Jesus' response shows he under-stood it as such. '*Woman, why do you involve me?*' *Jesus replied.* '*My hour has not yet come*' (4). That Jesus addresses his mother as

---

[17] J. Piper and W. Grudem, 'An Overview of Central Concerns', *RBMW*, p. 85.
[18] Matt. 1:20–21; Luke 1:26–38.
[19] Luke 2:13–14.
[20] Matt. 2:1–12; Luke 2:8–18.
[21] Luke 2:25–40.
[22] Matt. 2:13–18.

Woman seems designed to invite further investigation. Woman was a formal term of respect and not in any way derogatory, but equally it was not a term that would have been used in addressing one's mother and was not associated with close affection. It was Jesus' way of distancing himself from his mother and 'disengaging from her parental authority'.[23] Jesus is not, as Don Carson points out, 'rebuking his mother' but asserting his independence from any human advice or manipulation, even if the source of it was his mother. Carson continues:

> She had borne him, nursed him, taught his baby fingers elementary skills, watched him fall over as he learned to walk; apparently she had also come to rely on him as the family provider. But now that he had entered into the purpose of his coming, everything, even family ties, had to be subordinated to his divine mission.[24]

From this point on, Mary was required to make a costly adjustment in her relationship with her son. No longer could she act as other mothers might who exercised even in adulthood some proprietorial authority over their sons, but she was to adopt the role of the disciple. Mary begins that day to learn the hard and painful lesson that her calling was now to be his disciple first and foremost, not his mother who happened to be his disciple.[25] She needed to release him to fulfil his costly mission and her well-meaning attempts to promote his 'career' would only serve to frustrate it, like the well-meaning attempts of so many of his other friends who did not understand that God's kingdom is one where death is the way to life, humility the way to honour, and weakness the way to power. Mary's eagerness was to be admired, but her understanding was still at an elementary stage.

4. Mary: deeply bewildered (Mark 3:20–34)

It is difficult for us to imagine how bewildering Mary must have found the course her son followed in his life. We know the story from beginning to end, but she only knew it from the beginning and watched it gradually unravel in perplexing and unexpected ways towards its spectacular end. From the start she was caught up in the mystery of it all. Angelic visitors, ordinary, macho men, foreign

---

[23] B. Witherington III, *Women and the Genesis of Christianity* (Cambridge: Cambridge University Press, 1990), p. 89.

[24] D. A. Carson, *The Gospel According to John*, PNTC (Grand Rapids: Eerdmans and Leicester: IVP, 1991), p. 171.

[25] Witherington, *Genesis of Christianity*, p. 97.

aristocracy and godly prophets had all said strange things or behaved in puzzling ways when he was born. Simeon's comment that 'a sword will pierce your own soul too'[26] did nothing to clarify things. The hurried and unscheduled trip to seek safety in Egypt deepened the mystery. Jesus' 'precocious' behaviour in the temple at the age of twelve did nothing to solve the conundrum. Any mother would have done what Mary did when she 'treasured all these things in her heart'[27] and chewed over them internally, no doubt continuously.

According to Mark 6:3, Jesus was known in Nazareth as 'Mary's son', with no mention being made of Joseph, which suggests Joseph had already died.[28] Whether Mary wanted to be identified in this way is another matter. Mary's bewilderment had surfaced when early in his public ministry she and the rest of the family *went to take charge of him, for they said, 'He is out of his mind'* (21).[29] Their position in relation to him is artistically represented by Mark's comments that *standing outside* [the circle around him] *they sent someone in to call him* (31). Quite what Mary thought is not stated. She may have led the delegation, as one might expect a Jewish mother to have done, or merely been coerced into joining in the 'rescue mission' by her children. Collectively though it is clear that at this time the family were sceptical outsiders. Far from compliant, Jesus, astonishingly, brusquely repudiates the ties with his natural family.[30] For disciples the more important family was *whoever does God's will* (35).[31] Blood ties and opposition from one's natural kin could never be allowed to stand in the way of the work of the kingdom. Such comments would have proved a severe challenge to the place of the patriarchal family in the world of Jesus' day, especially as, when Jesus speaks of the family of faith to which his disciples belong, he noticeably omits any reference to the role of a human father within it but only 'brothers, sisters, mothers [and] children'.[32]

[26] Luke 2:35.

[27] Luke 2:51.

[28] This is preferable to the view that this is Mark's way of indicating that people knew Jesus was not Joseph's son. R. T. France, *The Gospel of Mark*, NIGTC (Grand Rapids: Eerdmans, 2002), p. 242; R. A. Guelich, *Mark 1-8:26*, WBC (Dallas: Word, 1989), pp. 177–178.

[29] Mary is specifically mentioned as being involved in v. 31.

[30] France, *Mark*, p. 178, argues that the terseness of the exchange is due to Mark's interest in teaching the necessity that loyalty to Jesus must take precedence over all other loyalties. Cf. Matt. 12:46–50 and Luke 8:19–21 which report the whole episode less confrontationally.

[31] Cf. Mark 10:28–31.

[32] Mark 10:30. See Matt. 23:9. E. S. Fiorenza, *In Memory of Her: A Feminist Reconstruction of Christian Origins* (New York: Crossroad, 1994), pp. 146–148.

These almost passing references to Jesus' family have occasioned much discussion regarding their actions.[33] Later in the New Testament we learn that they had become believers and disciples, with Mary and James assuming prominent roles in the church, but this was not their position during Jesus' lifetime. Like others they were trying to make sense of confusing pieces of the jigsaw. Others would have done exactly what they did in a culture that prized the importance of family honour. They were probably trying to remove Jesus from public view in order to spare their family from further embarrassment and retrieve its reputation.[34] Far from being in a specially privileged position, the family, Mary included, are presented as an ordinary family struggling to come to terms with the behaviour of an eccentric son.

Ben Witherington says that the synoptic Gospels 'show that Mary was fully human and struggled with the difficulties of placing her spiritual allegiance to Jesus over her motherly love for him and her other sons and daughters'.[35] This may well be true, but I suspect that Mary's struggles really lay elsewhere. Mary had shown great insight when she sang the Magnificat but it is apparent that she did not easily make connections between the claims about God's power and mercy she voiced there and what she saw her son doing and saying. The 'highly favoured' one had now become the deeply confused one. She was, after all, 'a simple Hebrew maid "engraced" by God. How could she understand all that was involved?'[36]

5. Mary: painfully faithful (John 19:25–27)

John alone reports that *near the cross of Jesus stood his mother . . .* (25).[37] Whatever her earlier opinions about Jesus she had not abandoned him but followed him to the place of crucifixion. It would seem that John intends us to see her standing there not only as a grieving mother but also as a convinced disciple. We are not made party to her inner thoughts but the conversation that ensues is about discipleship. Addressing his mother again as *'Woman'* – that respectful yet slightly formal way of speaking, already used by him in John 2:4, that indicates he is not subject to her as a normal Jewish son

[33] See discussion in Witherington, *Ministry of Jesus*, pp. 88–92.

[34] D. A. deSilva, *Honor, Patronage, Kinship and Purity: Unlocking New Testament Culture* (Downers Grove: IVP, 2000), p. 172.

[35] Witherington, *Genesis of Christianity*, p. 95.

[36] D. English, *The Message of Mark*, BST (Leicester: IVP, 1992), p. 90.

[37] On the historicity of this account and the difficulties of reconciling John's account with the Synoptic accounts of the crucifixion which do not mention Mary, see Bauckham, *Gospel Women*, pp. 218–23 and R. E. Brown, *The Gospel According to John XIII–XXI*, AB (Doubleday: New York, 1970), pp. 904–906, 913–916.

might be – he commits her into the care of *the disciple whom he loved,* who *from that time on . . . took her into his home* (26–27). Mary's natural children are absent from the scene, perhaps because they were still not yet believers,[38] but the principle Jesus had taught of the true family being the ones who did the will of God is now put into practice. She remains his mother but is now cared for by the family of faith.

Much has been made of Jesus' remark *'Here is your mother'* (27) to the disciple. If, given the way in which John constantly conveys spiritual truth symbolically, it is possible to make too little of the comment and see it as only the dying Jesus caring for his mother, it is also possible to make too much of it, as many have done.[39] But it is reasonable, with Ben Witherington, to see in this that Mary and the beloved disciples standing before the cross 'are depicted as representative male and female disciples',[40] standing as equals, although with different roles, before the crucified one.[41] The over-eager mother of John 2 had now become the submissive disciple of John 19. She was there to witness that the hour, which had not come in Cana, had now come at Golgotha.[42]

6. Concluding comments

As his mother, Mary is naturally the most important woman to play a part in the life of Jesus. She does so as a young woman of great faith 'engraced' by God to start with, before maturing through doubts and perplexities into a believer and devoted disciple of her son and eventually to receive a prominent place in the early church. She is neither to be denigrated nor venerated, but honoured as God's specially chosen one who bears his son and in due time becomes an exemplary disciple.

Yet Mary was not the only woman to figure in the life of Christ. Elizabeth and Anna have significant roles at the time of his birth. Several are mentioned in the course of his ministry and, strikingly, John points out that several were found with Mary standing at the cross. With her were *his mother's sister, Mary the wife of Clopas, and Mary Magdalene.*[43] Their presence at the cross and the absence of any mention of male disciples, with the exception of the beloved

[38] John 7:5.
[39] Brown, *John*, pp. 923–927.
[40] Witherington, *Genesis of Christianity*, p. 98.
[41] Witherington, *Ministry of Jesus*, p. 98.
[42] John 2:4, cf. 12:23, 27; 13:1; 17:1.
[43] Mark 15:40 gives a slightly different list. The commentaries discuss possible ways to reconcile these.

159

disciple, is particularly noteworthy, especially in Peter's case.[44] Whatever the explanation, the women's presence is a matter of comment and testifies both to their affection for Christ and courage in following him, since to identify closely with a convicted criminal would have been to come under suspicion oneself. Heedless of risk, they follow Christ to the cross and beyond it to the tomb, where they are rewarded by being the first witnesses to his resurrection.

The role the women play in the closing episodes of Christ's death and resurrection is, says R. T. France, also 'a pointer to something new in the movement Jesus had begun which contrasts strongly with the male domination of his . . . time'.[45] These women are pioneers who forge a path many would subsequently follow and discover grace and healing, liberty and significance, and forgiveness and transformation in Christ. At Pentecost, the Spirit would come on men and women and both male and female would become 'one in Christ'.[46]

[44] Apart from the subsequent account of Peter's denial of Christ, the last we read of the disciples before the crucifixion is that they had all deserted Christ 'and fled' (Mark 14:50).

[45] France, *Mark*, p. 665.

[46] Acts 2:17; Eph. 3:18.

Mark 5:22–34; Luke 7:36–50; John 4:1–42
12. Women in the encounters of Jesus

The Jewish historian Josephus neatly summarized the general attitude towards women by Jewish men in Jesus' day when he wrote that 'the woman . . . is in all things inferior to a man'.[1] Most Jewish males looked on women with disdain. To have a son was a cause of thanksgiving, to have a daughter a matter of regret. Men were creatures of reason while women were sensual creatures.[2] Women were seen to have little worth and their status constantly bracketed with that of children and slaves. Their place was chiefly one of seclusion in the home: 'best suited to the indoor life which never strays from the house', as Philo put it.[3] Even there they were subject to patriarchal authority and could be divorced without regard to their future well-being if they displeased their husbands. They were overwhelmingly thought to be not worth educating and mostly adjudged unteachable. Men blamed them for a whole host of ills and, not least, of being the source of sexual temptation. Since this was to be avoided at all costs, it was considered unwise to speak to a woman on the street, even if the woman in question was one's wife. Still greater care was needed when meeting with them in private.[4]

[1] Josephus, *Contra Apionem,* 24.201, cited by M. Evans, *Woman in the Bible* (Exeter: Paternoster 1983), p. 33.

[2] Philo, cited by J. B. Hurley, *Man and Woman in Biblical Perspective* (Leicester: IVP, 1981), p. 61.

[3] Philo, *De Specialibus Legibus*, 3.169, cited by Evans, *Woman*, p. 34.

[4] Numerous books have provided detailed support for this picture including K. E. Bailey, *Jesus Through Middle Eastern Eyes: Cultural Studies in the Gospels* (London: SPCK, 2008), pp. 189–190; Evans, *Woman*, pp. 33–37; Hurley, *Man and Woman*, pp. 62–74; and B. Witherington III, *Women and the Genesis of Christianity* (Cambridge: Cambridge University Press, 1990), pp. 3–9.

Jesus shows a wanton disregard for such strictures and adopts a revolutionary stance in his relationship to women. The Gospels report numerous encounters he has with them both in public and in private, and even records that women are included among his itinerant disciples.[5] He seems unembarrassed in their company and treats them with dignity and worth. He does not accuse them of being the source of sexual temptation but rather defends a woman caught in adultery against the accusations of men[6] and puts the onus on men to discipline their lust (Matt. 5:27–30).[7] He brings salvation and healing to them in the same way he does to men and they become valued sisters or mothers in his true, as distinct from his natural, family if they do God's will (Mark 3:34–35). They are capable, worthy of education (Luke 10:38–42). Furthermore, in flat contradiction to the respectable culture of the rabbis, he can even make the outrageous claim that 'tax collectors and prostitutes are entering the kingdom ahead of' priests and Jewish elders.[8]

People's claims are often one thing while their practice is another but in Jesus we find a perfect harmony between them. His appreciation of their worth was more than theoretical as can be seen from the several encounters the Gospel records where he ministers freely and lovingly to women. Among the several encounters recorded[9] we have selected three that may fairly have some claim to being representative.[10]

1. A woman in the crowd (Mark 5:21–34)[11]

The healing of the woman in the crowd at Capernaum is one of the most extraordinary healings recorded in the Gospels. It occurred while Jesus was on his way to the house of Jairus, *one of the synagogue leaders* (22) and therefore a man of standing. It would have been natural for him to assume he could command the attention of Jesus and enlist his services to cure his sick daughter. He stands in sharp contrast to the unnamed woman who had no confidence even to

---

[5] Luke 8:1–3.

[6] John 7:53 – 8:11. Assuming the text to be original.

[7] This is consistent with the teaching of Proverbs. See pp. 136–137.

[8] Matt. 21:31.

[9] Other encounters include those with Peter's mother-in law (Mark 1:29–31); the woman from Syrian Phoenicia (Mark 7:24–30); the widow of Nain (Luke 7:11–17); a crippled woman (Luke 13:10–17); and the woman caught in adultery (John 7:53 – 8:11).

[10] Other encounters will be covered in the following two chapters under a different heading.

[11] Also Matt. 9:18–26; Luke 8:40–56.

approach Jesus directly but who nonetheless drew on his power for her healing.[12]

a. Her condition

With a few deft brush strokes, Mark leaves us in no doubt about the desperate nature of her suffering. Her *bleeding* was long-standing, not a transient pain which would naturally pass in a day or so. In fact, she had been ill *for twelve years* (25), as long as Jairus' daughter had been alive (42). The illness had also proved stubbornly incurable. We do not know how wealthy this woman was but whatever assets she had once possessed had been spent in vain on seeking a cure through the normal medical channels.

The illness seems to be 'some sort of menstrual disorder'.[13] While its precise nature may be unclear, the implications are perfectly clear. Her illness meant she was a woman to be avoided at all costs. According to Leviticus 15:19–33 she was impure and would con-taminate anything or anyone she came into contact with.[14] She was condemned to live an isolated life socially and also spiritually since she would have been forbidden to worship in the synagogue. Her presence in the crowd was a violation of both the social code and the religious norms of her day. If the crowd had known she was present they would no doubt have turned on her, hence her quest for anonymity among the masses that followed Jesus.

All this meant she was desperate and in that desperation took a risk in reaching out to Jesus. Having heard of his reputation as a healer, she had nothing to lose by mingling with the crowd in the hope of touching him and drawing down healing from him. Her understanding may have been primitive but her faith was genuine, and would be rewarded.

b. His compassion

Healings often involved touch.[15] Jairus had begged Jesus to *put your hands on [my daughter] so that she will be healed and live* (23). But

---

[12] A miracle within a miracle story is typical of what has become known as a Markan sandwich.

[13] R. T. France, *The Gospel of Mark*, NIGTC (Grand Rapids: Eerdmans, 2002), p. 236.

[14] France also points out *tha Niddah*, a tractate in the *Mishna*, dealt with the issue (*Mark*, p. 236).

[15] F. J. Gaiser, *Healing in the Bible: Theological Insights for Christian Ministry* (Grand Rapids: Baker, 2010), pp. 165–176. Gaiser suggests touch is much more than physical contact and involves 'communication, sharing and insight', p. 168.

here a surprising reversal is in operation.[16] Jesus does not touch her; she touches him. Mark reports that she was healed *immediately* (29). All Jesus' healings in Mark are instantaneous[17] but here his point is a little different. The woman's touch leads not only to her instant healing but to Jesus' instant awareness that *power had gone out from him* (30). This way of putting it seems to indicate a physical transfer of energy, as if the battery that sustained Jesus' power to heal was run down as it empowered the healing in her body. Rather than her touch making Jesus unclean, the reverse happens. Healing power flows from Jesus to the haemorrhaging woman to make her clean.[18] By pointing out that many others in the crowd were in physical contact with him Mark counters the idea that it is mere touch that has led to her healing; rather, it is her faith (34).[19]

In the circumstances, Jesus' question, *Who touched my clothes?* (30), seems a trifle absurd to the disciples. It would have perhaps been just as sensible to ask, 'Who didn't touch me?' Even if he knew the identity of 'the culprit', he waits for her to identify herself. When she does so, she is nervous, perhaps for fear of the crowd's reaction, or in fear of losing the healing, or just because she is over-awed by Jesus. But Jesus' question is motivated by compassion, not by curiosity and still less by a desire to censure. 'He is not content to despatch a miracle; he wants to encounter a person.'[20]

Once she tells Jesus her story, we can see the wisdom of his not letting the matter drop. His response is to say to her *Daughter, your faith has healed you. Go in peace and be freed from your suffering* (34). In her wildest imagination she must never have thought she would hear such words. If she had been told by a doctor that she was healed it would have been enough. But how much more she hears from the lips of Jesus: *Daughter . . . faith . . . healed . . . peace . . . freed*. She is the only woman Jesus ever addresses as *daughter*. It is a term of tenderness that affirms she is a true member of God's family and is perhaps used by way of a conscious contrast to Jairus' natural daughter who is mentioned in the next verse.[21] Her healing is the result of her faith in him, not of magic or some other occult

---

[16] Mark 6:56 reports the practice became more widespread.

[17] With the exception of 8:22–26. 'Immediately' or 'at once' (*euthys*) is one of Mark's favourite words.

[18] Gaiser, *Healing*, p. 172, notes the contrast with 2 Sam. 6:6–7.

[19] France, *Mark*, p. 237.

[20] J. R. Edwards, *The Gospel According to Mark*, PNTC (Grand Rapids: Eerdmans and Leicester: Apollos, 2002), p. 165.

[21] Mary Ann Tolbert suggests that in calling her 'daughter', Jesus was placing her under his protection as her new Father, just as we see Jairus' daughter under his protection. In C. A. Newsom and S. H. Ringe (eds.), *Women's Bible Commentary* (London: SPCK and Louisville: Westminister/John Knox, 1992), p. 268.

power. Her healing was a true salvation and brought the blessings of God's *shalom* into her life.[22] It was a true liberation from her impurity and all that resulted from it.

This act of public identification and affirmation is no mere appendix to the story but the climax to it. Once a women had been 'cleansed from her discharge' she was required to bring a couple of doves or pigeons to the priest who would offer them to make atonement for her and then she would be restored to her normal place within her community, according to Leviticus 15:28–30. So in this public act of pronouncing her clean, Jesus acts as the priest who restores this woman to her rightful place in the community from which she had been banished for twelve years. He left others in no doubt that her ritual impurity and social stigma was ended and that she had a right to assume her full place among God's worshipping people. The tongues no longer had any cause to wag and the suspicions were denied their oxygen supply. Jesus gave her back not only her health but her human dignity, even her humanity, as well.

2. A woman in the house (Luke 7:36–50)[23]

The little town of Nain, twenty-five miles south of Capernaum, has a special place in the annals of Jesus' encounters with women. On entering the town Jesus encountered the funeral procession of a young man who was survived by his widowed mother (Luke 7:11–17). Without support of a husband, and now of her only son, she would have faced a very bleak future. In his compassion Jesus used his miraculous power to restore the son to life and 'gave him back to his mother'. Jesus was still apparently in Nain when his next encounter with a woman took place.[24]

a. Who she was

Jesus had been invited to a meal at the home of Simon, a member of the Pharisee party. Jesus was undoubtedly a figure of great intrigue to religious leaders and as a visiting rabbi he would have been a sought-after guest for dinner-table discussion. The Pharisees also had less honest motives and were always looking for a way of tripping Jesus up. Simon would have enjoyed rapid promotion up the ladder of Pharaisaic status if the trap had been set and sprung in his

---

[22] 'Go in peace' is a traditional blessing: Judg. 18:6; 1 Sam 1:17; 2 Sam. 15:9; Luke 7:50, etc.

[23] Similar but not identical stories are found in Matt. 26:6–13; Mark 14:3–9; John 12:1–8.

[24] J. B. Green, *The Gospel of Luke*, NICNT (Grand Rapids: Eerdmans, 1997), p. 305.

house. What honour would have been his! As it was, an incident occurred which shattered the decorum of the occasion and could only be considered embarrassing in the extreme.

A woman from the town who had a certain reputation entered the house. She would have easily been able to effect entry as the door would have been open for the many comings and goings of the guests and servants. She was known for having *lived a sinful life* (37). The Pharisee had the measure of her and had labelled her *a sinner* (39). That was all anyone needed to know about her. The term marks her out as 'a prostitute by vocation, a whore by social status, contagious in her impurity, and probably one who fraternizes with Gentiles for economic purposes'.[25] In other words, she was not the normal class of person you would have found on Simon's guest list. We do not know, of course, what led her into prostitution but many women were, and are, driven to it because of poverty. Almost certainly she would have had no parents to support her and no man to love her and provide her with any security.

Her presence would have provoked a crisis about ritual cleanness. The Pharisee would have been scrupulously careful about such niceties but the entry of a prostitute would put paid to any precautions he had taken and contaminated wholesale the purity of the event.

b. What she did

Having gatecrashed the dinner, she proceeds to behave in an outrageous and what would have been judged to be an offensive, manner. Jesus would have been stretched out on a couch at the table as was customary at such dinners, rather than sitting in an upright chair, so his feet would have been accessible to her. But that was no invitation for what followed.

As she stood behind him at his feet weeping, she began to wet his feet with her tears. Then she wiped them with her hair, kissed them and poured perfume on them (38). The action could only be interpreted in the culture of the day as 'erotic'. 'Letting her hair down in this setting would have been on a par with appearing topless in public', writes Joel Green.[26] Loose hair was the sign of a loose woman who was worthy of condemnation.[27] Her display of uncontrolled emotions and her flow of tears were nothing compared with

---

[25] Green, *Luke*, p. 309.

[26] Green, *Luke*, p. 310.

[27] See further K. E. Bailey, *Through Peasant Eyes* (Grand Rapids: Eerdmans, 1980), p. 9, who confirms Green's comment with the words: 'Clearly the rabbis considered uncovering the bosom and loosening the hair to be acts that fall in the same category.'

the way in which they would have interpreted her massaging of Jesus' feet. This was how a prostitute would treat one of her customers. Jesus' reputation, already in serious doubt, sank in Simon's eyes to new depths (39). This confirmed that Jesus was neither a holy man nor had an ounce of prophetic insight in him or he would have stopped such a disgusting charade.

c. How they reacted

Ironically, the moment the Pharisee determines that Jesus cannot be a prophet is the moment Jesus initiates a conversation that reveals how clearly Jesus understood what Simon was thinking. Simon's unspoken reaction is entirely conventional. The woman's behaviour was more than unacceptable and would have provoked hostility among the guests. Her action confirmed that she merited the label *sinner*. She was worthless and devoid of any qualities which could be admired. She was a woman to be avoided, not welcomed into your home!

With typical shrewdness, Jesus does not at first challenge his host directly but tells a story that removes his defences and enables him to see the truth. Two men owed a creditor money, one a little and the other a lot. When neither could repay him, *he forgave the debts of both*. 'Now', Jesus asked, '*which of them will love him more?*' (42). The answer is obvious – *the one who had the bigger debt forgiven* – and Simon gives it correctly, marching straight to the logical conclusion which Jesus wanted. Now Jesus explains, dramatically looking at the woman so as to force people to look at the real woman while still addressing the Pharisee (44), the same is true in relation to people's sins. Simon thought he had few sins to be forgiven, and so showed little love towards Jesus. Indeed, when Jesus entered his house he did not even observe the basic rules that governed how to entertain guests courteously. Simon condemned the woman for not observing social courtesies but he had failed to do so and was guilty of 'glaring omissions' and 'studied insolence'[28] as, according to Levison, he offered no refreshment for Jesus' feet, extended him no kiss of greeting and did not anoint his head.[29] In contrast, the sinful woman has more than made up for his neglect by washing his feet with tears, smothering his feet with kisses and pouring perfume on his head. Underneath it all, the difference was simply this: unlike Simon, she realized that she was a great sinner in need of great forgiveness. And such forgiveness resulted in the expression of great,

[28] Bailey, *Through Peasant Eyes*, pp. 5, 8.
[29] L. Levison, *The Parables: Their Background and Local Setting* (Edinburgh: T & T Clark, 1926), cited by Bailey, *Through Peasant Eyes*, p. 8.

167

even extravagant, devotion, that refused to be hemmed in by the respectability of religious niceness.

In case there should be any doubt that this woman was a recipient of God's extraordinary mercy,[30] *Jesus said to her, 'Your sins are forgiven'* (48) and added, *Your faith has saved you; go in peace* (50). We can only guess what impact that had on her subsequent life, although it is not unreasonable to assume her future was transformed by this encounter. Where would she go after this? She surely couldn't go back to the streets to earn her living as once she had done. She needed to belong and find support in a new 'community of forgiven and forgiving sinners'.[31] Whatever her future, she was just the sort of person for whom Jesus had been anointed to bring good news (Luke 4:18–19).[32] Such an affirmation of such a woman would have been a profound shock to the onlookers, many of whom could only continue to debate who Jesus was and what right he had to forgive sins, rather than benefit themselves from God's grace (49).

Contrary to the custom of the man's world in which he lived, Jesus engages with this sinful woman, in public. First, he accepts her scandalous actions as a sign of authentic devotion, secondly, he releases her from her sinful past, and then, thirdly, he singles her out as a model of faith and of the way God longs to furnish women with his *shalom*, however corrupted God's image had become within them.

3. A woman at the well (John 4:1–42)

Jesus' encounter with the woman at the well in Samaria is set immediately after his encounter with Nicodemus.[33] The contrast between them could not be greater and self-consciously serves to emphasize the extraordinarily unconventional nature of God's grace. Nicodemus was a respectable Jewish man of influence, steeped in the law and a member of the religious establishment, who came by night to quiz Jesus but found it hard to grasp his meaning. She was a less-than-respectable Samaritan woman, without influence, uneducated in the law and a member of an enemy people, who met Jesus at noon and came quickly to understand his meaning.

a. The setting

When Jesus left Jerusalem to return to Galilee, *he had to go through Samaria* (4). While many have argued that good Jews would have

---

[30] Luke 6:35.
[31] F. B. Craddock, *Luke*, Int (Louisville: John Knox Press, 1990), p. 106.
[32] Green, *Luke*, p. 309.
[33] John 3:1–15.

taken a long detour across the other side of the Jordan to avoid passing through the territory and, therefore, have interpreted the *had to* (*edei*) as a divine compulsion, the truth is probably more prosaic. It was the shorter route and avoided going into Gentile territory and so was the sensible road to take.[34] Even so, the meeting of the woman at the town well in Sycar was a divine appointment.

It was natural that after walking all that way Jesus, who was normal with respect to his human nature, would feel tired and hungry and so he *sat down by the well,* especially since *it was about noon,* the hottest part of the day (6). As he sits, while his disciples search for food, something surprising happens. *A Samaritan woman came to draw water* (7). Unless there was a special reason for doing so, no woman would have been found doing that at that time. Women avoided the heat of the day and collected water early in the morning or after sundown, but not at noon. And, given the heaviness of the jars they would carry on their heads when filled with water, they went as a group to assist each other in the task.[35] To any Jewish man who was concerned about keeping pure the alarm bells would have begun to ring. He could not be seen to talk to his wife or any Jewish woman in public, still less a Samaritan woman. Furthermore, drawing water alone at this time of day would obviously arouse suspicion. Any respectable Jew would probably have removed himself from the scene immediately. But far from doing so Jesus ignores the centuries-old hostility between Jew and Samaritan, rides roughshod over the battlements of entrenched gender-divide, and actually engages this woman in conversation.

b. The conversation

The conversation is full of surprises.[36] After the shock of Jesus actually speaking to this woman comes the surprise that he asks for a drink (7). In doing so he, the Jewish male, puts himself in the lower position, that of a person with a need she, the Samaritan woman, can supply. He is apparently willing to disregard any ritual purity rules and drink from a Samaritan bucket! No wonder she expresses surprise and probes further (9). Jesus' enigmatic reply only serves to confuse her further as he now offers her *living water* (10) which is further complicated by his saying that the water he supplies quenches a person's thirst for ever: *the water I give them will become in them a spring of water welling up to eternal life* (14).

[34] D. A. Carson, *The Gospel According to John*, PNTC (Leicester: IVP and Grand Rapids: Eerdmans, 1991), pp. 215–216.
[35] On the customs see Bailey, *Middle Eastern Eyes*, p. 202.
[36] Bailey, *Middle Eastern Eyes*, pp. 202–216, identifies ten surprises.

Having offered her this life-giving water, Jesus then appears to tease her by withholding it and telling her to call her husband (16). Was he, after all, a chauvinist who thought that a woman was only capable of acquiring such a life through her husband and was not worthy to receive it for herself? No. Before this woman could receive eternal life there were issues in her present life that needed addressing, as Jesus knows. Revealing that she currently had no husband, Jesus confronts her with the truth of her situation. She had *had five husbands* and her current live-in companion was at best a common-law husband, who would not have been recognized by any religious authorities (18). Her unfortunate marital track-record is not necessarily an indication of her immoral past. No explanation is given for it and it can be explained in many ways. Perhaps some of her husbands had died or had divorced her. It could be taken just as much as evidence of moral failure on the part of men as on her part.[37] Jesus does not explore the issue further and does not accuse her of sin or tell her she needs to repent.

The woman seeks to deflect the conversation from such a personal focus and introduces a discussion of theology about the legitimacy of the Samaritan centre of worship on Mount Gerizim, over which Jews and Samaritans had disagreed for centuries. Jesus uses the opportunity to teach a deeper truth about worship (21–24), to which she responds that the coming Messiah will make such matters clear (25). As Don Carson remarks, 'Jesus needs no further invitation' but reveals his true identity as the promised Messiah to her.

c. The outcome

At that point his disciples return and express astonishment that Jesus is talking to her (27). But she has other business than to stand around defending Jesus. The depth and authenticity of the conversation with him had raised the hope within her that he really was the Messiah. In a state of excited expectation she dashed back to her village where the neighbours could immediately see a change in her which persuaded them to enquire further of Jesus and to become believers in him for themselves (28–30, 39–42). So she becomes 'the first Christian female preacher'[38] and 'an evangelist to her own community [who] foreshadows the women who witness to the men regarding the resurrection'.[39]

[37] Carson, *John*, p. 221. Gail R. O'Day, 'John', in Newsom and Ringe, *Bible Commentary*, p. 296, suggests that she might even have been 'trapped in the custom of leverite marriage and the last male in the family refused to marry her'.

[38] Bailey, *Middle Eastern Eyes*, p. 212.

[39] Bailey, *Middle Eastern Eyes*, p. 215.

4. Concluding comments

We often speak of the need to judge a person, not by what they say but by what they do. In Jesus' case, what he says is perfectly consistent with what he does. Jesus treats women with dignity and respect, as having real value and significance in God's sight. He shows them to be capable of receiving the full blessings of God's healing and *shalom* for themselves without the need for it to be channelled through a man. Women can experience forgiveness in the same way as men in Jesus' kingdom. They are never treated as second-class citizens in his kingdom as they were elsewhere. Jesus lives in flagrant defiance of the regulations that governed relations between men and women in the Judaism of his day. In some cases, they became not only the recipients of grace, but also the channels of it to others. Their elevation is a sign of the inbreaking of the kingdom of God and demonstrates that the old order has ceased and a new quality of relationships has begun.[40] Contrary to the culture in which he lived, his actions demonstrate that women are in no way inferior to men.

[40] S. Grenz and D. M. Kjesbo, *Women in the Church: A Biblical Theology of Women in Ministry* (Downers Grove: IVP, 1995), p. 76.

13. Women in the teaching of Jesus

The novelist Dorothy Sayers said it brilliantly:

> They had never known a man like this Man – there never has been such another. A prophet and teacher who never nagged at them, never flattered or coaxed or patronized; who never made arch jokes about them, never treated them either as 'The women, God help us!' or 'The ladies, God bless them', who rebuked without querulousness and praised without condescension; who took their questions and arguments seriously; who never mapped out their sphere for them; never urged them to be feminine or jeered at them for being female; who had no axe to grind and no uneasy male dignity to defend; who took them as he found them and was completely unselfconscious. There is no act, no sermon, no parable in the whole Gospel that borrows its pungency from female perversity; nobody could possibly guess from the words and deeds of Jesus that there was anything 'funny' about women's nature.[1]

The way women are reflected in the teaching of Jesus when compared to the teaching of Jews in first-century Palestine is confirmation of the radical and shockingly counter-cultural nature of his message. In his parables, illustrations, direct teaching and teaching on family life and sexual ethics, Jesus shows a great respect for women and gives them a significance that the prevailing culture withheld. To focus on his teaching about women is to be confronted with the fact that the kingdom of God overturns conventional social structures and customary indicators of status and position. It is to be introduced to a kingdom which offers a very different kind of

---

[1] D. Sayers, *Are Women Human?* (Grand Rapids: Eerdmans, 1971), p. 47, cited in P. K. Jewett, *Man as Male and Female* (Grand Rapids: Eerdmans, 1975), p. 103.

relationships and community than that generally accepted in the cultures of either the first or twenty-first century.

1. Women in Jesus' parables

Jesus frequently used parables to instruct people about the kingdom of God. 'Told as kingdom-explanations for Jesus' kingdom actions',[2] they plainly indicate his mission to the powerless and marginalized, so it is no surprise that women figure frequently in these stories. Luke's Gospel has a particular emphasis on status reversal in the kingdom of God[3] and therefore women, who were generally considered to be of a very low status, receive particular attention and are clearly seen by Jesus as a valuable target audience for his teaching. Kenneth Bailey points out that, 'Jesus selected images and created parables with a deliberate concern to communicate his message to his women listeners on as deep a level as to his male followers'.[4] In stark contrast to,

> rabbinic parables [which] pointedly avoided mentioning women, [Jesus] spoke of using yeast in bread-making, of child birth, of grinding meal, of wedding attendants, of housewives and of widows. He used pictures of women to illustrate themes of vigilance, of perseverance in prayer, of divine mercy and of the joy of God over the salvation of a lost sinner.[5]

Parables reflected real and ordinary life and Jesus took his illustrations and images from the perspective of the women as well as from the men of the day. It is noticeable that when Jesus taught in parables he regularly coupled male with female examples to reinforce his points; women's work was equally as valid as men's in giving insight into the kingdom of God, and he was equally concerned that women as much as men should identify with his teaching.

a. The parable of the persistent woman (Luke 18:1–8)

The parable of the woman who kept bothering the local judge until she got justice is notable for a number of reasons. Bailey comments on how it balances the illustration of the male 'Friend at Midnight', in Luke 11:5–8, both by its place in the structure of Luke's Gospel

[2] N. T. Wright, *Simply Jesus* (London, SPCK, 2011), p. 91.
[3] E.g., 1:5 – 2:52. See pp. 152–155.
[4] K. E. Bailey, *Jesus through Middle Eastern Eyes: Cultural Studies in the Gospels* (Illinois: IVP and London: SPCK, 2008), p. 194.
[5] M. Evans, *Woman in the Bible* (Exeter: Paternoster, 1983), p. 48.

and through its many points of contact with it.[6] In this parable 'a woman is the hero of the story . . . The woman is presented as a model to emulate in regard to confidence and persistence in prayer'.[7] Contemporary Jewish writers would never have used a woman to serve as the hero in such key teaching. Furthermore, as Witherington notes, the very quality Jesus commends '(her perseverance and persistence) is a characteristic that in a patriarchal society was often seen as a negative attribute in a woman'.[8] The parable is positive about the very qualities of audacity and a refusal to be ignored, which then as now are not usually regarded as appropriate in females. Yet Jesus presents her as an ideal role model of faith for disciples, both men and women, when they pray to God.

b. The parable of the ten virgins (Matt. 25:1–13)

This parable is one the rare occasions when Jesus uses women in part at least as a negative illustration. Five of the women in the parable were prepared and ready for the bridegroom's arrival, but five were not. Jesus clearly does not present women in an idealized fashion and can use women as important examples in teaching truth even when they not portrayed positively. It serves to remind us to keep a genuine balance between male and female when presenting matters of truth.

In Matthew's Gospel this parable immediately follows teaching about two male servants, one good and one 'wicked' and their different states of readiness at their master's return, further demonstrating Jesus' concern to balance male and female perspectives.[9] Bailey suggests that in this way Jesus is 'trying to compensate for the gender gap in the religious culture of the day'.[10] He points out further that ten men were required to establish a synagogue in Jesus' day and some thought that ten men were required for a valid celebration of a marriage.[11] By contrast, the mention in this parable of ten unmarried women involved in the celebration of a marriage indirectly recognizes the different place women would occupy in his new kingdom community. Stressing the need for all, women as well as men, to be prepared for the arrival of the bridegroom, that is, the future coming of the Son of Man,[12] it warns that some, sadly, will not be ready.

[6] Bailey, *Jesus*, p. 263, n. 3.

[7] Bailey, *Jesus*, p. 266.

[8] B. Witherington III, *Women in the Ministry of Jesus*, SNTSMS 51 (Cambridge: Cambridge University Press, 1984), p. 37.

[9] Matt. 24:45–51.

[10] Bailey, *Jesus*, p. 274.

[11] Bailey, *Jesus*, pp. 273–274.

[12] Matt. 24:26.

c. Female and male parallelism in the parables of Jesus

The balancing of females and males in Jesus' parables has often been a matter of comment and it is helpful to see how frequently this occurs. The parallels of the persistent woman and ten virgins are noted above but it is worth also noting:

- Luke 5:36–39: mending a garment (women's work) and making of wine (men's work).
- Luke 13:18–21: planting a mustard seed (men's work) and kneading leaven into bread (women's work).
- Luke 15:3–10: the lost coin (women's concern) and the lost sheep (men's concern).

Other parallels are found in Jesus teaching outside of the parables:[13]

- Luke 4:25–27: in Jesus' first sermon he mentions the woman of Zarephath alongside Naaman the Syrian.
- The rejected woman of Luke 7:36–50 is complemented by the rejected tax collector in Luke 18:9–14.
- Luke 12:51–53: men and women will be divided by their response to the kingdom of God.
- Luke 14:26–27: men and women are both required to respond to the call to follow Christ above all else.
- Luke 20:27–36: women and men both have a place in teaching about the resurrection.
- Luke 21:1–4: a woman is praised over a man; an exceptional occurrence in the context of contemporary teaching.

Alongside his other teaching, the parables of Jesus emphasize the importance of valuing women as good examples of God's dealing with humankind, of using imagery relevant to women, and of balancing female and male stories in our teaching. As models for contemporary preachers they demonstrate the need to work hard at illustrative material to ensure it connects to all their listeners.

2. Women as unexpected examples in Jesus' teaching

In a broad sweep of his teaching, allusions to women can be found not as the exception but as a routine way of expressing kingdom teaching.

Jesus refers to himself as a mother hen, who longs 'to gather [the] chicks under [his] wings' as he looks over Jerusalem and sees how

[13] Bailey, *Jesus*, pp. 194–195.

far from God its inhabitants are.[14] As Witherington suggests, the saying reminds us 'of the lament of God over his wayward children in Hosea, or, since feminine imagery is used here, Rachel weeping for her lost children'.[15] Jesus, indicative of his supportive and affirming view of women in their role as nurturers, takes for himself the most gender-distinctive role of women and acknowledges his own nurturing instinct for Israel.

A further incident that gives insight into Jesus' teaching occurs when he receives the laments of the women of Jerusalem as he walks the path to the cross.[16] Jesus advises the women not to weep for him but for themselves, as they will face the destruction of their city in the not-too-distant future. If he, an innocent man, finds himself condemned in such a way, then the 'dry tree' with no life in it – a reference to Israel – should expect similar or worse. Jesus identifies with their plight and uses them to highlight the seriousness of the situation. He takes their chorus of lament seriously; not dismissing or ignoring their remarks as contemporary rabbis would have done, but using them to teach further truth.

Jesus makes no attempt in any of his teaching to conceal the sinful nature of women or the future destiny of those who reject the kingdom of God. In his apocalyptic teaching Jesus reflects women as equal in both grace and disgrace. The listener is reminded of Lot's wife who disobeyed God and suffered the consequences, but is also told of some women finding safety 'on the day when the Son of Man is revealed'.[17] Women share with men the full and direct consequences of their responses to God and their commitment to Christ.

Despite the compelling evidence that Jesus fully affirms the humanity of womanhood and is sensitive to women, it is difficult to ignore the fact that much of the language of Jesus' teaching is male in its orientation.[18] On occasions, Jesus avoids using the natural masculine form of the word, as, for example, when he refers to a child in the neuter[19] to illustrate the values of God's kingdom. But much of his teaching is masculine. The Beatitudes, for example, use masculine forms throughout: the key term *makarioi*, 'blessed is', is in the masculine. According to Evelyn and Frank Stagg, such examples could be multiplied across the discourses of the Gospels and they surmise that 'in the light of his radical affirmation of woman

---

[14] Matt. 23:37.

[15] Witherington, *Ministry of Jesus*, p. 47.

[16] Luke 23:28–31.

[17] Luke 17:30–35.

[18] E. Stagg and F. Stagg, *Woman in the World of Jesus* (Philadelphia: Westminster Press 1978), p. 126.

[19] Mark 9:33–37.

in his manner and teaching it is tempting to see the heavy hand of traditional language here'.[20] However radical his teaching, Jesus also reflects the culture of his time.

3. Women in Jesus' teaching on family life

Jesus delivers a number of lessons on family life; from children and parenting to widows, sex, celibacy and divorce. The values he presents introduce women as individuals of significance, worth and deserving of equal respect to men. In his kingdom women enjoy the same privileges and respect as men but are also subject to the same expectations and responsibilities as its male citizens.

a. Parenthood

In Mark 7:9–13 and 10:19 a person's duty to both father and mother is reinforced and both are said to be deserving of care and support. In spite of the Old Testament law, 'some rabbis taught that one should honour father more than mother'.[21] Witherington believes that in overturning the oral tradition and the rabbis' ideas about the vow of corban, which prevented parents from benefitting from their children's property because it was dedicated to the temple, he makes 'a strong affirmation of the traditional family structure' with its emphasis on children caring for both their aging parents.[22] In doing so, Jesus provides a stronger basis than normal for women being protected and esteemed alongside men.

b. Widows

In the story of the 'Widow's Mite' (Mark 12:41–44) a poor woman, who makes the smallest possible offering in the temple, is commended by Jesus. In doing so, 'Jesus is stepping forward as a strong advocate of oppressed or abused widows'.[23] His concern and regard for women in marginalized and powerless roles is an exact reflection of the character of God as seen in the Old Testament.[24] Jesus calls his disciples to him with the intention of using the example of this poor widow to teach them about following him and what it means to be part of the kingdom of God. Her willing sacrificial act serves as a

---

[20] Stagg and Stagg, *World of Jesus*, p. 128.
[21] Witherington, *Ministry of Jesus*, p. 12.
[22] Ibid.
[23] Witherington, *Ministry of Jesus*, p. 18.
[24] Exod. 22:22; Deut. 10:18; 24:19–21; 26:13; Pss. 68:5; 146:9; Isa. 1:17; 9:17; Jer. 7:6; 22:3; Zech. 7:10; Mal. 3:5.

model for God's people where such extraordinary generosity should be a natural expression of being a member of his new community. So kingdom values are taught through a powerless woman while powerful men stand condemned. As Witherington concludes, 'Jesus' special concern and admiration for women is perhaps nowhere more strikingly juxtaposed with his disgust over certain groups of privileged and supposedly pious men than here'.[25]

c. Marriage

Jesus' wisdom on marriage is as radical to the ears of the first-century Jew, male or female, as any of his other teaching. In presenting marriage in the context of the kingdom of God he overturned cultural assumptions and demanded a fundamental re-evaluation of domestic relationships and behaviour. In his teaching on marriage women are portrayed as equal in rights and responsibilities to men.

Jesus reinforces marriage as God's plan for humankind and the intention that it should be an unbreakable union of faithfulness and commitment. In Matthew 19:6, where he does this, Jesus appeals 'to God's will in creation, building upon the Priestly narrative in Gen 1:27; 5:2 where male and female are created together and for one another, with no subordination as in the rib passage'.[26] It is evident in Jesus' teaching that women and men are equally accountable and have equal entitlements within marriage.

d. Sex

In Matthew 5:27–28 and John 7:53 – 8:11 there is implied recognition that women were most often the vulnerable and the victims in sexual relationships. Stereotypes of the temptress and the wanton woman were overturned as Jesus implicitly rejects the right to blame women for the sexual failure of men, which 'is provocative and stands in contrast to many commonly held views of His day'.[27]

As in many places today, so then, women were reduced to simply being an object for sexual gratification. With few rights of their own, their purpose would be regarded as satisfying men. 'Adultery in Judaism was a sin against the rights of man.'[28] Adultery in Jesus' teaching was a sin against both man and woman. The lust of a man for a woman was equated with adultery and the woman was shown

---

[25] Witherington *Ministry of Jesus*, p. 18.
[26] Stagg and Stagg, *World of Jesus,* p. 135. Ch. 1 argues 'the rib passage' does not suggest subordination.
[27] Witherington, *Ministry of Jesus*, p. 50.
[28] Stagg and Stagg, *World of Jesus*, p. 128.

to have rights in sexual relationships.[29] Jesus sets a new standard as he teaches husbands that if they committed adultery they did so not only against their wives but against God and, moreover, that they could betray their wives not only by their actual practice but in their minds as well.

As in his other teaching on family relationships Jesus affirms women as whole persons and not just sex objects. The episode of the woman caught in adultery in John 8:2–11 reflects Jesus' teaching on sexual ethics in relation to women. The woman is held responsible for her failure to be faithful to her husband and Jesus never suggests she is innocent. However, Jesus rejects the discriminatory judicial processes of his day which held the woman guilty without equally holding the male partner to account. Jesus engages fully with the woman as a person and demands that she go and live differently, telling her 'to leave her life of sin', while indicating that the men are as guilty as she. Witherington sums it up well: 'Jesus does not approve of a system wherein man's lust is not taken as seriously as a woman's seduction.'[30]

e. Divorce

Jesus' teaching on divorce, in Matthew 5:31–32; 19:1–12, upholds the covenantal view of marriage that was God's original intention for humankind. It offers a firm basis for society and the protection of the wife in a culture where women were valued far less than men. Jesus' teaching against divorce again speaks up for the powerless victim in the marriage (inevitably the wife in his day) and indicates that she is not an object to be traded but a person who needs saving from the serious moral and spiritual consequences which would follow divorce. As Stagg and Stagg put it, in divorce 'she is victimised in being cast out, as an adulteress is cast out'.[31] She would have been left without any rights, a damaged reputation and without obvious means of support. Anyone who married her would himself be committing adultery.

This would have sounded an unacceptably jarring note to men of the day. It warned them that they could not act against women as they might like even if their culture thought it acceptable, since it was unacceptable in God's kingdom. In saying this Jesus raises the status of women in marked contrast to the customs of the day[32] and by affirming marriage and the commitment it involves, counters

---

[29] Matt. 5:28.
[30] Witherington, *Ministry of Jesus*, p. 23.
[31] Stagg and Stagg, *World of Jesus*, p. 132.
[32] Witherington, *Ministry of Jesus*, p. 28.

stereotypical attitudes to women as either temptresses or merely as part of her husband's belongings.

Jesus' teaching on divorce does not draw an unrealistic portrait of women that would prove false in the light of their full humanity. Mark 10:12 teaches there is no double standard between women and men in their failure before God. A woman becomes an adulterer if she divorces her husband and marries another man, just as much as a man does when he divorces and remarries.

f. Jesus' true family

Through the generations women have been valued in the eyes of many because they are mothers and their role as nurturers and family carers has given them an honoured spiritual status. Yet, Jesus does not support this common attitude in his teaching in an unqualified way. Two brief insights show that Jesus overturned sentimentality as far as family relationships are concerned and declared that the first call on a woman's life was to respond to the call of God and follow in his ways.

In Matthew 12:46–50, Jesus responds to the comment, 'Your mother and brothers are standing outside, wanting to speak to you', by saying, 'Here are my mother and my brothers. For whoever does the will of my Father in heaven is my brother and sister and mother.' True family members are those related to each other by their obedience to God. All biological or social ties of ethnicity, gender, social status and culture, are secondary to the critical factor of belonging to God. This principle liberates women whose whole lives were determined by others, and remains a liberating principle for all who find their worth not through their position in a family, or place in society, or by an 'accident' of birth but by doing God's will.

Jesus relates comfortably to the women who listen to his teaching and seek God, since they are his sisters. The inclusion of 'sisters' in verse 50 is striking. Only Jesus' mother and brothers were 'standing outside', not his sisters, so the reference to them in this gender-inclusive way 'is the more significant'. [33] It shows there were already women among Jesus' band of disciples. This statement alone was revolutionary for women in its day and still declares today that women are significant, not because of anything society might say or the way they are judged by others, but because of their response to Christ.

[33] R. T. France, *The Gospel of Matthew*, NICNT (Grand Rapids: Eerdmans, 2007), p. 498.

Luke 11:27–28 gives a second insight into Jesus' attitude to women as the moral torchbearers of society simply by virtue of the fact that they are mothers. Luke records that 'a woman in the crowd called out, "Blessed is the mother who gave you birth and nursed you"'. Jesus replied 'Blessed rather are those who hear the word of God and obey it'. As Mary Evans comments, even by responding to her, 'Jesus showed that the opinions of women mattered, in a way that Judaism rarely acknowledged'. It shows how important he thought them to be. Yet, in dismissing her comments as 'sheer sentimentality' he also treats women as responsible and rational human beings worthy of being educated.[34] Their role as mothers is secondary to their choosing to do God's will. Once again Jesus reinforces the part women have in seeking God and living in obedience to him as the basis for their true value within the family or community.

g. Celibacy

In Jesus' day, women would inevitably follow the path of marriage. It was not socially possible to remain single since a woman would need the support and protection of a man, which meant, with few exceptions, a husband. However in Matthew 19:11–12, Jesus offers another option to those who find the requirements of marriage unacceptable, and that is the path of celibacy. Jesus makes the point that not all are able to marry, some because they were born that way, others because life has made it so, and still others because they have renounced marriage for the sake of the kingdom of heaven. While in the original context the reference to singleness related to men, there is no reason to apply this saying exclusively to men. Indirectly, Jesus is offering women liberation from suffocating social pressures. They, as well as men, can turn their back on the social obligation of marriage and follow the call of the kingdom of God to serve in a celibate capacity. This is neither an easier nor a more difficult path to follow, but it is a novel one that offers women a way of finding their personal place in God's kingdom.

4. Women as recipients of Jesus' teaching (Luke 10:38–42; John 11:17–37)

The account of Martha being too busy with the housework and Mary sitting piously at Jesus' feet to learn from him has been used many times to encourage women to have right priorities. Yet the question remains as to whether people have understood and applied this

---

[34] Evans, *Woman in the Bible*, p. 49.

teaching accurately. In many churches the provision of food and hospitality continue to be more significant than hearing the word of God. As with Martha and Mary, relationships become tense over catering and power continues to be brokered in the church kitchen rather than the church genuinely being concerned to hear the teaching of Jesus. It is possible for church leaders to meet to discuss everything from catering to finance and buildings and yet forget actually to apply the word of God to their community.

Jesus made close friendships with women like Martha and Mary, just as he did with men, and he did not reject the anointing by Mary at their home in Bethany.[35] The fact that Jesus was willing to teach women such as Mary is of crucial significance in itself. He teaches them just as a rabbi would teach his male pupils and he was not afraid to risk scandal by doing so in private.[36] His actions in entering a woman's house, befriending and teaching her would have been unheard of in first-century Jewish culture.

The language of Luke 10:39, *Mary, who sat at the Lord's feet listening to what he said,* is a clear formula for being a disciple of and learning from Jesus. Joel Green explains that the language of listening or hearing God's word, which Luke uses frequently,[37] is a way of saying that Mary 'has joined the road to discipleship'.[38] Women were not generally educated or considered worth teaching in first-century Palestine; they undertook the domestic roles so that men might study. The presence of Mary at Jesus' feet is a radical departure from contemporary social convention. While Jesus never directly said that women should have the right to study, he showed it by his actions in the home of Mary and Martha.

If Mary listens intently to Jesus and so shows that she has begun the path of discipleship, when Martha asks for help and questions whether Jesus cares that *my sister has left me to do the work by myself* (40), she is gently censured for not being moulded by the priorities of the kingdom of God. Service and hospitality are important in the kingdom, but are to be carried out in the context of first hearing and applying the message of the word of God.

Luke's Gospel places this incident after the parable of the Good Samaritan as a reminder about what it means to genuinely hear God's word. Green points out that even though he knew the law, 'the lawyer did not act' and so is condemned.[39] Yet it is neither

[35] John 12:1–8.
[36] Witherington, *Ministry of Jesus*, p. 114.
[37] E.g., in 6:47; 8:11–12, 21; 11:28; also in Acts 22:3.
[38] J. B. Green, *The Gospel of Luke*, NICNT (Grand Rapids: Eerdmans, 1997), p. 435.
[39] Green, *Luke*, p. 434.

Martha's activism which is condemned, nor Mary's passivity which is commended. What Jesus declares as unacceptable is any 'service grounded in moral intuitions other than those formed through hearing the word'.[40] Jesus does not attack Martha, but gently instructs her and suggests that he is not best welcomed by 'distracted, worrisome domestic performance', but by giving attention to his teaching.[41] In responding in this way, he defends 'Mary's right to learn'.[42]

John 11:17–37 records a later incident with Mary and Martha following the death and burial of their brother Lazarus. As Jesus arrives four days after the body had been interred, the dialogue between Jesus and the sisters reinforces their close relationship and how much Jesus is concerned to bring spiritual understanding to them through this crisis experience, as well as in their routine domestic experiences. 'This time,' as Mary Evans observes, 'even in her grief, Martha is ready to listen.'[43]

So Jesus reveals more about himself saying, *I am the resurrection and the life* (25). This profound and direct revelation of himself is made to a woman, just as the earlier disclosure of his Messiahship had been made to the woman of Samaria.[44] And he receives an honest and heartfelt response in return. *'Yes, Lord,' she replied, 'I believe that you are the Messiah, the Son of God, who is to come into the world'* (27). For many, including the author, who grew up being taught that Peter's confession[45] was the first and only (or so the impression was given) confession of the Messiahship of Jesus, it was quite a discovery to learn that Martha also makes a clear confession of Jesus as the Christ. In this way, 'The fourth evangelist intimates that women have a right to be taught even the mysteries of the faith and that they are capable of responding in faith with an accurate confession'.[46] And she serves as a model encouraging women to confidently confess him.

Jesus reorganizes priorities for both women and men. Martha is at fault not because of what she is doing but because her concern was to engage Jesus in her agenda rather than the other way round. Mary is positively commended because she has put Jesus and his word first, letting other things fall into place.[47]

---

[40] Green, *Luke*, p. 434.
[41] Ibid.
[42] Witherington, *Ministry of Jesus*, p. 101.
[43] Evans, *Woman in the Bible*, p. 52.
[44] John 4: 26–39.
[45] Matt. 16:16.
[46] Witherington, *Ministry of Jesus*, p. 109.
[47] Matt. 6:33.

5. Concluding comments

It is an understatement to say that Jesus' teaching was very different to that of his contemporaries. His teaching reveals that he valued women, made friends with women, taught women, challenged women, inspired women, protected women and encouraged women to fulfil their potential as equal human beings in his kingdom. Unlike Jewish first-century writers, 'we do not find negative remarks about the nature, abilities and religious potential of women'.[48] Evans, citing Forster, puts it clearly, 'Jesus' approach to women is "without precedent in contemporary Judaism"'.[49]

Jesus' teaching shows that he is a radical reformer of the place of women in the family and in the community. Women, who were largely marginalized and undervalued in his society, were granted rights to full participation in the family of faith which they did not enjoy in the male preserve of Judaism or in most pagan cults. The teaching of Jesus communicated to women in ways with which they could identify and asserts their significance as equal to that of men in his kingdom.

[48] Witherington, *Ministry of Jesus*, p. 127.
[49] Evans, *Woman in the Bible*, p. 44, citing W. Forster, *Palestinian Judaism in New Testament Times* (Edinburgh: Oliver and Boyd, 1964), p. 127.

Luke 8:1–3; Luke 23:44 – 24:12
14. Women as disciples of Jesus

The Galilean women 'achieved their goal, which was to follow Jesus on his Way and minister to him. In doing so they provided a model of true discipleship. They heard the call of Jesus to follow him, they attached themselves to him in his ministry and suffering, they gave faithful witness to his resurrection victory.'[1]

Women were involved in Jesus' itinerant ministry from its earliest stages. While they are not numbered among the Twelve, they are present and play a significant role as Jesus starts out preaching and healing in Galilee and moves on towards Jerusalem. It is the women whose discipleship demonstrates an astonishing commitment and courageous faithfulness at the cross and women who are the first at the empty tomb. They are models of true discipleship and of those who are willing to give up all for the kingdom of God.

1. Women on the road with Jesus (Luke 8:1–3)

a. The women who became disciples

In three significant verses Luke gives an unexpected insight into the place of women among the itinerant disciples of Jesus. There were obviously a number of them including some he had *cured of evil spirits and diseases.* Three of them are mentioned by name: Mary Magdalene, Joanna and Susanna. Mary was a common name, and several of them appear in the gospel story, so Luke clarifies that the *Mary* he is referring to is *called Magdalene.* Each of the three was well known enough to be named but Mary Magdalene heads the list and seems especially prominent either because of the remarkable

---

[1] R. Ryan, 'The women from Galilee and discipleship in Luke', *BTB* XV (1985), p. 59.

healing that she had received when Jesus had cast *seven demons* out of her or, more probably, because of the pivotal role she plays later as a witness to the resurrection. *Joanna* was *the wife of Chuza* who was the administrator of Herod's estate. She was almost certainly wealthy and may well have come from one of the important families of Galilee. Being married to a courtier in the inner circles around Herod, Richard Bauckham speculates, quite reasonably, that she may have been one of the key inside sources Luke used in writing his Gospel.[2] We know nothing further of *Susanna*, who is not referred to again by name in the New Testament but was presumably known to the early Christians. These three are not the only women and are joined by *many others* in Jesus' travelling band.

The mere mention of these women says a huge amount about how inclusive the early followers of Jesus were. Those who had struggled with poor health and demon possession, with all the implications that had for impurity in Israel's religion, walked sided by side with those who were wealthy and from the upper echelons of their small nation. Jesus was good news for all.

This record of the women who followed Jesus as members of the earliest group he gathered around him is not something the later community of Christians would necessarily have wanted to emphasize. In seeking to gain credibility with the wider world such information might have been omitted in order to avoid provoking the moral suspicions that their place at the heart of the Gospel story would almost certainly have aroused. This was not the kind of record that would have been invented by a Christian community anxious not to put any obstacle in the way of the acceptance of their message.

In saying, *the Twelve were with him and also some women,* Luke indicates that there is nothing distinctive about the nature of being a disciple as a woman compared to that of being a man. They were not treated differently or in any way as a second-class band of disciples. The essence of discipleship was to accompany Jesus on the way and to be witnesses to his ministry and Luke makes it clear that these women did just that, alongside the men, from the beginning.[3]

How was it possible that women could leave their homes and follow when, in the culture of the day, their family obligations would have been considerable? It may have been that many of the women who responded to Jesus and followed him were single either because they were widowed or divorced or, more unusually, had never married. Some were clearly married but as women of independent

---

[2] R. Bauckham, *Gospel Women* (Eerdmans: Grand Rapids, 2002), p. 119. On Joanna generally see pp. 109–165.

[3] Bauckham, *Gospel Women*, p. 113.

financial means, as was not unknown, had the self-determination and independence to leave their domestic duties in the hands of others and follow.

These women who were with Jesus from the start of his ministry and heard his teaching throughout, were well qualified to be both witnesses to and, even more importantly, interpreters of the resurrection. John Nolland comments that their mention so early in Luke's Gospel, not only serves the purpose of setting the women in parallel to the men as disciples but also prepares the way for the significant role they were to play in the passion and resurrection story.[4]

b. Women as supporters

These women were helping to support them [Jesus and his entourage] *out of their own means.* Some have chosen to understand this as saying that the women continued in a domestic role among the band of disciples in a way similar to the way they would have acted in the family or at home. But this is not what Luke means. He is referring to a financial arrangement whereby they funded the mission team out of their personal assets.[5] Some of these female disciples were wealthy women who used their resources for the benefit of God's work. To claim that these words suggest they fulfilled a more domestic role is to misread what Luke is saying. There are no gender-specific roles and no hierarchy of service mentioned by Luke,[6] with the men preaching while the women supported them domestically.

Kenneth Bailey points out what an astonishing revelation this is about the Jesus movement. For women to sponsor a teacher was one thing, but for them to leave home and have a significant measure of control over the money with which the movement is funded on the road was quite another. It would have been considered scandalous by many, especially as it would mean stopping in villages overnight and receiving hospitality from those who were not relatives.[7] The intertestamental writer, Ben Sirach, is much more representative of the culture of the time when he advises men not to trust their wives, to be careful about the supplies issued to her, and to avoid letting her be the means of supporting her husband, saying, 'There is wrath and impudence and great disgrace when a wife supports her

---

[4] J. Nolland, *Luke 1-9:20*, WBC (Word: Dallas, 1985), p. 365.

[5] Luke 8:3.

[6] Bauckham, *Gospel Women*, p. 114.

[7] K. E. Bailey, *Jesus through Middle Eastern Eyes: Cultural Studies in the Gospels* (London: SPCK, 2008), p. 193.

husband'.[8] Against this background, the Jesus movement was profoundly counter-cultural and engaged in a hugely risky enterprise.

All who followed Jesus would have left their families and households behind. The male disciples would have had to leave their financial resources behind, since their families would need them, but the women could give their money more freely as their families were unlikely to be dependent on them. Both female and male disciples demonstrate in their different ways that material possessions are to be forfeited, either because they were left behind or used to support the community on the road.

Significantly, Luke has placed his report of the wealthy women using their resources for the purpose of the kingdom as a lead-in to the parable of the sower (8:4–15). Perhaps he intended us to see that the women were examples of the seed sown on good soil that produced an abundant harvest for the benefit of many.

c. Women and the meaning of discipleship

Jesus makes it clear that to be a disciple is to follow him: 'Whoever wants to be my disciple must deny themselves and take up their cross and follow me.'[9] The essence of discipleship is simply following Jesus, albeit on a costly and demanding road. As followers the women modelled true discipleship, from the first days to the last, in a number of ways:

- They heard the word of God that Jesus spoke and taught, and responded to him.
- They used their personal resources to sustain the mission and work of Jesus.
- They left behind family and other social relationships to be a part of God's kingdom work.
- They faced a life of sacrifice and hardship as they travelled with Jesus.

Ryan explains their discipleship was composed of a threefold response to him. First, the women responded to a call to leave home and follow the way of the kingdom; secondly, it involved a personal attachment to Jesus; and, thirdly they showed their discipleship in a willingness to share the life, destiny and reaction of others to Jesus the Christ.[10]

---

[8] Ecclesiasticus 25:22 (NRSV). Other references to Ben Sirach are found in Bailey, *Jesus*, pp. 189–190.

[9] Matt. 16:24.

[10] Ryan, 'Women from Galilee', p. 56.

Our understanding of discipleship is sharpened when we realize that the phrase 'to be with him'[11] is a technical expression that holds levels of meaning which can easily be missed. It means to willingly support and follow.[12] It means a conscious detachment from other priorities such as family and material possessions,[13] and a forgoing of personal plans and ambitions, whether one is a woman or a man.[14] Discipleship involves a radical severing of ties with the social structures and values of the day and full participation in the work and life of Jesus. It necessitates 'laying down one's life', experiencing persecution,[15] facing trouble with authorities,[16] and betrayal by friends[17] but always with the hope of God's kingdom promises being fulfilled.[18] There is nothing to suggest in all this that women did not embrace these challenges as fully as the male disciples did or were anything less than full disciples.

d. Women and the ministry of preaching

As disciples travelling with Jesus, did the women have involvement in preaching and the proclamation of the Good News as did the men? Heine[19] refutes those who would say they did not, pointing out that the text of Luke 8:1 says *Jesus proclaimed the Good News of the Kingdom of God and the twelve were with him and some women who* . . . She argues that the connection between discipleship and preaching is forged in the opening words of this chapter and is applied to both men and women equally. Bauckham is less persuaded about whether these verses indicate whether the disciples preached or not, as they were later to do, but, in his view, if the men were preaching alongside Jesus then so too were the women.[20] However, when the seventy-two were sent out, as mentioned in Luke 10:1–20, 'it is surely natural for readers to assume that women were included'[21] and so presumably participated in preaching and healing alongside the men.[22]

[11] Luke 8:1.
[12] See Luke 8:1; 8:38; 9:18; 22:56. Ryan, 'Women from Galilee', pp. 56–57 cites S. Brown, *Apostasy and Perseverance in the Theology of Luke*, Analecta Biblica 36 (Rome: Pontifical Biblical Institute, 1969).
[13] Luke 14:25–26; 18:29.
[14] Luke 9:57–62.
[15] Luke 12:4.
[16] Luke 12:11.
[17] Luke 21:16–17.
[18] Luke 22:27–30.
[19] S. Heine, *Women and Early Christianity* (SCM: London, 1987), p. 61.
[20] Bauckham, *Gospel Women*, p. 111.
[21] Bauckham, *Gospel Women*, p. 112.
[22] Origen certainly assumed they were included. See L. L. Belleville, *Two Views*, p. 45.

It would be easy to be unaware of the importance of the women in the mission of Christ since the apostles were all men, but the women's presence amongst Jesus' followers was critical for the development and expansion of his work. The picture of them being treated as full disciples is confirmed elsewhere. In Luke 10:39 the language Luke uses of Mary is that of a rabbi with his acolyte. In Luke 11:27–28, in a seemingly passing comment, Jesus includes women in theological discussion, which could also be said to be true of his conversations with the woman at the well and the Syro-Phoenician woman.[23]

As disciples of Jesus, then, women listened and responded to his teaching, engaged in ministry alongside men, and served as ambassadors of the kingdom of God. Moreover, they illustrate how radical the kingdom was and how much it overthrew social conventions that insisted the woman's place was confined to the home.[24] They epitomized the truth that the kingdom of God was an inclusive kingdom and had a particular place for the marginalized, powerless and vulnerable.

e. Women disciples not part of the Twelve

Among the larger, diverse group of disciples which included the women, twelve men were chosen as apostles in a class of their own. The question has to be asked why no women were included in the Twelve. Some build a great deal on this and argue that since only men were apostles then, so today only men can serve as priests or authoritative teachers. But we might similarly ask why Gentiles were not included in the Twelve and whether their absence disqualifies them from serving in those capacities today? Jesus taught so that that people might hear and respond to his message. He was revolutionary enough. To have made women or Gentiles more central to his movement would have made it harder for the people of Israel even to begin to hear and understand what he was saying. As Linda Belleville says, 'He was simply a realist in terms of the amount of change Palestinian culture could accommodate at that point in time'.[25] To have appointed women to the Twelve would have been 'too provocative in his world to gain any adherents for his movement'.[26] In the rest of his ministry Jesus shows such compassion to women and Gentiles that it is impossible not to think that

---

[23] John 4:7–26; Mark 7:24–30.
[24] S. Grenz and D. M. Kjesbo, *Women in the Church, A Biblical Theology of Women in Ministry* (Downers Grove: IVP, 1995), p. 77.
[25] Belleville, *Two Views*, p. 45.
[26] C. Blomberg, *Two Views*, p. 145.

this was an action intended to avoid unnecessary offence (there was sufficient necessary offence!) and aimed at maintaining an openness to his message. Besides this, there is an obvious symmetry between the twelve tribal heads in the old covenant, all of whom were men, and these twelve close companions as the founding apostles and foremost leaders of the new covenant age.

For women to be known as his disciples was astonishing enough in itself in first-century Middle East culture. Bailey, with his extensive knowledge and experience of those cultures concludes, 'I know of no place in traditional society where the social scene presented in this text is possible'.[27] For women to even be part of the wider travelling group would have been scandalous enough and it would have therefore been unthinkable for a woman to be part of the Twelve at this formative stage of the new kingdom communities.

2. Women at the cross of Jesus (Luke 23:44–56)

The women not only followed Jesus during his lifetime but played a critical role as witnesses to the cross and the resurrection. The women observed Jesus' execution (49); they were witnesses to the burial (55); they were the first to see the empty tomb (24:3) and were originally the exclusive recipients of the message that Jesus was alive again (24:4–8). Joel Green points out that Luke seems to draw particular attention to the women.[28] They are significant because they provide the continuity of memory from the early preaching of Jesus, through his itinerant ministry, to his passion, and through the resurrection on into the Acts of the Apostles. The role they play as eyewitnesses throughout is crucial.

The women are said to have *followed him from Galilee* (49). The word used for follow, *synakoloutheō*, is the same word which is used in Luke 5:11 of the disciples who left everything and followed Jesus. The word is used only in the Gospels and on one other occasion in Revelation 14:4. The fact that it is not used more widely suggests that it had become synonymous in the early church with discipleship and that its specific meaning was of following Jesus wherever it might take them – for the women, from Galilee to Jerusalem, from celebration to crucifixion, from the cross to resurrection – whatever the cost or circumstances.

All the Gospel writers emphasize the presence of the women at the cross. Were the male disciples present? If so, they seem to have been sheltering behind the women. Matthew 26:56 speaks of all the

[27] Bailey, *Jesus*, p. 192.
[28] J. B. Green, *The Gospel of Luke*, NICNT (Grand Rapids: Eerdmans, 1997), p. 828.

disciples deserting Jesus and fleeing from the Garden of Gethsemane with no mention of them returning to witness his crucifixion. Mark mentions only women as being present at the cross, otherwise Jesus died surrounded by opposition and hostility.[29] Luke possibly includes male disciples among the acquaintances who *stood at a distance.* And only one (unnamed) male disciple is specifically cited as being present by John.[30] Yet several women are repeatedly named. John refers to Mary the mother of Jesus, Mary the wife of Clopas and Mary Magdalene being there.[31] Mark refers in addition to Mary the mother of James and Joseph, and Salome,[32] while Matthew in addition to these refers also to the mother of Zebedee's sons.[33] It was the women not the men who stayed with Jesus to the last, prompting Witherington's comment that 'the trained male leadership fails at the Cross'.[34]

They were courageous to be there at all. The role of spectators at the crucifixion was to mock and jeer the victim. To have shown any sign of support or devotion to a person being executed as an enemy of the state would mean the authorities would keep their eye on them and regard them as suspects themselves. No wonder they *stood at a distance, watching these things.* For all that, their discipleship was both faithful and courageous.

The women witnessed and experienced the violence and pain of the crucifixion. They were not shielded from the appalling picture of their friend and Lord being brutally beaten and raised on a cross. The graphic portrayal of the violence of the beatings in the film *The Passion of the Christ*, directed by Mel Gibson,[35] is perhaps closer to the reality of the occasion than many of the sanitized or sentimental-ized versions which have come to the screen or are suggested by the polished crosses in our churches. The women disciples were women of courage, prepared bravely to face the most horrific scenes and yet maintain their devotion and care.

Suffering is no respecter of gender, age or culture and women have often found themselves facing the cruellest of situations because of

---

[29] Mark 15:40–41.
[30] John 19:26–27. Jesus passes his filial responsibility to 'the disciple whom he loved' and affirms his mother's maternal relationship to him. In doing so Jesus reflects that the biological family no longer has primary significance and affirms Mary as a woman of faith and a disciple of Jesus the Christ, who also happened to be her biological son. See pp. 158–159.
[31] John 19:25.
[32] Mark 15:40.
[33] Matt. 27:56.
[34] B. Witherington III, *Women in the Ministry of Jesus*, SNTSMS 51 (Cambridge: Cambridge University Press, 1984), p. 114.
[35] *The Passion of the Christ*, Icon Productions, USA, 2004.

their discipleship. Down through the centuries, as the history of world mission testifies, women have replicated the courage and endurance of the women at the cross. Mary Slessor, who followed David Livingstone in the continent of Africa, was an explorer, missionary and evangelist. Her discipleship proved significant in taking the gospel to many communities and bringing hope to the lost and despairing. In 1966, Jackie Pullinger travelled to Hong Kong without connections, support or a clear plan, but simply in obedience to the call of God. There she established, in the unpoliced area of Kowloon's Walled City, which was dominated by Triad gangs, projects to offer the love of Christ to opium addicts and the homeless. The St Stephen's Society continues to offer hope and God's strength to those most in need. More recently Emily Chalke went to Bangkok to offer love and hope to women trapped in the sex industry. Her courage in confronting the men who sustain the industry by visiting the city as sex tourists was extraordinary, as was her nerve in rescuing women from the powerful masters for whom violence is a regular tool of employment. It is the only place I have seen a genuine sign 'all guns to be left outside' as we entered a hotel where Emily was working and where pimping and criminal activity prevailed.

Luke only mentions one male 'disciple' by name during the days of the crucifixion. Joseph of Arimathea was a dignified and godly man who responded to Jesus' execution with both generosity and audacity. He sought permission to bury Jesus and facilitated his burial in a tomb he possessed. John mentions 'he was accompanied by Nicodemus'.[36] However, even their gracious acts are complemented by those of the women whom Luke mentions. As women traditionally would have done, they prepared the burial ointments and spices that they had not had time to get ready to anoint the body of Jesus. The women are not merely spectators of the burial but have work to do as well.

3. Women at the tomb of Jesus (Luke 24:1–12)

As the first witnesses to the resurrection the women become 'the first ambassadors of the "age to come"'.[37] None of the Gospels gives a definitive list or full account but they all agree the women were the first to be present at the tomb. This suggests the writers were using a common basic tradition alongside some independent sources to which each Gospel writer had access. Luke records that *Mary Magdalene*, who had been given prominence earlier, *Joanna, Mary the mother of*

---

[36] John 19:39.
[37] G. Osborne, cited in Grenz and Kjesbo, *Women in the Church*, p. 77.

James and the others (10) were present when they went to care for the body of Jesus but found the tomb both open and empty.

They were certain of what they witnessed. They heard the angels announce Christ's resurrection and were the first to *remember his words* (8) that had prophesied his death and resurrection. Their remembering was not merely a recalling, but a making sense of them. At long last the pieces fitted into place and the mystery was resolved. They were able to make the connections and to link the evidence of the empty tomb before their eyes to his earlier words and understand their significance. Jesus had kept his improbable promise to die and *on the third day be raised again* (7).

The women were not only instructed to *remember* Jesus' teaching but, according to Mark 16:7 and John 20:17, commissioned to tell the men – Peter and the other apostles – that Jesus had risen from the dead. Their first, independent attempt to announce the resurrection was received as *nonsense* by the *Eleven* and the other disciples with them. The male apostles, who should have been anticipating it but were not, considered their news a ridiculous story. Perhaps they should not have expected otherwise, since women were not considered reliable witnesses at the time. When Peter does at last go to the tomb he returns confused and not yet with the excitement and faith of the female disciples (12).

The crucial role the women play as witness to and heralds of the resurrection, which is confirmed by all four Gospels, is extraordinary.[38] In an age where the testimony of women was not considered credible, God chose to disclose the news to the women first and make them the initial bearers of the good news. In a culture where the Gospel writers would have wanted to give as much weight to testimonies about the resurrection as possible it is clear that these women would not have been the first people to choose to put in the witness box, unless it truly happened. Still today some discount reliable testimony simply because it comes from a woman's lips. Yet God announces the good news of the risen Christ from whoever's lips he chooses.

Their witness of the resurrection would have conferred a measure of authority on them in the early church where they 'acted as apostolic eyewitness guarantors of the tradition about Jesus'.[39] Their story would have been well-known and no Gospel writers would have been able to suppress it, even if they had wanted to do so.[40] This provides the most affirmative evidence of the value of women as disciples of Christ and of their role as messengers of the gospel. Why, then, does

[38] See Bauckham, *Gospel Women*, pp. 257–310.
[39] Bauckham, *Gospel Women*, p. 295.
[40] Bauckham, *Gospel Women*, p. 260.

Paul not refer to them in 1 Corinthians 15:1–7? It may well be no more than a sign that in an overwhelmingly patriarchal culture the early missionaries were 'not entirely comfortable'[41] with the part they played at the resurrection. The fact that the gospel makes so much of it, therefore, is further evidence of the credibility of the stories. Furthermore, as Bauckham adds, they are not in fact absent from Paul's concise summary in 1 Corinthians 15 since he refers, in verse 7, to Christ appearing 'to all the apostles'. Since Paul is clearly using 'all the apostles' to distinguish them from the Twelve, mentioned earlier, this wider sense of apostle would have included the women.[42]

The discipleship of the women which had taken them from the outset of Jesus' ministry in Galilee to the final chapters of his ministry in crucifixion and resurrection meant the women were the continuity factor through all the events. They were the ones entrusted with the privilege of sharing with the men that Jesus was no longer dead but resurrected and alive. They had listened to his teaching and were able to make sense of the empty tomb in the light of his teaching along the way. The full discipleship they model includes journeying and serving, hearing and remembering, and, applying and announcing the words of the Christ.

4. Women at Pentecost

The women continued their discipleship in the confusing and perplexing days following the ascension. They waited in fear and trepidation in Jerusalem for the coming of the Holy Spirit and they were recipients of God's gift of that Spirit on the Day of Pentecost. Their presence fulfils the prophecy of Joel 2:28–29. They shared in the worship, service, proclamation and miracles and were fully a part of the community which had visions, dreams and prophesied in the power of the Spirit. The forces of patriarchy may subsequently have sought to curtail their freedom or devalue their role. But nothing could detract from the privilege that God had bestowed on these faithful disciples, that of being the first to grasp the good news of resurrection and to be among the first group to experience the power of the Spirit descend on the church.

5. Concluding comments

Both before and after the crucifixion of Jesus women participated fully in the community of faith alongside men as disciples. The

[41] Bauckham, *Gospel Women*, p. 259.
[42] Bauckham, *Gospel Women*, p. 310.

contemporary context of Jewish as well as much pagan culture would have excluded women from any serious role in their religious practices, but in the kingdom of God they were given a central role in serving alongside men, not underneath them, and were even entrusted with the greatest news of all, that of the resurrection, before the men. Women received the most significant affirmation of all when, as the incontrovertible report in all four Gospels records, they were the ones to find the tomb of Jesus empty, giving them 'priority' 'in knowing and proclaiming this foundational fact to Christian faith'.[43]

Many women, as Witherington points out,[44] may have been attracted to become disciples because they had benefitted personally from Jesus' healing and found forgiveness and new life through him. However, becoming a disciple had other attractions too. It offered the possibility of being the follower of a great teacher, of travelling with others, of remaining single, and of being teachers and evangelists themselves.

Discussions, often highly charged ones, continue about the role of women in Christian communities and often the biblical texts quoted portray women in a less favourable light or a stereotypical role. If the women's role was put in the context of the women who were the disciples of Jesus then a different conclusion might be drawn. As Ryan indicates:

A long and sometimes heated debate is taking place today about the role of women in the Church. The tradition for those who would limit the position of women in the church has been to point to Biblical figures like Eve as a sinful prototype or Sarah as a strong matriarch. It would seem that the example of Jesus and his Galilean women disciples provides a better model of faithful, active, full discipleship for women in the Church.[45]

---

[43] Evelyn Stagg and Frank Stagg, *Woman in the World of Jesus* (Philadelphia: Westminster Press, 1978), p. 144.
[44] Witherington, *Ministry of Jesus*, p. 128.
[45] Ryan, 'Women from Galilee', p. 59.

Part Four
Women in the new community

Acts 16:13–15; 18:18–28; Romans 16:1–16; Philippians 4:2–3
15. Women in action

With the coming of the day of Pentecost Peter announced that Joel's long-standing prophecy had been fulfilled.[1] In this new age, the Spirit would be poured out on both sons and daughters, men and women, and people of both genders would prophesy, without distinction. What follows in the Acts of the Apostles provides ample evidence to support this and demonstrates women had a very active and varied role to play in the early church.

Besides the named individuals we will discuss below, women were among the disciples in the upper room in Jerusalem who awaited the coming of the Spirit[2] and were frequently found among those who became believers.[3] Dorcas, otherwise known as Tabitha, the clothes-maker, who was renowned for 'doing good and helping the poor', was raised from the dead on Peter's visit to Joppa.[4] Mary, the mother of John Mark, hosted at least some of the believers in Jerusalem in her house.[5] And Philip's four daughters were recognized as prophets.[6] Paul's writings support this picture of their active involvement in the life and mission of the early church. One third of the individuals he greets in his letters are women,[7] several of whom he refers to as fellow servants or co-workers in the gospel, just as he would of his male colleagues. All these women

---

[1] Joel 2:28–32.

[2] Acts 1:14.

[3] Acts 5:14; 8:3, 12; 9:2, 16:1, 13–15; 17:4, 12, 34; 21:5.

[4] Acts 9:36–42.

[5] Acts 12:12. Acts 12:17 suggests another group met elsewhere. See R. W. Gehring, *House Church and Mission: The Importance of Household Structures in Early Christianity* (Peabody: Henrickson, 2004), pp. 69–74.

[6] Acts 21:9.

[7] L. L. Belleville, *Two Views*, p. 36.

were active in ways that were appropriate to the gifts God had given them.

Several receive more extended treatment and these are the ones to which we turn in this chapter.

1. Lydia, the converted businesswoman (Acts 16:13–15)

In the absence of a synagogue in Philippi, Paul made his way to *a place of prayer* by the river. A synagogue could only be constituted if ten male householders came together but a less formal gathering for prayer, without a building, could take place in the absence of a sufficient number of men. In Philippi, the prayer group seemed mainly to be composed of women, among whom was Lydia, a God-fearing Gentile woman. The exact meaning of her being *a worshipper of God* is debated, but is probably equivalent to being a God-fearer, the description given to Cornelius. Although from outside the Jewish people, she identified herself with them in worship and was devoted, in so far as a Gentile woman could be, to following the Jewish God.

Lydia, was *a dealer in purple cloth* from Thyatira in Asia Minor, a place which was a centre for the production of this material. Her business, either as a manufacturer or trader, took her to Philippi where a trade guild of purple dyers is thought to have been active.[8] Several factors combine to suggest she was a woman of some standing. First, the trade in which she was engaged was a luxury trade. Purple cloth was expensive and worn by the elite in the Roman Empire. In fact, 'if Lydia dealt in true purple cloth, she would have been under imperial control and may even have been a member of the emperor's household (Phil. 4:22)'.[9] Secondly, she is named, which suggests she was either of high status or at least well-known in the church.[10] Thirdly, she presided over a sizeable household and was able to offer Paul and his entourage hospitality (15).

As an independent, and possibly reasonably wealthy, businesswoman she would not have been unique. In the first century women in the Roman world were emerging from the shadows and interacting more freely in the pubic world and attending social occasions in their

---

[8] R. S. Ascough, *Lydia: Paul's Cosmopolitan Host*, Paul's Social Network (Collegeville, Liturgical Press, 2009), p. 80.

[9] Ascough, *Lydia*, p. 75. It is curious that Lydia is not mentioned in Philippians but there may be several explanations for this, including the most likely that she was no longer in Philippi when Paul wrote to them.

[10] D. G. Peterson, *The Acts of the Apostles*, PNTC (Grand Rapids: Eerdmans and Nottingham: Apollos, 2009), pp. 460–461.

own right.[11] In commerce and business, they functioned 'in pretty much the same way as men' with wealth and social status determining their place in society rather than gender.[12] Some of these women may have been widowed or divorced, but others were clearly single and had never been attached to a man. In the public sphere, then, Lydia was no 'also-ran' to a man.

As Paul was preaching *the Lord opened her heart to respond* to the gospel (14). God's initiative meant her mind was open to the gospel Paul preached and she came to believe with the result that *she and the members of her household were baptised*.[13] Paul and his companions were then *persuaded* to accept hospitality at her house during their remaining time in Philippi. Her offer was typical of the generous hospitality Luke commends among the early believers. The fact that Paul needed persuading suggests nothing more than they were adopting the normal rules of social etiquette whereby such an invitation was resisted when first issued.[14] Not to have accepted would have been to contravene the ancient rules of hospitality, while doing so provided the assurance that Paul believed her conversion to be genuine. There seem no implications for gender either in the offer or its acceptance, and ideas that some form of on-going relationship developed between Paul and Lydia has absolutely no basis. But it did mean that Lydia, at least to a limited extent, became a patron of Paul's work and offered him material assistance in his mission.[15]

What is of note is that Paul's first convert in Philippi was a woman and the embryonic church in that city was formed among women. As a householder she became a significant figure in the leadership of this new community just as possibly Chloe did in Corinth,[16] Nympha did in Laodicea,[17] and Apphia, with her husband Philemon, in Colossae.[18] This stands in marked contrast to the inability of the Jewish population to form a synagogue there, presumably because of the absence of men.[19]

[11] See *inter alia*, Ascough, *Lydia*, pp. 65–69; B. W. Winter, *Roman Wives, Roman Widows: The Appearance of New Women and the Pauline Community* (Grand Rapids: Eerdmans, 2003); B. Witherington III, *The Acts of the Apostles: A Socio-Rhetorical Commentary* (Grand Rapids: Eerdmans and Carlisle: Paternoster, 1998), p. 492.

[12] Winter, *Roman Wives*, p.175.

[13] On household baptisms see Witherington, *Acts*, p. 493 n. 102.

[14] Witherington, *Acts*, p. 493.

[15] G. D. Fee, *Paul's Letter to the Philippians*, NICNT (Grand Rapids: Eerdmans, 1995), p. 390; *contra* Ascough, *Lydia*, p. 53.

[16] 1 Cor. 1:11.

[17] Col. 4:15.

[18] Philm. 2.

[19] B. Witherington III, *Women and the Genesis of Christianity* (Cambridge: Cambridge University Press, 1990), p. 215.

2. Priscilla, the fearless teacher (Acts 18:18–28)

Of the six occasions when Aquila and Priscilla are mentioned, always as a couple, it is noteworthy that Priscilla's name is mentioned first on four occasions.[20] Whether this means she came from a more prestigious social background than Aquila or was more prominent in the church we cannot say. But, as Mary Evans claims, 'there is not the slightest hint of anything other than an equal partnership in every aspect of their relationship'.[21] Paul describes this couple as 'fellow workers in Christ Jesus [who] risked their lives for me [and] not only I but all the churches of the Gentiles are grateful to them'.[22] Our interest, however, lies not in the particular event that lay behind this commendation, but the role they are reported to have played in teaching Apollos *the way of God more adequately* (26).

Apollos was evidently an intelligent and inspiring teacher who spoke with passion about Jesus as accurately as he knew how. In knowing only the baptism of John, however, he fell short of full knowledge and there was more for him to learn. So *when Priscilla and Aquila heard him, they invited him to their home and explained to him the way of God more adequately* (26). Priscilla was obviously involved in teaching Apollos alongside her husband. We are given no indication of how the teaching was apportioned but the wording cannot be construed to mean Aquila did the teaching while Priscilla cooked the meal. No one seems to doubt that Priscilla played an intelligent and explicit role in instructing Apollos in doctrines of the faith.

Those who have reservations about the appropriateness of women having a teaching role in the church suggest that there is a difference between the type of teaching Priscilla undertook here and that which Paul seems to forbid in 1 Timothy 2:12.[23] The difference, it is argued, is that here Priscilla teaches privately in her home, whereas the prohibition in 1 Timothy refers to public teaching in the church. The former is described as *'unofficial guidance'* while the latter is official teaching.[24] But the private/public distinction is hard to maintain since much of the life of the early church centred around the home and Paul himself speaks of having 'taught [the Ephesians] publicly

---

[20] Acts 18:2–3, 18, 26; Rom. 16:3; 1 Cor. 16:19; 2 Tim 4:19.

[21] M. Evans, *Woman in the Bible* (Exeter: Paternoster, 1983), p. 123.

[22] Rom. 16:3.

[23] E. g. G. W. Knight III, *The New Testament Teaching on the Role Relationship of Men and Women* (Grand Rapids: Baker, 1977), pp. 52, 67; C. Blomberg, *Two Views*, p. 147.

[24] J. Piper and W. Grudem, 'An Overview of Central Concerns', *RBMW*, p. 84. See also p. 218 and T. R. Schreiner, *Two Views*, p. 279.

and from house to house' (Acts 20:20). Houses, with their workshops, were often the venues for teaching in the ancient world.[25] The distinction is not really sustainable. Even the official/unofficial distinction is anachronistic in the light of the fluidity of patterns of leadership and teaching in the New Testament. Linda Belleville is right in asserting, 'Such distinctions . . . are decidedly modern ones'.[26] The reason for inviting Apollos to their house has probably more to do with the discretion Priscilla and Aquila sought to exercise. As F. F. Bruce commented, 'How much better it is to give such private help to a preacher whose ministry is defective than to correct or denounce him publicly!'[27]

Priscilla has had many successors down through the history of the church. Women have consistently played a formative role as pioneering missionaries and teachers of the church's doctrine. It is unconvincing (to say the least) to argue, as some do, that it is legitimate for them to do so in the initial stage of church formation but that once the church is established and regular patterns of government are in place, they cannot continue to serve in the same way and their mission is over and they are required to make way for male elders.[28] Foundations matter. Faulty foundations lead to defective buildings. So why is any continuing teaching ministry considered more significant (and so only worthy of men) than that of the pioneering ministry that lays the foundations of the church in the first place?

Priscilla played a crucial role in instructing Apollos and then, although her activities are never detailed in the same way, she evidently continued to play a courageous role in missionary advance and in the leadership of the church which met in their house, no doubt using her gifts as a teacher.[29]

3. Phoebe, the generous deacon (Romans 16:1–2)

The first person to be named in Paul's long list of personal contacts in Romans 16 is Phoebe. There is no mention of a husband, leading to the speculation that Phoebe was either widowed or a single woman of some independent means. In commending her to the church Paul describes his *sister* in two ways: she is *a deacon (diakonon) of the*

---

[25] See R. F. Hock, *The Social Context of Paul's Ministry: Tentmaking and Apostleship* (Philadelphia: Fortress Press, 1980), pp. 37–42.

[26] Belleville, *Two Views*, p. 59.

[27] F. F. Bruce, *The Book of Acts,* NICNT (Grand Rapids: Eerdmans, 1988), p. 360, cited by Peterson, *Acts*, p. 526.

[28] This is argued by J. B. Hurley, *Man and Woman in Biblical Perspective* (Leicester: IVP, 1981), p. 250.

[29] 1 Cor. 16:19.

church at Cenchreae, the eastern seaport of Corinth, and *the benefactor (prostatis) of many people, including me.* Unfortunately the commendation tends to be suffocated by controversy over the meaning of both terms.

Thinking that Paul could not be referring to Phoebe as the holder of the position of deacon, some translations refer to her as 'servant' of the church in Cenchreae.[30] Paul does use the word in a general sense to refer to himself and his co-workers as servants or ministers of Christ and the gospel without any implication that they were occupying the office of a deacon in a church.[31] But the phrase *deacon of the church at Cenchreae* seems to imply something more particular than this. The *office* of deacon was still embryonic, but the *role* of deacon was already clear. Deacons provided 'practical service to the needy' and were purveyors of material Christian compassion.[32] Philippians 1:1 and 1 Timothy 3:8–13 demonstrate that the church recognized deacons, even if they were yet to become holders of an institutional office. Women were recognized as deacons both in Philippi[33] and Ephesus, if, as is likely, 1 Timothy 3:11 refers to women who were deacons rather than deacons' wives in the church there.[34] There was no feminine form of the word *diakonos,* which meant that the word either was avoided, so as to avoid confusion with male deacons as in 1 Timothy 3:11, or could embrace women, as here. If Paul had simply wanted to commend her for her 'service' there would have been other ways he could have done that; his words suggest something more specific. The term does not imply that she was the leader, preacher or minister (in the contemporary sense) of the church but she was clearly 'more than an ordinary believer'.[35] On balance, then, it would seem Phoebe was publicly recognized as a full deacon, on a par with any male deacon.[36]

The second term Paul uses of her is equally debated. The word *prostatis (benefactor)* usually means 'patron'.[37] In its masculine form

---

[30] KJV, ESV and NIV. RSV used 'deaconess'.

[31] 1 Cor. 3:5; 2 Cor. 3:6; 6:4; Eph. 3:7; 6:21; Col. 1:7, 23, 25; 4:1; 1 Tim 4:6. D. Moo, *The Epistle to the Romans,* NICNT (Grand Rapids: Eerdmans, 1996), p. 913, esp. n. 7.

[32] C. E. B. Cranfield, *The Epistle to the Romans,* vol. 2, ICC (Edinburgh: T & T Clark, 1979), p. 781.

[33] See below on Euodia and Syntyche.

[34] See discussion in I. H. Marshall, *The Pastoral Epistles,* ICC (Edinburgh: T & T Clark, 1999), pp. 492–495; A. Perriman, *Speaking of Women: Interpreting Paul* (Leicester: Apollos, 1998), pp. 63–67.

[35] Moo, *Romans,* pp. 913–914.

[36] Cranfield, *Romans,* p. 781; J. G. G. Dunn, *Romans 9-16,* WBC (Dallas: Word, 1988), pp. 886–87.

[37] See J. C. Campbell, *Phoebe: Patron and Emissary* (Collegeville: Liturgical Press, 2009), pp. 78–92.

it referred to a wealthy individual who acted as patron and, under Roman law, as protector and guarantor of a religious group. 'The word was applied to the leader of worship in a Graeco-Roman temple as well as to a governor, a chieftan, and a leader of a democracy.'[38] It was a term that carried some authority and certainly prestige and status.[39]

Cranfield commented that, 'It could hardly have any technical legal sense such as the masculine form *prostatēs* could bear'.[40] But a decade later James Dunn would comment that, 'The unwillingness of commentators to give *prostatis* its most natural and obvious sense of "patron" is most striking', and pleaded that 'the word should be given its full weight'.[41] In the intervening decade there had been much fresh discovery about the role of women in the public and religious life of the Roman world, with knock-on effects on the Jewish religious world as well. Their emergence into the public arena from the hidden world of domestic life is well-attested and their acting as patronesses of religious groups is well documented.[42]

Among Christians, the prestige of the patron had been 'converted' to use Bruce Winter's term.[43] Patrons were usually conscious of their position, expected people to ingratiate themselves to them, and had an eye to how they would benefit from their position. Christian patrons and patronesses, by contrast, served people 'without respect for their *persona*' or for how they might benefit in doing so.[44]

As patroness, Phoebe would not necessarily have presided over the assembly, although the evidence does not rule that out. But as Paul makes explicit, she used her resources to support many people, including his own mission, akin to the women mentioned in Luke 8:1–3. Some have even speculated that she is mentioned first in Romans 16 in the hope that she would be the chief financier of Paul's Spanish mission.[45]

[38] K. E. Bailey, 'Women in the New Testament: A Middle Eastern Cultural View', *Anvil* 11 (1994), p. 10.

[39] E. C. Stewart, 'Social Stratification and Patronage in Ancient Mediterranean Society', in D. Neufeld and R. E. DaMaris (eds.), *Understanding the Social World of the New Testament* (London and New York: Routledge, 2010), pp. 156–167; A. D. Clarke, *Serve the Community of the Church: Christians as Leaders and Ministers* (Grand Rapids: Eerdmans, 2000).

[40] Cranfield, *Romans*, p. 782.

[41] Dunn, *Romans 9-16*, p. 888.

[42] C. Osiek and M. Y. MacDonald (eds.), *A Woman's Place: House Churches in Earliest Christianity* (Minneapolis: Fortress Press, 2006); B. W. Winter, *Roman Wives*.

[43] B. W. Winter, *After Paul left Corinth: The Influence of Secular Ethics and Social Change* (Grand Rapids: Eerdmans, 2001), p. 203.

[44] Winter, *After Paul*, p. 203.

[45] See discussion in Osiek and MacDonald, *A Woman's Place*, p. 216. Others suggest, more reasonably, that she was the bearer of the letter to Rome.

Be that as it may, Phoebe remains a significant figure in the church at Cenchreae, who used her wealth to support Christian believers widely and Paul's mission specifically. She had the rare distinction of balancing beautifully the serving role of deacon with that of the leading role of patroness and merited the warm acceptance of God's people as a result.

4. Junia, the well-known apostle (Romans 16:7)

The most arresting of Paul's greetings in Romans 16 is that in verse 7 to *Andronicus and Junia* who were *outstanding among the apostles*. They were Christians before Paul was converted and had shared a prison term with him.

The first conundrum about this verse is to identify if Junia is a man or a woman. Some argue that the name could be a contracted form of the man's name Junianus, while others maintain it refers to a woman's name, Junia. Piper and Grudem represent the complementarian position and state that we cannot know whether the person was a man or a woman and claim that 'the evidence is indecisive'.[46] But the overwhelming weight of evidence and the consensus among contemporary scholars suggests otherwise. The evidence seems quite decisive in favour of Junia being a woman.

What is that evidence?[47] It was not until the thirteenth century that the masculine form Junias was introduced into the biblical manuscripts, on the basis of an assumption that a woman could not be *outstanding among the apostles*. The early church fathers, including Chrysostom who was known to express reservations about women as priests, had no hesitation in accepting it referred to a woman. The female name, Junia, is well-attested, whereas Junias is not attested at all. Furthermore, it makes natural sense to read *Andronicus and Junia* as a husband-wife team, like Priscilla and Aquila in verse 4. Unless, then, one wants to impose a dogmatic

---

[46] Piper and Grudem, *RBMW*, p. 79.

[47] This paragraph is dependent on R. Bauckham, *Gospel Women: Studies of the Named Women in the Gospels* (London: T & T Clark, 2002), pp. 166–169; Cranfield, *Romans*, p. 788; Moo, *Romans*, pp. 921–923; and Dunn, *Romans 9-16*, p. 894, who comments, 'The assumption that it must be a male is a striking indictment of male presumption regarding the character and structure of earliest Christianity'. For a recent lively, if combative, account see S. McKnight, *Junia is Not Alone: Breaking our Silence about Women in the Bible and the Church Today* (Englewood: Patheos Press, 2011). McKnight blames the 1927 Nestle edition of the Greek text for 'stealing' Junia and 'burying her alive by changing the name from a feminine to a masculine form', and Kurt Aland's 1979 edition for dropping the feminine even in the footnote.

interpretation on these verses the evidence leads us to understand Junia as a woman.

Resolving her gender in this way only accentuates, however, the next conundrum in this verse. What does it mean to say that she and Andronicus were *outstanding among the apostles?* It could mean that they were outstanding in the eyes of the apostles, that is 'well respected by the apostles' or 'esteemed by them'.[48] Or it could mean that they were 'outstanding among the group who may be designated as apostles'.[49] Cranfield speaks for many in saying that although the former sense is grammatically possible the latter is 'more probable – we might say virtually certain'.[50]

They were obviously not members of the original Twelve but they were members of the larger group, who like the Twelve were witnesses to the resurrection (they were, after all, *in Christ* before Paul), and were the original itinerant missionaries and church planters, instrumental in the spread of the gospel immediately after Pentecost. Dunn may be pushing the case too far in arguing that 'they belonged most probably to the closed group of apostles appointed directly by the risen Christ in a limited period following his resurrection'.[51] The evidence for such an official group is thin.[52] Nonetheless, there is no reason to deny that Junia, with her husband Andronicus, played an exceptional role in the formation of the early churches and was therefore acknowledged as 'an outstanding apostle'. Even if all it means is that she was a 'travelling missionary',[53] it places her among the preachers of the early gospel, among the guarantors of the Christian tradition, and among those who exercised leadership gifts in the early churches.

Richard Bauckham, noting that Junia may be the Latin form of Joanna, raises the intriguing question as to whether the Junia of Romans 16 is the same person as Joanna who was a disciple of Jesus, mentioned in Luke 8:3. His scintillating argument certainly lends texture to a number of New Testament passages, but ultimately it cannot be more than fascinating speculation and it must not distract us from the astounding claim that in the early church they recognized a woman as an apostle, and an *outstanding* one at that.

---

[48] NIV mg.

[49] Cranfield, *Romans*, p. 789. For a careful consideration of the opposite argument which, he concludes, is ultimately unpersuasive, see Bauckham, *Gospel Women*, pp. 172–180.

[50] Cranfield, *Romans*, p. 789. *Contra* Moo, *Romans*, p. 923.

[51] Dunn, *Romans 9-16*, p. 895.

[52] 1 Cor. 15:7 speaks of 'all the apostles' as distinct from the Twelve, mentioned in v. 5.

[53] Moo, *Romans*, p. 924.

5. Euodia and Syntyche, Paul's fractious co-workers (Philippians 4:2–3)

While Lydia disappears from view, women continue to be significant in the church at Philippi. Paul names two women, Euodia and Syntyche, who were long-standing friends and significant figures, perhaps even deacons, in the church, who were both an asset and a liability.[54]

On the one hand Paul commends them as women who *have contended at my side in the cause of the gospel*. In doing so he brackets them without distinction 'as full members of his mission team'[55] alongside *Clement and the rest of my co-workers*. Paul does not specify the precise task they undertook, whether as those who preached, testified or helped support and organize the work in other ways. In using the word *contended*, a word drawn from the athletic stadium or gladiatorial ring, he conveys that they were no mere onlookers in his mission but fully entered into the struggle and the suffering of it alongside the rest. They were women of courage.

On the other hand, they 'had fallen on some bad times'[56] and were now not contending for the gospel but contending with each other. It was a quarrel that could affect the whole church and therefore needed to be resolved rather than allowed to fester. After pleading with them to *be of the same mind in the Lord* Paul is realistic enough to know that this would be difficult and they would need help in being reconciled.[57] So he asks an unidentified *true companion* to assist them.[58] Philippians was perhaps the happiest church in the New Testament but it was not perfect and there is more than one hint in the letter that it was threatened with division due to pride on the part of some of its members. Perhaps this very conflict between Euodia and Syntyche lay behind the emphasis Paul places on unity and humility earlier in the letter.

The vignette of life in the Philippian church gives us a window onto the real-life experience of the early church. Women had an incredible contribution to make and yet were never to be idealized. Like men, they were fallible and could behave in sinful ways, even

---

[54] Fee, *Philippians*, p. 389, suggests he names them precisely because they are his friends. Fee, p. 69, and M. Bockmuehl, *The Epistle to the Philippians*, BNTC (London: A & C Black, 1998), p. 238 argue they may have been deacons, which is why deacons receive special mention in Phil. 1:1.

[55] G. W. Hansen, *The Letter to the Philippians*, PNTC (Grand Rapids: Eerdmans and Nottingham: Apollos, 2009), p. 285.

[56] Fee, *Philippians*, p. 389.

[57] G. F. Hawthorne, *Philippians*, WBC (Waco: Word, 1983), p. 179.

[58] On the various suggestions as to who this person was see Hawthorne, *Philippians*, pp. 179–180.

while courageously serving the Lord. The picture is painted 'warts and all'.

6. Concluding comments

Whatever the meaning of the apparently more restrictive verses found in some of Paul's letters, their practice demonstrates that women played a range of prominent roles in the early church. They did so according to their gifts and circumstances, as witnesses, teachers, hostesses, patroness, missionaries, and one even earned the title 'apostle'. They did so without any hint that their ministry was restricted to females or that they did so under the authority of men. Given the largely patriarchal context of their day and male-orientation of the early writings, they play a remarkably expansive role alongside men in contending for the gospel. But the New Testament is no idealistic feminist tract and it recognizes their failings, as it does the failings of men, as well as their contribution. Gender is not the primary issue, only commitment to Christ and the formation of a Christ-like character.

1 Corinthians 11:2–16
16. Women in prayer

We might have thought the story apocryphal except my mother claims to have been present when it happened. A group of women met for coffee and decided to spend some time in prayer. Fearing that they might be contravening the teaching of 1 Corinthians 11 if they did so with their heads uncovered, they solemnly proceeded to place cushions on their heads before they prayed. 1 Corinthians 11 has certainly given rise to an immense amount of discussion and been responsible for all sorts of zealous, if not always well-informed, spiritual practices, especially about hats and headship.

The passage introduces a long section of 1 Corinthians (chs. 11–14) in which Paul is concerned with the question of propriety in worship. The first and last segments in this section concern the behaviour of men and women. The segments next to them deal with irregularities at the Lord's Supper (11:17–34) and the use (or rather misuse) of spiritual gifts (12:1–30; 14:1–25). The segment in the centre deals with the paramount need for love (12:31 – 14:1).[1] To begin with Paul is concerned about how men and women who speak in the church should dress, especially with regard to what they wear on their heads. What people wear on their heads, then as now, often has symbolic significance and certain headgear is appropriate in some circumstances but inappropriate in others. To wear a baseball cap to a football match is entirely suitable, to wear it at a wedding would be another matter.

Whatever the complexities, and they are many, Paul's essential

---

[1] On the composition of 1 Cor. 11:2 – 14:40 see K. E. Bailey, *Paul Through Mediterranean Eyes: Cultural Studies in 1 Corinthians* (London: SPCK, 2011), p. 295. See also the next chapter, esp. p. 226.

concern is clear. When taking part in public worship[2] men and women should sport different styles of headcovering. What is appropriate for men is not appropriate for women and vice versa. The crucial difference is that when men pray or prophesy they should do so with their heads *uncovered*, whereas women should speak with their heads *covered*. While the passage is often considered as directed at women (and we must plead guilty to discussing it from this perspective here) the truth is that it is directed equally to men and women. Even so, it is true that, 'Within the larger question of the place of women in the New Testament,' as Kenneth Bailey asserts, 'this passage is of critical importance'.[3]

As ever, Paul grounds his pastoral admonition in theology and he mentions three interlocking principles to support his argument that it is important to maintain a distinction between the genders when women and men participate in worship. They concern male headship, creation and *the very nature of things* (14).

1. Headship theology (2–6)

a. Theory

Paul's first argument for gender-specific headdress at Corinth is that of headship: *I want you to realise that the head of every man is Christ, and the head of the woman is man, and the head of Christ is God* (3). He does not explicitly explain why this means men should not cover their heads when they pray whereas women should, but his reasoning becomes clearer as his discussion develops.

Many would be surprised to discover that this is one of only two places where men are referred to as *the head of a woman*, the other being Ephesians 5:23.[4] The significance of a concept is not established by the number of times particular words are used, nonetheless, the emphasis that some place on the headship of the man, interpreted as male authority, seems out of proportion to the number of times Scripture mentions it. It can only be made to serve as a foundation for understanding the relationship between the genders if a good number of other verses that do not mention it are forced through its filter. And it begs the question as to what male headship means.

---

[2] Some resolve the apparent contradiction between Paul permitting women to pray and prophesy here with his command to them to keep silent in church (1 Cor. 14:34) by saying this refers to a private meeting as opposed to public worship. But Paul gives no hint of such a distinction which, in any case, is unsustainable given that the early churches met in private households.

[3] Bailey, *Paul*, p. 297.

[4] See ch. 18.

Before discussing what *the head of the woman is man* means, we should note that Paul places the idea in the context of Christ being the head of man and God being the head of Christ. This cannot imply that the Son is in any way inferior to the Father and any idea of the Son being subordinate to the Father has to be handled with precision and great care.[5] Yet, the world was seen as having a sense of order in which people had their correct place, with God in the place of supremacy, and chaos and disorder threatened when people abdicated their place for another. Paul's use of headship relates to the similar, if wider, concept of 'submission' that is mentioned elsewhere in the New Testament and again is discussed in chapter 18.[6]

There are four ways in which the meaning of 'head' has been interpreted.

First, and most obviously, 'head' literally refers to that part of a person's anatomy that is above the neck and contains the brain, eyes, ears, nose and mouth. The word is used in this literal sense repeatedly in verses 4, 5, 6, 7, 10 and 13.[7] But this cannot be its meaning in verse 3 where its use is obviously metaphorical.

Secondly, as a metaphor it may refer to the source, origin or what comes before. For example, we speak, about the source of a river as its head. Several advocate this meaning here and point out that Paul connects his discussion with creation in verses 8–9.[8] If so, it fits the relational tone of the argument and the absence of any suggestion of the man having 'authority over' a woman.[9] However, there are several problems with this view. It would imply that God is the source of Christ, which cannot be. More particularly, the evidence for *head* being understood in this way is weak and Wayne Grudem's extensive research found no examples of this meaning in ancient literature and finds the interpretation totally unpersuasive.[10]

---

[5] K. Giles, *The Trinity and Subordinationism: The Doctrine of God and the Contemporary Gender Debate* (Downers Grove: IVP, 2002).

[6] E.g., Rom. 13:1, 5; 1 Cor. 15:27–28; 16:16; Eph. 5:21, 24; Col. 3:18; Heb 12:9; 13:17; Jas 4:7; 1 Pet. 2:13, 18; 3:1, 5; 5:5.

[7] The word does not occur in verses 5b, 6 and 13 in the Greek but is necessarily implied.

[8] L. L. Belleville, *Two Views*, pp. 99–101; M. Evans, *Woman in the Bible* (Exeter: Paternoster, 1983), p. 75–77; G. D. Fee, *The First Epistle to the Corinthians*, NICNT (Grand Rapids: Eerdmans, 1987), pp. 503–505 and 'Praying and Prophesying in the Assemblies, *DBE*, pp. 149–155; P. B. Payne, *Man and Woman One in Christ* (Grand Rapids: Zondervan, 2009), pp. 113–139.

[9] The only reference to 'authority' in the passage is in v. 10 which says 'the woman ought to have authority over her own head'.

[10] W. Grudem, 'Does *Kephalē* mean "Source" or "Authority Over"?', *TrinJ* 6 (1985), pp. 38–59 and 'The Meaning of *Kephalē* ("Head"): A Response to Recent Studies', *RBMW*, pp. 425–468. See the more moderate critique in A. Perriman, *Speaking of Women: Interpreting Paul* (Leicester: Apollos, 1998), pp. 25–30.

Thirdly, 'head' is viewed as the seat of authority.[11] This is often said to be the 'natural' or 'self-evident' interpretation of the word and the way in which, for example, it is plainly used in Ephesians 1:22. In spite of this, the evidence for this meaning is not quite as simple as is often suggested. Reviewing the way 'head' is used in the Old Testament, Perriman concludes that although there is 'some scope for confusion' 'the evidence strongly suggests that the figure was not used in the Septuagint to denote a position of authority'.[12] The context does not suggest that authority is the focus of the discussion and the only reference to authority refers to women, not men, having authority (10). Extra-biblical use of the word 'head' is much more varied than those who argue it must mean authority admit.[13]

Fourthly, 'head' might simply refer to a position of prominence. It means 'foremost, uppermost, pre-eminent' which, as Perriman says, 'is the simplest, most obvious, most natural, most elegant metaphorical sense'.[14] The head, after all, is the most prominent part of the body, the visible part by which we recognize one another. It suggests 'visibility, eminence, social superiority, not the other dimension of authority and subservience'.[15] We recognize each other because of our heads, without it carrying overtones of supremacy. This is the most frequent way it is used in the Septuagint and while at times it may carry connotations of authority, it frequently does not and the two should not be necessarily equated. Unless there are other reasons in the context to take it as meaning authority, which there are not, it should not be understood as meaning that the man is in authority over the women in 1 Corinthians 11:3. Thiselton's magisterial commentary pronounces in favour of head meaning prominence, if only just, not least because it does justice to the multivaried meaning of the idea.[16]

This fourth understanding of 'head', certainly fits the context well and lends coherence to the rest of Paul's argument. Paul builds his argument for distinctive head coverings on the fact that men were more prominent than women in the social and church cultures of the day.

[11] G. W. Dawes, *The Body in Question: Metaphor and Meaning in the Interpretation of Eph. 5:21-33*, *BibInt* 30 (Leiden: Brill, 1998), pp. 122–149; J. A. Fitzmeyer, 'Another look at *KEPHALĒ* in 1 Corinthians 11:3', *NTS* 35.4 (1989), pp. 503–511; Grudem, 'Does *Kephalē*' and 'The Meaning of'; J. B. Hurley, *Man and Woman in Biblical Perspective* (Leicester: IVP, 1981), pp. 163–168.

[12] Perriman, *Speaking of Women*, p. 20.

[13] Fee, 'Praying and Prophesying', pp. 149–152.

[14] Perriman, *Speaking of Women*, p. 32.

[15] Perriman, *Speaking of Women*, p. 33.

[16] A. C. Thiselton, *The First Epistle to the Corinthians*, NIGTC (Grand Rapids: Eerdmans and Carlisle: Paternoster, 2000), pp. 811, 816–820.

b. Practice

From the theory, Paul turns to the practice, which also contains a number of difficulties. Speaking first of the men, Paul says it is shameful if they *kata kephalēs echōn*, which literally means 'having down the head', and is usually (and reasonably) translated in terms of having something hanging from the head, that is, having the head covered.[17] The opposite instruction applies to women, whose behaviour is shameful if they speak with their heads *uncovered*. The question is, covered with what? Does Paul mean with one's hair or is it a reference to a prayer shawl or perhaps, for women, a veil. (Whatever it means, he is not referring to a modern woman's hat, still less a cushion!)[18]

Paul might mean that men should not have long flowing hair when taking part in public worship as, in his day, this sent out signals of an effeminate or homosexual lifestyle: honourable, heterosexual men had short hair.[19] This interpretation fits with his comments in verses 14 and 15, although there may have been more obvious ways to say it. Thiselton considers this view as 'strong' but not 'conclusive'.[20]

It could be that Paul was advising against the Roman and Jewish practice of men covering their heads when praying, which might be considered shameful for several reasons.[21] Other meanings are possible as well, such as the way in which men covered their heads when mourning or in the cult of Isis, and obviously Paul would wish to dissociate Christian worship from such practices.[22] Even if we

---

[17] Fee, *First Corinthians*, p. 506.

[18] For details see R. E. Ciampa and B. S. Rosner, *The First Letter to the Corinthians*, PNTC (Grand Rapids: Eerdmans and Nottingham: Apollos, 2010), pp. 512–522; Hurley, *Man and Woman*, pp. 168–171; C. S. Keener, *Paul, Women and Wives* (Peabody: Hendrickson, 1992), pp. 22–31, 85–102; Perriman, *Speaking of Women*, pp. 103–108; T. R. Schreiner, 'Head Coverings, Prophecies and the Trinity', *RBMW*, pp. 125–127; Thiselton, *First Corinthians*, pp. 823–826; B. Witherington III, *Conflict and Community in Corinth: A Socio-Rhetorical Commentary on 1 and 2 Corinthians* (Grand Rapid: Eerdmans, 1995), pp. 232–235.

[19] J. Murphy-O'Connor, 'Sex and Logic in 1 Cor. 11:2-16', *CBQ* 42 (1980), pp. 482–500; Payne, *One in Christ*, pp. 141–145; B. W. Winter, *After Paul Left Corinth: The Influence of Secular Ethics and Social Change* (Grand Rapids: Eerdmans, 2001), pp. 132–133.

[20] Thiselton, *First Corinthians*, p. 825.

[21] Payne, *One in Christ*, pp. 141–142. Fee, *First Corinthians*, p. 507, cites Lightfoot as advocating this as a way of Paul distancing himself from Jewish customs, especially in the light of 2 Cor. 3:12–18. Winter, *After Paul*, pp. 121–123, discusses high-status Roman men wearing a head covering at sacrifices and suggests Paul is saying that accepting such status markers is to obscure the status marker that really counts, i.e., God's image.

[22] Fee, *First Corinthians*, pp. 507–508.

cannot, Paul's readers would readily decode the symbolic meaning of the different hairstyles or headdresses so that they could avoid behaving in a way that brought dishonour to the church and to Christ. That, after all, is Paul's primary reason for the distinction between men and women here.

Women brought shame on their heads by uncovering them when speaking. Again this could either mean that they were to wear a prayer shawl of some kind or be a reference to the way they wore their hair. Most do not think it refers to a veil, which was not normally worn in Greek and Roman cultures; being unveiled in worship would not have been considered shameful.[23] It is certainly not referring to the kind of veil worn by some contemporary Muslim women as there is no evidence of such a practice, except among a small minority of ultra conservatives.[24] Since Paul goes on to suggest that for a woman to have her head *uncovered* is like having *her head shaved* (5), and then later says that the glory of her *long hair is given to her as a covering* (15), it is probable that he is referring to her hairstyle rather than any material head covering.[25]

The explanation again involves us understanding the various cultural signals that would be sent out by different hairstyles.[26] A woman whose head was shaved was likely to be a convicted prostitute or perhaps a despised slave. Long flowing hair denoted a sexually loose lifestyle.[27] In the cult of Dionysius, which was prominent in Corinth, women engaged in sexually immoral rituals and prophesied with their hair hanging loose.[28] No wonder Paul wished to distance the young Christian community from sending out such messages. To display either a shaved head or flowing hair would have sent out the wrong signals to men and been sexually provocative. Hence, Paul insists, they keep their long hair, which is their *glory*, but tie it up, covering their head with it, rather than letting it hang loose. These women may have been thinking that since they were members of the eschatological community the normal social conventions and symbols no longer applied to them. But Paul encourages them not to overturn those conventions and so bring shame on the church.

Bruce Winter's recent researches suggest a variation on this theme.

---

[23] Part of our difficulty in interpretation is that practices varied from time to time, across cultures and between rural and urban settings.

[24] Hurley, *Man and Woman*, p.179.

[25] For extensive evidence see Payne, *One in Christ*, pp. 147–173.

[26] Fee, *First Corinthians*, pp. 508–510; Thisleton, *First Corinthians*, pp. 828–833.

[27] It is interesting how the device of a prim and proper lady being transformed into a sexually attractive or seductive woman by letting her hair down is still frequently found in contemporary films.

[28] Payne, *One in Christ*, pp. 163, 169–171.

Arguing that Paul was referring to a veil, rather than long hair, Winter believes he was likely to be admonishing the women at Corinth not to adopt a 'gesture of solidarity' with the 'new women' who were emerging in Roman society at the time.[29] They removed their veils 'to ridicule the much-prized virtue of modesty which epitomized married women' and to flout the conventional symbols of marriage and assert their independence from their husbands.[30] It was shameful behaviour in a society where 'you were what you wore' and where dress codes were legally prescribed and socially enforced. In arguing this, Winter reaches the same conclusion by a different, and perhaps more convincing, route. Paul is concerned that the Christians, both male and female, do nothing to bring the gospel into disrepute by adopting styles that indicate the distinctions between men and women no longer mattered and that marriage was no longer significant.

2. Creation theology (7–12)

In the next section, 'Paul raises the theological stakes by introducing a new line of argument based on his reading of the Genesis creation story'.[31] It is designed to explain more fully what lay behind Paul's thinking.

a. The distinction between men and women (7–10)

(i) Image and glory

Paul goes back to the creation story in Genesis 1:26–27 and 2:18–22, to point out that there is a gender difference between men and women. In using the creation accounts he gives precedence to the second account, which enables him to stress the difference between the genders and to highlight the temporal priority of man in the sequence of creation.[32] He speaks of man not only as the image but also as the glory of God (7). Genesis does not refer to man as the glory of God, but Psalm 8:5, from which Paul takes his cue, says that God 'crowned them with glory and honour'. Glory is often associated with image 'and counterbalances the notion of "shame"' that he had already mentioned.[33]

[29] This is discussed more fully in ch. 19.

[30] B. W. Winter, *Roman Wives, Roman Widows: The Appearance of New Women and the Pauline Communities* (Grand Rapids: Eerdmans, 2003), pp. 77–96; *After Paul*, pp. 123–131.

[31] R. B. Hays, *First Corinthians*, Int (Louisville: John Knox, 1997), p. 186.

[32] Fee, *First Corinthians*, p. 515.

[33] Ciampa and Rosner, *First Corinthians*, p. 523.

In saying that *woman is the glory of man* (7) he is not denying that she is also born in the image of God.[34] That was a given. Paul's interest simply lies elsewhere, in the idea of *glory* rather than *image*. By saying that *woman is the glory of man* he may be expressing the simple idea that a woman is man's 'pride and joy',[35] the one in whom man glories. A man takes delight in a woman and finds that 'of all creation, woman is the most beautiful'.[36]

God had placed his glory in Adam so that Adam would bring praise and honour to him in the world. It was not for Adam to distract people from seeing God's glory by living a dishonourable life. So now, women were neither to distract men from worshipping God, in whose image they were made, by tempting them to lust, nor draw attention to themselves by their scandalous dress code.[37] Such behaviour would jeopardize the relationship that was intrinsic to God's creation.

Again, Paul may well be saying that just as Eve was the crowning glory of Adam by becoming his companion and bringing wholeness to him he would otherwise have lacked, so it is still.[38] The verses that follow support this, especially if we do not read them in the traditional, but probably erroneous, way. Paul says that not only did woman come from man but that *neither was man created for woman, but woman for man* (9). Traditionally this has been taken to mean that woman was created to serve and bring pleasure to man who is her superior. But such an interpretation is by no means obvious and the word *dia* could well mean 'because of' rather than 'for the purpose of'.[39] Paul might rather be saying: 'Woman was created because of a need in man. He was lonely and in need of help and companionship. Thus woman was created as the strong one to help the weak one.' Woman then becomes the summit and 'glory' of creation rather than an afterthought or an anti-climax after man.

All these interpretations have one thing in common. They are based on the conviction that the distinction between the genders, represented by hairstyles or headcovering, brought a depth and richness to human relationships that was lost if the genders merely sought to resemble each other. Paul instructs them, then, to affirm

---

[34] Ciampa and Rosner (*First Corinthians*, p. 524) suggest that all born after Adam, including Eve, 'inherit' the image through Adam rather than derive it directly from God. But Gen. 1:27 seems to contradict this as far as Eve is concerned.

[35] Payne, *One in Christ*, p. 180.

[36] Payne, *One in Christ*, p. 179.

[37] Ciampa and Rosner, *First Corinthians*, pp. 528–529; Keener, *Paul*, pp. 37–38.

[38] Fee, *First Corinthians*, p. 516; Payne, *One in Christ*, p. 179.

[39] Bailey, *Paul*, pp. 309–310.

the distinction not as a matter of hierarchy or headship (in the sense of authority) but as a matter of relationship.[40]

(ii) Authority on her head

'Lest the readers should not be sufficiently confused already,' writes Richard Hays, 'Paul abruptly interjects a sentence that has remained almost completely bewildering to subsequent interpreters.'[41] *It is for this reason that a woman ought to have authority over her own head, because of the angels* (10). The problems in this verse concern whose authority and why angels.

A helmet is a symbol of a police officer's authority and a crown is a symbol of a sovereign's authority, worn on the head. So, wearing the proper hairstyle, or head covering, was a sign that a woman had authority to pray or prophesy in pubic worship. But what that means more precisely has led to much debate. Several older translations, as well as commentators, assume the authority belongs to the husband, although the verse does not say so. They take it, therefore, to mean that a woman should wear a symbol on her head, like a veil, which indicates she is 'under' the authority of her husband.[42] It is, they argue, her relationship to him that gives her the right to contribute. Those who interpret *head* (3) in terms of authority, or argue that the creation logic of verse 7–9 speaks of a hierarchy in creation, would say this is the correct meaning.[43]

However, this interpretation is 'full of difficulties' and begs the question why Paul speaks of 'a sign of authority'; rather than 'a sign of submission', if that was what he meant?[44] The traditional interpretation is questionable because '"to have authority" in Greek always means, just as it does in English, to exercise authority, not to submit to it'.[45] Its natural meaning is that if her head is dressed properly, a woman has authority to pray and bring a prophetic message to the church, without any need to justify her action further. To get from this that she is somehow subordinate to a man is to read into the text what is not there.[46] The most recent NIV translates it as *a woman ought to have authority over her own*

---

[40] Thisleton, *First Corinthians*, p. 833.

[41] Hays, *First Corinthians*, p.187.

[42] RSV translated it as, 'That is why a woman should have a veil on her head', but 'veil' does not occur in the Greek. *Living Bible* and J. B. Philip's equally unjustifiably insert 'male' before authority.

[43] For a sustained exposition of this view and a rebuttal of alternative views see Schreiner, 'Head Coverings', pp. 132–137.

[44] Fee, 'Praying and Prophesying', pp. 155–156.

[45] Hays, *First Corinthians*, p. 187.

[46] M. Hooker, 'Authority on her Head: An Examination of 1 Cor. 11:10', *NTS* 10 (1964), pp. 410–416.

head,[47] so as to emphasize a woman has freedom to choose whether to pray and prophesy in public worship or not, in fulfilment of Joel's prophecy.[48] This implies a degree of independence from men.

Yet even this is not a perfect fit to Paul's argument and so some have taken it to mean simply that a woman needs to take control of her hair rather than let it be dishevelled or hang loose, so as to maintain gender differentiation and ensure respectability in the eyes of the wider community.[49]

(iii) Because of the angels

But where do the angels fit? Paul mentions angels several times in 1 Corinthians, so it is perhaps not an entire surprise they are introduced here.[50] There are several reasons why Paul might have appealed to their presence but we cannot be sure which specifically he had in mind.[51] First, it was a common Old Testament and later Jewish belief that holy angels were present at worship, as guardians of order and protectors of the purity of worship. Paul is concerned that they would be offended if they encountered a lack of propriety. This is perhaps the most likely reason. Secondly, angels might be tempted by a woman's uncovered head and find it sexually provocative. Paul wants to avoid a repetition of Genesis 6:2–4. Thirdly, Paul may mention them because, according to 1 Corinthians 6:3, women would one day judge the angels, and therefore should demonstrate their ability to exercise control over a small matter like their hairstyle now. Fourthly, Paul might be referring to guardian angels, as mentioned in Matthew 18:10, although it is not clear why this should be a reason for adopting a certain dress code. There is no way ultimately to choose between these or the other suggestions. Whatever interpretation is adopted, it is a reminder that when people gather for worship it is not merely a meeting of visible human beings but that there are unseen beings present as observers as well. Philip Payne sums it up like this: 'It ought to be embarrassing enough for a woman to be seen by others in the church with her hair let down, but knowing she is being observed by God's holy angels should be reason enough for even the most foolhardy woman to restrain her urge to let her hair down.'[52]

---

[47] esv and nrsv translate it as the niv mg.: 'a symbol of authority on her head', which is neutral.

[48] Joel 2:28–29.

[49] Hays, *First Corinthians,* p. 187; Thisleton, *First Corinthians*, pp. 800, 839.

[50] 4:9; 6:3; 13:1.

[51] Details are found in Ciampa and Rosner, *First Corinthians*, pp. 529–531; Fee, *First Corinthians*, pp. 521–522; Keener, *Paul*, pp. 42–45; Perriman, *Speaking of Women*, pp. 99–101; Thisleton, *First Corinthians*, pp. 839–841.

[52] Payne, *One in Christ*, p. 186.

b. The relationship between men and women (11–12)

While the distinction between the genders is important and needs to be maintained, Paul immediately balances this by stressing that they now relate in an entirely mutual way to each other. Whatever a crude interpretation of the creation story might imply, *in the Lord* (11), there is a complete symmetry between them. Neither is sufficient in isolation and both are dependent on each other, summed up in the truism that if woman came from man in the first place, men have come from women ever since.

Even here, Paul's choice of word presents some exegetical difficulties. The word *chōris*, which is translated as *independent*, conveys the idea of being 'separate from' or 'different from'.[53] Some say this word points to the essential equality of men and women and stresses that no one gender has any special privilege or greater authority, but this may be stretching its meaning somewhat. It is clear, however, that there is no room for competitiveness and Christians of both genders were equally free to contribute in worship, provided they were sensitive to both the created differences and the cultural signals they were transmitting in doing so.

3. 'Natural' theology (13–16)

Paul's third argument for men and women maintaining different dress codes in worship makes visible what has been present below the surface throughout. He speaks of what is *proper* (13), of what *the very nature of things teach[es]* (14) about the way women should wear their hair.

a. In society (13–15)

Paul is not using *nature* in terms of what is biologically determined. After all, nature decrees that a man's hair grows whereas Paul says, *Does not the very nature of things teach you that if a man has long hair, it is a disgrace to him?* (14) Rather, as the context demonstrates, he is appealing to what is generally considered proper (13), to custom (16), and to 'the way things are' (14).[54] All cultures recognize a distinction between the genders that was inherent at creation and in Corinth it was marked by a clear dress code. Observing the dress code brought honour and respect whereas ignoring it provoked shame and disrespect (14–15). Paul did not want the Corinthian

---

[53] Payne, *One in Christ*, p. 192–193; Thisleton, *First Corinthians*, p. 841.
[54] Fee, *First Corinthians*, p. 527.

believers to cause offense because they ignored a social convention which, however superficial in itself, was based on a genuine creation principle. If they were to cause offense it was to be because they preached Christ crucified, a message which was offensive and shameful enough in itself.[55]

The way cultures mark the distinction between men and women is variable, and changes over time. Cultures are capable of great 'beauty and goodness' and equally, because of the fall, they are 'tainted with sin' and some may even be 'demonic'.[56] All cultures need to be critiqued rather than merely adopted. Nonetheless, for all their imperfections a culture often strives, unknowingly, to express what God determined at creation. The way in which some cultures have expressed the distinction between the genders has been evil. Yet the recognition that God created men and women differently so that they could complement each other is a distinction we should observe, but not misinterpret. To use it to argue that women are members of the church but can only participate in a restricted sense if under the authority of a man, is a misinterpretation of Paul's argument, as verses 13–16 make clear. To use it to say there are some social markers that the people of God should continue to observe out of respect for creation and the society in which they live, is to understand Paul aright.

b. In the church (16)

Paul points out that it is not only in society that such customs are observed but in *the churches of God* as well. He had previously tried to restrain the individualistic tendencies of the Corinthians by an appeal to the wider practice of the church and would do so again.[57] The Corinthian believers were not loners, free to behave according to their own personal preferences, but part of a global movement where respect for others was essential. The high-octane spiritual experiences of the Corinthians led them to adopt a certain arrogance towards others[58] and they seemed to think that their possession of the Spirit exempted them from living within normal social constraints. To throw over the symbols of distinction between men and women, as some were doing, was 'a denial of the "not yet" dimension of [their] present eschatological existence'.[59] It was also to isolate themselves from their fellow believers and deviate from the *traditions* which Paul had *passed on* (2).

[55] 1 Cor. 1:18 – 2:5.
[56] Lausanne Covenant, clause 5, 'Culture and Leadership'.
[57] 4:17; 7:17; 14:33.
[58] 1 Cor. 4:1–13.
[59] Fee, 'Praying and Prophesying', p. 159.

4. Concluding comments

Underneath all the complexities and uncertainties of 1 Corinthians 11:2–16 Paul is teaching some important truths.

1. Men and women are equally welcome to participate in public worship, contributing in prayer and in the speaking of prophetic messages.
2. Both are required to dress appropriately which means (a) not in a salacious way, (b) according to their gender, (c) out of respect for each other's place in creation, (d) so as not to distract or tempt others, and (e) so as not to suggest marriage is no longer a God-ordained way of life.
3. The essential gender distinction inherent in the creation of male and female should be respected. The distinction was one of difference not hierarchy.[60] Men should not seek to behave or dress like women and women have no need to imitate men to exercise their gifts in the church.
4. The distinction must be held in tension with their essential equality *in the Lord.*
5. Though members of an eschatological community, Christians still need to live within the social mores of their culture, unless, obviously, those customs are sinful.
6. Care should be taken to understand the meaning of dress codes, and other patterns of behaviour, so that no shame is brought on the church. For Corinth this particularly related to hair styles or head coverings. For other cultures and other times the symbolic markers of honour and shame may be different.

In short, throughout, Paul balances the order of creation with the order of the new creation in Christ. If creation stressed gender distinction, the new creation stresses mutuality.[61] Neither of these should be privileged over the other, or assumed to tell the whole story. Both are necessary to make up the complete picture. Like the Corinthians, we are still called to live in the tension of being part of this creation, while living in real anticipation of the new creation that is yet to come. But for the moment, 'We are what we wear.'[62]

---

[60] On the difference see E. Storkey, *Created or Constructed? The Gender Debate* (Carlise: Paternoster, 2000), esp. p. 64.

[61] J. Gundry-Volf, cited in Thisleton, *First Corinthians*, p. 811.

[62] Winter, *Roman Wives*, p. 85.

1 Corinthians 14:26–40
17. Women in worship

Some Christian churches forbid women to participate in worship on the basis that Paul said *Women should remain silent in the churches* (34). It looks like a straightforward-enough command and seems to settle any dispute. Unfortunately, however, the text bristles with problems.

The most obvious problem is that a few chapters earlier, in 1 Corinthians 11:5, Paul had acknowledged that women prayed and prophesied in the assembly without expressing any reservation about their doing so. Surely he would not contradict himself in such a short space by issuing a blanket ban on their speaking? So, in what sense were they to keep silent? Is he prohibiting all speech or just a particular form of speech? Secondly, Paul backs up his injunction to women to keep silent with the words *as the law says*. There is no obvious Old Testament law that says this, so what did he have in mind? Moreover, Paul does not usually speak of *the law* in this way. Thirdly, he tells women that *if they want to enquire about something, they should ask their own husbands at home* (35). So, does this apply only to married women and, if not, what are the unmarried women to do? Fourthly, how do these verses fit with Paul's discussion of the gifts of tongues and prophecy earlier in the chapter? Do they continue that discussion or is this a separate issue? Fifthly, many see verse 34 as an abrupt interruption to the flow of the chapter, but is it? Sixthly, once we read on from these verses and read Paul asking *Or did the word of God originate with you? Or are you the only people it has reached?* (36), the mysteries deepen.

1. Interpretation: false trails

The subject of Paul's teaching in 1 Corinthians 14 is the handling of the gifts of tongues and prophecy in Christian worship. Some argue that the verses enjoining women to keep silent (34–35) do not relate to that topic and seem to abruptly introduce a new subject. This view has even more force if verse 33 – *God is not a God of disorder but of peace* – satisfactorily concludes the discussion of tongues and prophecy. In addition, some point out that verse 33 links naturally to verse 36, with the intervening verses seeming to be something of a digression. So how may we account for the inclusion of the verses here? Three major explanations have been offered.[1]

a. The verses are not original

Some argue the text was not originally written by Paul but was added later by an editor and so, presumably, does not have the canonical status of Paul's genuine apostolic writing. This has the advantage of removing the difficulty of the apparent contradiction with 1 Corinthians 11:5 and brings it into line with 1 Timothy 2:11–12, although the wording is not 'sufficiently close' to require this.[2] Even several conservative scholars adopt this position.[3]

The arguments for and against such a view are complex but the fact that all the early manuscripts contain these verses weighs heavily against it. The main evidence for the argument is contextual rather than textual and that can be better resolved in other ways.

b. The verses have been displaced

A more common and nuanced way of resolving the problems, on the basis of the flow of the argument, is to argue that these verses have been displaced and came originally either after verse 40, or were a marginal note by Paul himself.[4] The former has some early manuscript support, although not much, but the latter seems dubious as

---

[1] More detail regarding the complexity of the arguments in this section are found in: D. A. Carson, 'Silent in the Churches: On the Role of Women in 1 Corinthians 14: 33b-36', *RBMW*, pp. 140–145; G. Fee, *The First Epistle to the Corinthians* (Grand Rapids: Eerdmans, 1987), pp. 699–705; D. G. Horrell, *The Social Ethos of the Corinthian Correspondence* (Edinburgh: T & T Clark, 1996), pp. 184–195; C. S. Keener, 'Learning in the Assemblies', *DBE*, pp. 161–171; A. Perriman, *Speaking of Women: Interpreting Paul* (Leicester: Apollos, 1998), pp. 103–108; A. C. Thisleton, *The First Epistle to the Corinthians*, NIGTC (Grand Rapids: Eerdmans and Carlisle: Paternoster, 2000), pp. 1146–1162.

[2] B. Witherington III, *Conflict and Community in Corinth: A Socio-Rhetorical Commentary on 1 and 2 Corinthians* (Grand Rapid: Eerdmans, 1995), p. 288.

[3] Notably, Fee, *First Corinthians*, pp. 699–705; P. B. Payne, *Man and Woman, One in Christ: An Exegetical and Theological Study of Paul's Letters* (Grand Rapids: Zondervan, 2009), pp. 214–267.

[4] Witherington, *Conflict and Community*, p. 288.

it would have been a long marginal note.[5] Earl Ellis, who is open to the possibility of displacement, says, 'In any case it is part of the original letter and should be treated as such'.[6] However, whether such an argument is necessary at all is doubtful.

c. The verses contain a quotation

At several points in 1 Corinthians, Paul is evidently quoting a slogan of the Corinthians and then answering it.[7] The absence of quotation marks in the original makes it difficult to be always certain when the Corinthians are speaking and when Paul is speaking, even if it is mostly clear. Some suggest that verses 34–35 express the Corinthians' view that Paul then refutes in verse 36 onward. Once more, however, the evidence for this is weak. As Craig Keener points out, usually when Paul adopts this approach he at least partly agrees with the Corinthians' statement before qualifying it and leading them to a deeper understanding of the issue, which is not the case here.[8] Furthermore, the words Paul uses here concerning speaking, silence and order are all words Paul has himself used earlier in the chapter and so seem to come from him rather than them.[9]

None of these approaches to the interpretation of these verses are convincing, or really necessary. Like a good lawyer who is paid to be professionally suspicious, some scholars see difficulties where they do not actually exist. As Andrew Perriman says, 'properly understood, they are not out of place in the discussion in chapter 14 and are consistent with Paul's general concerns in the letter'.[10]

2. Explanation: key issues

Placed in their proper context these verses make a great deal of sense but do not amount to a blanket ban on women speaking in church.

---

[5] R. E. Ciampa and B. S. Rosner, *The First Letter to the Corinthians*, PNTC (Grand Rapids: Eerdmans and Nottingham: Apollos), p. 718.

[6] E. E. Ellis, *Pauline Theology: Ministry and Society* (Grand Rapids: Eerdmans and Exeter: Paternoster, 1989), p. 68.

[7] E.g., 6:12–14; 7:1–5; 8:1–3.

[8] C. S. Keener, *Paul, Women and Wives* (Peabody: Hendrickson, 1992), p. 76.

[9] Thisleton, *First Corinthians*, p. 1152.

[10] Perriman, *Speaking of Women*, p. 107.

a. The verses in the context of 1 Corinthians 11 – 14

Kenneth Bailey argues convincingly that 1 Corinthians 11 – 14 is 'a single essay'.[11] Composed of seven sections in a ring cycle, it deals with the question of men and women in the church's worship and is particularly concerned with how to overcome disorder in worship. Paraphrased, his outline is:

1. Men and women: leading in worship, appropriate dress (11:2–16).
2. Disorder at the Lord's Table (11:17–34).
3. Spiritual gifts and the body (theology) (12:1–30).
4. The paramount importance of love (12:31 – 14:1).
5. Spiritual gifts and the body (practice) (14:1–25).
6. Disorder in using tongues and prophecy (14:26–33).
7. Women and men: contributing in worship, no chatting (14:33b–40).

Seen in this light, far from being an abrupt departure, these verses are an entirely appropriate step in the discussion that mirrors the concern about men and women at the start of the essay and brings it full circle.

b. The verses in the context of 1 Corinthians 14:26–40

The last two parts of this essay on worship deal with the concern for order in worship where everyone, irrespective of whether they are male or female, contributes with *a hymn, a word of instruction, a revelation, a tongue or an interpretation* (26). Any pastor who encourages participation in worship services knows the potential for disorder when the participants are scripted (at least as far as time is concerned!), let alone when the worship may be more free-flowing, as here. The concern for order is overt in verse 33a – *God is not a God of disorder but of peace* – and is again explicit at the end of the section in verse 40 – *But everything should be done decently in a fitting and orderly way.* The reference to women keeping silent fits this wider discussion.

In fact, women are the third group of people who are told to keep silent within the short space of ten verses. First, the speakers in tongues, both men and women, are told to *keep quiet (sigatō) in the church* if no interpreter is present (28). Secondly, the prophets, again

---

[11] K. E. Bailey, 'Women in the New Testament', *Anvil* 11 (1994), p. 16. See also K. E. Bailey, *Paul through Mediterranean Eyes: Cultural Studies in 1 Corinthians* (London: SPCK, 2011), pp. 295–96.

both men and women, are told to stop speaking *if a revelation comes to someone who is sitting down* while they are speaking (30). Women, then, follow a sequence of people told to *remain silent (sigatōsan)* when their speaking is going to disturb worship. It should be noted that Paul uses the same word in reference to tongue speakers as he does about women. So the context suggests that this is an admonition that women should not participate in a way which leads to chaos and confusion, rather than a blanket ban on their saying anything in worship. This removes any contradiction with 11:2–6, where Paul accepts without reservation that women can pray and prophesy in the church.

Because of the immediate context it has become popular among some to argue that what Paul is forbidding is that women should take part in judging prophecies.[12] It relates, so the argument goes, to the instruction in verse 29 that *others should weigh carefully what the prophets say*, but qualifies it by stipulating that women should not engage in this process. Some of these prophecies may have been given by their husbands and they would then be publicly calling into question what their husbands had said. Don Carson supports this view and then expands it, turning it into a general prohibition on women teaching. He writes, 'a strong case can be made that Paul refused to permit a woman to enjoy a church-recognized teaching authority over men (1 Timothy 2:11ff.), and the careful weighing of prophecies falls under that magisterial function'.[13] Others, too, interpret it in the wider framework of women not being permitted to teach and George Knight even imaginatively suggests that these verses are designed to prevent women from circumventing this restriction by protesting that they are not teaching but only asking questions![14] But, as Craig Keener protests, 'the one view that has *no* support in the context is that Paul's requirement that women be silent just means that they are not allowed to teach'.[15]

While the view that it relates to the interpretation of prophecy has the merit of taking the context seriously, it does not really stand up to scrutiny as explaining the interdict. Women were permitted to give a prophecy, so why should they not be involved in weighing them? Is weighing a prophecy really a significantly different exercise of

---

[12] Ellis, *Pauline Theology,* pp. 69–70; J. Hurley, *Man and Woman in Biblical Perspective* (Leicester: IVP, 1981), pp. 188–193; W. Grudem, *The Gift of Prophecy* (Eastbourne: Kingsway, 1988), pp. 220–224; Thisleton, *First Corinthians,* p. 1158; B. Witherington III, *Women and the Genesis of Christianity* (Cambridge: Cambridge University Press, 1990), pp. 175–176.

[13] Carson, 'Silent in the Churches', p. 153.

[14] G. W. Knight III, *The New Testament Teaching on the Role Relationship of Men and Women* (Grand Rapids: Baker, 1977), p. 37; Grudem, *Gift of Prophecy,* p. 253.

[15] Keener, *Paul, Women and Wives,* p. 79.

authority from giving one? If Paul had really wanted to ban women from being involved in the process of discernment there were more natural ways in which he could have made that clear. With Perriman, I conclude that this interpretation 'lacks intrinsic credibility'.[16] Paul actually refers to their asking questions, *enquir[ing] about something* (35), which is not the obvious way of talking about evaluating prophesies. The link with the previous verses is not specifically to prophecy but to speech of several kinds that are disruptive.

c. The verses in the context of the early church's culture

What Paul has in mind, then, is simply that women were disrupting the Corinthian assembly by noisily asking their husbands questions during the course of their meetings. Their manner may have displayed arrogance or disrespect to their husbands, but, in any case, it was certainly disrespectful to their fellow worshippers and hence they were not *in submission.* Acting like this was *disgraceful* or shameful, a word which carries particular connotations in their culture, on which see below. Understanding Paul's prohibition like this fits both the context and his choice of words, as well as being supported from our knowledge of the wider religious and social context of the Mediterranean world.

There would have been a variety of reasons why women may have behaved in this disruptive way. Some might have lacked education and their enquiry may have been a genuine desire to learn, but even this pure motive could be pursued in the wrong way. From his long experience of Middle Eastern cultures, Kenneth Bailey suggests a number of other reasons for the ban in Corinth.[17] Corinth was a cosmopolitan city in which many languages were spoken and the church was composed of many from the lower status groups in the city (1:26). Participants in worship, especially visitors, may have spoken in a more classical dialect rather than the colloquial language that would have been readily understood by the common people and their messages difficult to grasp because of foreign accents. In those circumstances attention spans could be limited and it would be common for 'a low buzz' to break out as people chatted in an attempt to clarify meaning. Or perhaps, as Bailey conjectures,

Paul had just affirmed that the Corinthians were getting drunk at the Lord's Supper and that the prophets and tongues speakers were all talking at once! It seems that some of the women gave up and

[16] Perriman, *Speaking of Women*, p. 112.
[17] Bailey, *Paul*, pp. 412–415.

started chatting. Who could blame them? Yet all needed to work together to create the required 'decency and order' necessary for meaningful worship.[18]

Paul's point is pastoral but, as always, grounded in theology. His theology of the conduct of church worship concerns the nature of God and of the body of Christ, where mutual submission was required, rather than being about the authority of men over women. Paul's theology was not ideology and is generated for much more down-to-earth reasons than some of the theologians who struggle to explain these words suggest.

The church at Corinth was not living in a vacuum and their social context would inevitably have influenced them. While the role of women in the public assembly and Jewish synagogue was still carefully circumscribed, women were enjoying greater and greater liberty in the newer cults, some of which, like that of Isis, explicitly promoted the equality of women. The interjection of ecstatic messages and prophecies by women in these rites was common.[19] It would be extraordinary if these developments did not have an impact in the new Christian assemblies and if there was no need for them to work out how to handle such behaviour in their early years.

More than likely, then, Paul was not banning women from speaking in church at all but forbidding the undisciplined inter-ventions and chattering that turned orderly worship into liturgical chaos. The former served all whereas the latter pandered to the needs of a few individuals. So, 'Paul is correcting an abuse of a privilege, not taking back a woman's right to speak in the assembly, which he has already granted in ch. 11'.[20]

3. Motivation: diverse reasons

An unusual number of reasons are packed into these verses to buttress Paul's command, all of which lend support to the interpret-ation that he was forbidding disruptive speech.

a. An ecclesiological reason

Whether the paragraph about women speaking begins at verse 34 or halfway through verse 33 is debatable. The phrase *as in all the*

[18] Bailey, *Paul*, p. 415.
[19] W. Meeks, *The First Urban Christians: The Social World of the Apostle Paul* (New Haven: Yale University Press, 2003), pp. 24–25; Perriman, *Speaking of Women*, pp. 117–119.
[20] Witherington, *Conflict and Community*, p. 287.

congregations of the Lord's people could either conclude what is said about the prophets or introduce what Paul goes on to say about women. The weight of evidence is perhaps in favour of it being linked with the previous verses, but its meaning applies to both the prophets and the women. Maybe it is unnecessary to choose and the phrase is a hinge, serving to connect the two groups and attaching equally to them both.

Throughout 1 Corinthians Paul shows himself concerned about the wider customs and traditions of the churches and evidently wants to bring the Corinthians into line with others.[21] Verses 26–27, that immediately follow, rebuke their sense of independence from the wider church and encourage them to think more carefully about their relationship to himself as an apostle and to other Christians. The basis for Paul's appeal to conformity lies in the character of God. God is a God of order, as creation itself testifies (although he does not mention it here[22]), and that order should be reflected in the way the churches conduct their worship. Disorder is ruled out, not on the pragmatic ground that it leads to poor communication and would prove an unsatisfactory experience for worshippers, but on the theological ground that it is inconsistent with the God who is being worshipped. The Corinthians 'are marching to their own drum; Paul is urging them not only to conform to the character of God, but also to get in step with the rest of his church'.[23]

b. A social reason

Added to the common and well-based custom of the churches, Paul now turns to *the law* (34) to provide a second reason for women keeping silent in church. Here, again, we encounter a major problem since there is no obvious law, certainly no Old Testament law, which prohibits them from doing so. What 'law', then, does Paul have in mind? Two broad answers suggest themselves.

First, Paul might be using 'law' in the rather looser sense of 'the Law and the Prophets' rather than having a specific Old Testament statute in mind. The general tenor of several passages of the Old Testament might support the silence and submission of women, but this seems rather vague. Others have suggested Paul is thinking of the law of creation, although they differ over whether it is Genesis 2 or 3, the creation of Eve after Adam, or the judgment of Eve following the fall (especially 3:16), that he has in view. None of this seems satisfactory, nor is it the way Paul would usually make use of

[21] 4:17; 7:17; 11:16, 23–26; 15:3.
[22] 1 Cor. 11:7–12.
[23] Fee, *First Corinthians*, p. 698.

the Old Testament Scriptures. Hence many have looked for a different explanation.

The second approach, which takes various forms, is to understand 'the law' not as a biblical law but as a law of the culture and of custom. Women were forbidden from participating in the city's assembly and contemporary social norms would certainly have frowned on women interrogating men in public in the way Paul prohibits here. In the Roman world it was acceptable for a women to ask their husbands questions at home, just as Paul recommends, but not by intervening in a public assembly.[24] Commentators often quote a similar sentiment in Plutarch who wrote that 'a woman ought to do her talking either to her husband or through her husband' and argued that for a woman to speak personally was for a woman to expose herself, as if she were exposing her nakedness.[25] In officially recognized Roman religions, in contrast to the uninhibited behaviour of women permitted in oriental cults, 'women who participated were carefully organized and their activities strictly regulated'.[26]

Those accustomed to synagogue worship would certainly have regarded such behaviour as scandalous. Perriman relates it specifically to the unity of Christians and thinks that it has to do with the way Jewish Christians would interpret the law and that Paul is anxious that the Gentile Christians in Corinth do not offend their fellow believers. For him, it is not so much the wider social context that explains Paul's comments but the more immediate religious context.

Explaining it by reference to social 'laws' rather than biblical law makes sense. We know that Paul is concerned about the way 'unbelievers or enquirers' would view what went on in a worship service (see 14:22–25). So these verses could well be seeking to rule out behaviour that would place an unnecessary stumbling block in the path of those who were not yet believers.

Paul's use of the words *but must be in submission* (34) fits this interpretation. They are taken by those who want to argue for male headship and for the subordination of women as referring to a woman's specific and unalterable role in relation to their husbands. But Paul does not say that they must be *in submission* to their husbands, even though husbands are referred to in the next verse. In fact, he does not stipulate what they must be in submission to and, given the flow of the argument, it is more probable that this means they must be in submission to others in the worship service and to the orderly way in which Christians conducted worship elsewhere rather than trying

---

[24] Ciampa and Rosner, *First Corinthians*, p. 730.
[25] The quotation comes from Plutarch's *Advice to Bride and Groom*, as cited in Ciampa and Rosner, *First Corinthians*, p. 726.
[26] L. L. Belleville, *Two Views*, p. 77.

to further their own interests in a self-centred way. The concept of submission, which we explore more fully in chapter 18, is a common concept in Paul's writings and applies to both genders and people in many different roles and relationships. Above all, in the church, Christians need to 'Submit to one another out of reverence for Christ'[27] and that seems to be what Paul is saying here, and no more.[28]

c. A pragmatic reason

A third reason Paul instructs women to stop disrupting worship is that it is unnecessary since there is another way in which they can learn. Paul's reference to their *enquir[ing] about something* shows that he is specifically concerned about their education. Asking questions was a core method of education in his day[29] and Paul is keen for these women to learn. But they should not learn at the expense of others, turning services 'into a question-and-answer session'[30] but rather *ask their own husbands* (35) in the privacy of their own homes, just as Plutarch and others recommended. Enquiring at home would certainly be safer and avoid any possibility of undermining or embarrassing their husbands in public, or still worse, embarrassing another woman's husband.[31]

It may be safely assumed that most women would have been married and could seek answers from their husbands, but what if they were single? In that case, we can assume that with few exceptions, like perhaps Lydia, they would be part of a patriarchal household and could ask their fathers or brothers at home.[32]

d. A cultural reason

The NIV's translation *disgraceful* (35) in reference to women speaking in the church is harsh and open to misunderstanding. At the heart of the value system of the ancient world were the values of honour and shame.[33] There was a clearly defined social code that

[27] Eph. 5:21.
[28] Witherington, *Genesis of Christianity*, p. 177.
[29] Keener cites Plutarch's *On Lectures* in 'Learning in the Assemblies', p. 165.
[30] Witherington, *Conflict and Community*, p. 287.
[31] Ciampa and Rosner, *First Corinthians*, p. 725.
[32] Perriman, *Speaking of Women*, p. 123.
[33] See D. A. deSilva, *Honor, Patronage, Kinship and Purity: Unlocking New Testament Culture* (Downers Grove: IVP, 2000); B. J. Malina, *The New Testament World: Insights from Cultural Anthropology* (Louisville: John Knox Press, 2001), pp. 27–57; R. L. Rohrbaugh, 'Honor: Core Value in the Biblical World', in D. Neufeld and R. E. DeMaris (eds.), *Understanding the Social World of the New Testament* (London and New York: Routledge, 2010), pp. 109–126.

labelled certain behaviour as honourable and other behaviour as shameful. It was not primarily moral as much as social. The Western world has largely moved away from such a value system though remnants of it continue to exist when we talk about the implications of a soldier's conduct for 'the honour of the regiment', or when we talk about 'honour among thieves'. The Eastern world still exhibits a much greater sensitivity to the honour of the family or the race and the need to defend it and avoid shame, than the Western world.

Such values were part of the warp and weft of Paul's world and he would, and does, use such language quite naturally. David deSilva explains the concepts like this: 'If honor signifies respect for being the kind of person and doing the kind of things the group values, shame signifies, in the first instance, being seen as less than valuable because one has behaved in ways that run contrary to the values of the group'.[34] It is behaviour that causes one to 'lose face' or reflects badly on the group (often a kinship group), causing it to be dishonoured in the eyes of others. It is more complicated than that but that is the essence of it.

As mentioned, Paul is concerned throughout with encouraging Christians, both male and female, to behave in such a way that they will not bring dishonour on the Christian community and on Christ. His rebuke to women who called out their questions across the Christian assembly is a particular example of this concern. He wants them to cultivate a more conventional social ethos in their worship, one characterized by more decorum, so that the scandalous message of the cross[35] is not eclipsed by what is perceived as unnecessary socially scandalous behaviour.

4. Application: radical implications

Social values change over time and cultures are transformed. What is acceptable at one time is scandalous at another, and what is scandalous at one period becomes natural and unobjectionable at another, and not always for moral reasons. We no longer live in a culture where it is considered honourable for women to keep quiet in public, except in some religious communities. Far from it! Modern cultures consider it scandalous if women are denied education on a par with men, are not permitted equal opportunities with men, and are not able to use their gifts unhindered for the benefit of others. What was scandalous in Paul's time is now taken as a basic human right. What

---

[34] deSilva, *Honor*, p. 25.
[35] 1 Cor. 1:18–31.

was thought honourable in regard to women's vocal restraint in Paul's time, would now be considered scandalous.

So we face the ironic situation, to which Ciampa and Rosner call attention, that 'In much of the world today such a recommendation [that a woman should ask their husband at home] would only discredit the person making such a statement, given the fact that the husband is hardly more likely to understand the issues better than the wife'.[36] And, we might add, discredit their gospel too.

To be faithful to what Paul is teaching, and so to Scripture, we must ask two questions, one theological and one social. The theological question is not about male authority but 'How does our practice of worship reflect the nature of the God we are worshipping?' That rules out much that society might find acceptable. But we must also go on to ask, 'What is it that the social ethos of our world would find unseemly and how can we remove cultural barriers that may become unnecessary obstacles to our preaching of the gospel?' The relation between male and female gender, then as now, might be a key issue, even though, ironically, it will work out in exactly the reverse of the way Paul uses it.

5. Concluding comments

1 Corinthians 14:34–35 cannot be an outright or principled prohibition on women participating in worship, since Paul had just a little earlier commented on their fitness to do so. In its context it seems Paul is asking them to *remain silent* if their interventions are disruptive, just as he asked prophets and tongue-speakers to *keep quiet* a few verses earlier. The silence he encourages becomes even more significant when placed in the cultural context where women were not expected to participate in public assemblies and where their doing so might prove a stumbling block to people hearing and receiving the gospel of Christ. Here as elsewhere, they were encouraged to learn, but to do so in a more socially-acceptable manner.

[36] Ciampa and Rosner, *First Corinthians*, p. 730.

1 Corinthians 7:1–7;
Ephesians 5:21–33; 1 Peter 3:1–7
18. Women in marriage

The English marriage service has traditionally expected the bride and groom to use different words when making their promises to each other. The bride alone has been required to 'love, honour *and obey*'. A wife's obedience is a biblical imperative, or so many have argued, even though the word is not to be found as such in the New Testament. The word obey owes more to *The Book of Common Prayer* than to Scripture.[1] The constant replaying of this note to the exclusion of others present in the New Testament has trivialized its rich melodic harmony until it sounds like a young child picking out a tune with a single finger on a piano.

This chapter examines three New Testament passages which teach about the wife's role in marriage.

1. Surprising mutuality (1 Cor. 7:1–7)

In 1 Corinthians 7, where Paul addresses the life of the married and the single, he is not only building on the previous chapters, which have set out a theology of sexuality, but addressing issues the Corinthians themselves have raised (1). While he appears personally to prefer the single life he does so because of the freedom it gives to single-mindedly serve Christ in the current circumstances ('because of the present crisis', v. 26[2]) rather than as a matter of theological

---

[1] Tyndale had previously translated 1 Pet. 3:5 as 'For after this maner in the olde tyme dyd the holy wemen which trusted in God tyer the selves and were obediet to their husbades', which may be the origin of the Prayer Book's use of the word. But in the Greek the word is 'submit', although the word 'obey' is used in the following verse.

[2] B. W. Winter, *After Paul Left Corinth: The Influence of Secular Ethics and Social Change* (Grand Rapids: Eerdmans, 2001), pp. 215–225, suggests this referred to three severe grain shortages Corinth suffered which resulted in social unrest and may have been seen by Christians as the beginning of the eschaton and so they concluded that they should avoid procreating children.

principle. 'Paul appears to think that marriage is the normal state of affairs and that remaining single requires a special "gift".'[3] To those who are married, Paul argues that their commitment to each other must be unreserved and the desire to be spiritual must never be used to avoid intimacy. In that context he writes somewhat surprisingly.

Paul countermands the Corinthians' statement[4] which promoted sexual abstinence: *'It is good for a man not to have sex with a woman'* (1). There were some in Corinth, among them possibly some women,[5] who appeared to think marriage belonged to the old order of things and that as Christians living in the new age of the Spirit they were no longer confined to the ordinary ways of life on earth.[6] The really spiritual person would abstain from sexual relations whether married or not.

Paul strongly refutes this in the case of marriage saying, *each man should have sexual relations with his own wife and each woman with her own husband* (2). The heart of his rebuttal, in verses 3–4, lies in a doctrine of marriage, but that heart is bracketed by more pragmatic reasoning. With the opening bracket, Paul realistically observes that sexual immorality is common (2) and does not want to give anyone an incentive to add to it. With the closing bracket, Paul acknowledges that men and women are creatures who have powerful sexual drives and there are limits to how long one can endure abstinence before Satan exploits their human weaknesses (5). Any abstinence, then, should occur *by mutual consent and for a time* (rather than being open-ended), *so that you may devote yourself to prayer.* The exercise of 'spiritual discipline must not lead to a permanent separation'.[7]

The heart of Paul's argument however lies in verses 3–4 and shows that marital relations are a God-given gift and not a concession to inadequate self-control or simply a means of avoiding immorality. Paul's words display a remarkable symmetry about the rights and duties of the husband and the wife. Both are called to fulfil their

[3] B. Witherington III, *Women and the Genesis of Christianity* (Cambridge: Cambridge University Press, 1990), p. 138.

[4] This could be read as a question rather than a statement, or as Paul's view rather than the Corinthians' view. Reasons for taking it as a statement by the Corinthians which Paul rebuts are found in R. A. Ciampa and B. S. Rosner, *The First Letter to the Corinthians*, PNTC (Eerdmans: Grand Rapids and Nottingham: Apollos, 2010), pp. 272–278 and A. C. Thisleton, *The First Epistle to the Corinthians*, NIGTC (Grand Rapids: Eerdmans and Carlisle: Paternoster, 2000), pp. 498–500.

[5] This is argued strongly by M. Y. MacDonald, 'Women Holy in Body and Spirit: The Social Setting of 1 Corinthians 7', *NTS* 36 (1990), pp. 161–180.

[6] G. D. Fee, *First Epistle to the Corinthians*, NICNT (Grand Rapids: Eerdmans, 1987), p. 269.

[7] K. E. Bailey, *Paul through Mediterranean Eyes: Cultural Studies in 1 Corinthians* (London: SPCK, 2011), p. 202.

marital duties to their partners and both are said to *have authority over* their partner's bodies. Neither has precedence in their relationship. The rights do not fall on one side and the duties on the other. Intimacy is completely mutual.

At first sight verse 3 appears to give one partner the right to demand that the other satisfy their desire, especially as the language of *fulfil* [one's] *duty* is the language of paying a debt.[8] It would seem as if Paul is picturing marriage as a legal contract in which either partner is in a position to require the other to have sexual relations, whether they want it or not. But this is not so. People took the idea of owing an obligation extremely seriously at the time[9] but the obligation Paul sets out is an obligation to give love, not demand it. And this is emphasized even more once verse 4 is taken into account. Marriage has involved the voluntary yielding of one body to one's partner. As Bailey explains,

> The marital relationship is now presented as a positive 'right' that each partner is expected to *give as a gift* to the other. The husband and wife are equal in this regard. Neither partner is to demand those rights, rather each is to *give gifts* to the other. Gifts given in love are always seen by the giver as valuable, otherwise they would not be given. Furthermore, by definition, a gift is always offered as a result of free choice. If it is coerced, it is not a gift.[10]

The surprising element in this is the equal status given to the wife. The common understanding was that the wife was the property of the husband and the assumption was that he had authority over her body, but not vice versa.[11] By saying they have authority over each other's bodies, Paul is giving the remarkable right of control to the wife over her husband. He is no longer free, as would have been thought normal in the ancient world, to fulfil his sexual desires as he chooses, but is restrained by a prior obligation. The common assumption that it was acceptable for a man, but not a woman, to commit adultery is overturned by Paul's saying.[12]

Even the more enlightened writings, such as the *Midrash Rabbah*, stated there was a differential involved in a husband and wife's place in marriage.[13] A man who denied his wife conjugal relationships was penalized far less than a woman who denied her husband. His suffering was adjudged the greater and his compensation was therefore

[8] Fee, *First Corinthians*, p. 279, n. 56.
[9] Winter, *After Paul*, p. 227.
[10] Bailey, *Paul*, pp. 201–202.
[11] Ciampa and Rosner, *First Corinthians*, p. 281.
[12] For evidence see Winter, *After Paul*, pp. 228–230.
[13] See Bailey, *Paul*, pp. 202–203.

greater. Her obligation was greater, but her privileges lesser. For Paul to advocate such an equal partnership in marriage, as he clearly does, was nothing short of astonishing.[14]

2. Christlike submission (Eph. 5:21–33)

The idea of mutuality is equally prominent in what Paul says about the relationship between the husband and the wife in the 'household code' of Ephesians 5. Discussing relationships within the household was common currency among philosophers of Paul's day since the household was a major building block of Roman society. Some have argued that Paul patterned his household code on Aristotle and the Stoics, but it seems unnecessary to posit such a source since regulating relationships in households was a regular topic of the time. Looking at the codes found in the wider Hellenistic culture provides us with a benchmark by which to measure the distinctiveness of those found in the New Testament.[15]

It would be surprising if there was not much in common between the household codes in the New Testament and those found elsewhere, since they were all affected by the same social and cultural context. Even so, the New Testament codes have a number of distinctive features about them. Like most codes they concern the three primary pairs of relationships, namely, those between husband and wife, parent and child, and master and slave. Unlike most codes they address both parties in these pairings directly and equally, treating even the 'subordinate' partner as a person in their own right and not just as the property of the household owner. Most codes instruct the male householder as to his authority and rights and, in so far as they address the 'subordinate' partner at all, they do so through him.[16]

Here Paul instructs members of Christian households as to how they are to conduct themselves in the 'new creation communities' and in the light of the spiritual conflict in which they live.[17]

[14] E. S. Fiorenza comments 'It is not only remarkable that Paul insists on equality and mutuality in sexual relationships between husbands and wives, but even more that he advises Christians, especially women, to remain free from the marriage bond' since remaining unmarried was 'quite exceptional' in the first century. *In Memory of Her: A Feminist Reconstruction of Christian Origins* (10th Anniversary Edn, New York: Crossroad, 1994), p. 224.

[15] Household codes are also found in Col. 3:18 – 4:1; 1 Tim. 2:8–15; 5:1–2; 6:1–2; Titus 2:1–10; 1 Pet. 2:13 – 3:7. For an overview see C. E. Arnold, *Ephesians*, ZECNT (Grand Rapids: Eerdmans, 2010), pp. 369–372; P. H. Towner, 'Household Codes', *DLNTD*, pp. 513–520.

[16] B. Witherington III, *Women in the Earliest Churches*, SNTS Monograph 59 (Cambridge University Press, 1988), pp. 42–47.

[17] T. G. Gombis, 'A Radically New Humanity: The Function of the *Haustafel* in Ephesians', *JETS* 48 (2005), pp. 317–330.

a. 'Out of reverence for Christ'

The primary motivation for mutual submission is respect for Christ. To submit to another is not a natural reaction for sinful humanity, yet Christians do so in recognition of the whole tenor of the teaching of Christ, whose disciples they are and to whom they are accountable. A refusal to live in this way is in effect to disrespect him.

As with Colossians, where seven out of fourteen references to 'the Lord' occur in the instructions to households, the longer and more detailed instructions in Ephesians are shot through with Christ. Within each pair of relationships mentioned there is, in fact, a third partner, Christ himself. Non-Christian versions of the household code obviously do not mention Christ and Paul's doing so puts a totally different construction on the outworking of these instructions than is found elsewhere. All that follows needs to be read through the lens both of Christ's presence in the relationship and of his position as Saviour and Lord. He who came to serve not be served[18] and 'who made himself nothing'[19] is the pattern for all relationships and his teaching governs them all. His life of grace, love and 'self-abasing service' defines the qualities which are to be evident and the behaviour which is to be practised. His presence will encourage the household to relate in humility, service, patience, forgiveness and love to one another. On the other hand, whatever is incompatible with him is ruled out for both partners, whether it is self-seeking assertiveness on the part of the weaker partner or abusive authoritarianism on the part of the household head.

b. Submission

The idea of submission is 'surprisingly prominent in the New Testament'.[20] It was originally a hierarchical term but came to have 'a considerable range of meaning' and did not 'immediately carry with it the thought of obedience'[21] by New Testament times. In general it has to do with 'order', and so 'a proper social ordering of people'[22] which was prized in the ancient world as the antidote to chaos and anarchy. Citizens, it was argued, owed a duty of submission to political authorities, just as soldiers did to their commanders,

---

[18] Mark 10:45.

[19] Phil. 2:7.

[20] R. T. France, *Women in the Church's Ministry: A Test Case for Biblical Hermeneutics* (Carlisle: Paternoster, 1995), p. 33.

[21] G. Delling, '*hypotassō*', *TDNT*, vol. 8, p. 41.

[22] Arnold, *Ephesians*, p. 356.

and the low born to the higher born. The term did not carry any of the negative overtones that it often carries today and did not imply inferiority on the part of the one submitting, since people were caught in a complex web of relationships in which they might play different roles.

Submission was not to be identified with obedience, even if on occasions this is how it would have demonstrated itself. Wives are not told to obey their husbands, unlike the children, who are told to obey their parents. 'Paul avoids the nuances of "obedience" and "ruling",' Craig Keener believes, 'but he does not mind calling wives to submit or husbands to love, because this was the behaviour that should indeed characterize all Christians'.[23] One can obey without submitting since submission is a broader and different concept which defines the attitude of heart and mind, and requires one to let go of being in control or a desire to be dominant.

(i) Mutual submission

Paul invites wives to submit themselves to their husbands in the context of inviting all, both men and women, to *submit to one another out of reverence to Christ* (21). It is not, therefore, something wives have to do but from which husbands are exempt. It defines all relationships among Christ's followers. Some[24] have tried to argue that 'one another' in verse 21 applies only to the wife submitting herself to her husband and not vice versa, but such a position is indefensible for several reasons. The word 'submit' does not actually occur in verse 22, but is only implied, from verse 21. So verse 22 is tightly tied into verse 21 where 'submitting' is a participle rather than an active verb ('submit') which indicates that this is a continuation of what it means to live the Spirit-filled life mentioned in verse 18.

There is no indication that the meaning of 'one another' is tied to select members of the household, and it is not usually used in a restricted fashion. Throughout Paul's writings he teaches the need to live in submission to one another by demonstrating humility and by deferring to others.[25] Even where the actual word 'submit' is not used the concept is widespread and, in Howard Marshall's words,

---

[23] C. S. Keener, *Paul, Women and Wives* (Peabody: Hendrickson, 1992), p. 156.

[24] E.g., S. B. Clark, *Man and Woman in Christ: An Examination of the Roles of Men and Women in Light of Scripture and the Social Sciences* (Ann Arbor: Servant, 1980), p. 74–76; G. Knight III, 'Husbands and Wives as Analogues of Christ and the Church: Ephesians 5:21-33 and Colossians 3:18-19', *RBMW*, p. 167, n. 6; P. T. O'Brien, *The Letter to the Ephesians*, PNTC (Grand Rapids: Eerdmans and Nottingham: Apollos, 1999), pp. 398–405.

[25] Gal. 5:13; Phil. 2:3–4; Eph. 4:2, 32; 5:1.

'If it is true of Christian relationships in general, it must surely include the marriage relationship'.[26] Ephesians 5:22–24 is a call to observe in marriage the basic principle of all Christian living since a Christian was one who had renounced their 'own will for the sake of others . . . and to give precedence to others'.[27]

(ii) Voluntary submission
The form of the participle used for 'submitting to one another'[28] means that Christian are called to voluntarily submit to others. As the church has voluntarily submitted herself to Christ so the wife is invited to voluntarily submit herself to her husband. The husband is never commanded to make her submit and the issue here is not about a husband exercising authority over the wife.[29]

(iii) Comprehensive submission
Paul's final words to wives are that they *should submit to their husbands in everything* (24). 'This means that a wife should cultivate an attitude of affirming, supporting and respecting her husband's leadership in the marriage without holding back certain areas where she wants to assert or maintain control.'[30] But since submission is mutual, and since Christ himself defines it, this is not a licence for the husband to demand obedience, to require that the wife act sinfully or submit to abuse.

In the Christian community, then, submission was essentially voluntary and mutual, even if worked out within the context of an ordered structure.

b. Head

The reason for submission is given as *for the husband is the head of the wife as Christ is the head of the church, his body, of which he is the Saviour* (23). Paul's concern is focused on the particular relationship between husband and wife. His instructions are not to be taken as teaching that every relationship between a man and a woman is one of submission.[31]

Again we confront the meaning of the word 'head'.[32] Paul speaks

[26] I. H. Marshall, 'Mutual Love and Submission in Marriage: Colossians 3:18-19 and Ephesians 5:21-33', *DBE*, p. 197.

[27] Delling, '*hypotassō*', p. 45.

[28] It is in the middle or passive voice.

[29] Arnold, *Ephesians*, pp. 357, 380.

[30] Arnold, *Ephesians*, p. 383.

[31] Knight, 'Husbands and Wives', *RBMW*, p. 169.

[32] In a representative traditional exposition of this passage, Knight 'assumes' that head 'implies authority' and interprets the passage from this perspective (ibid.).

of Christ as 'head' three times in Ephesians,[33] each time highlighting the connection between the head and the body of the church. A body is dependent on its head for direction and guidance, but equally to provide it with strength and sustenance.[34] Inherent in the metaphor here, then, is 'the dual notion of leadership and provision' rather than it standing for source or emphasizing authority. It also makes perfect sense in terms of 'head' meaning prominence as argued earlier.[35] To be prominent meant to be in the position of honour and to be more noticeable, as a man was in the ancient world, especially of the family.

Paul roots his understanding of the male headship of the family here not in any creation mandate but by analogy with Christ's headship of the church *of which he is the Saviour* (23). So this is a new creation principle not just the old one, and Christ serves as the pattern for male headship in the family, as is explained further in verses 25–33. Christ became the Saviour of his church by himself voluntarily submitting his body to torture and death, as verse 25 states, not by being self-assertive, or self-protective, nor by standing on his status and demanding obedience, but by sacrificial self-giving love.

When women in the Christian household submit to their husbands they might expect to be met with a reciprocal submission, patterned on Christ himself, rather than an arrogant authoritarianism which has been moulded by the non-Christian values of their culture. Even if Paul accepts the normal social structure of his day,[36] he invests that skeleton with an entirely new and counter-cultural body. His vision for each marriage partner 'is counter-cultural to the core' and 'would have been difficult for couples in the Roman world to live out apart from the enabling grace of God',[37] as it still is.

Paul's final word to wives is, *Now as the church submits to Christ, so also wives should submit to their husbands in everything* (24). But in submitting to Christ, the church submits to 'a beneficial and loving

[33] 1:22; 4:15–16; 5:23.

[34] C. E. Arnold, 'Jesus Christ: "Head" of the Church', in M. M. B. Turner and J. B. Green (eds.), *Jesus of Nazareth: Lord and Christ: Essays on the Historical Jesus and New Testament Christology* (Grand Rapids: Eerdmans, 1983), pp. 346–366; *Ephesians*, p. 382; Marshall, 'Mutual Love', p. 198.

[35] See discussion on p. 213.

[36] Acknowledging Paul adopts the patriarch structure of marriage of his day, Marshall asks, 'Does it, however, *require* this structure?' and argues that the general trajectory of Scripture requires us to answer 'No' and uphold the legitimacy of the greater equality husbands and wives enjoy today. He compares the issue to the comparable developments that have taken place in industrial relations which no longer require us to insist on the obedience of slaves to their masters ('Mutual Love', pp. 200–204).

[37] Arnold, *Ephesians*, p. 399.

rule that enables growth'.[38] In submitting to her husband, the Christian wife may expect to encounter the same.

c. Has Paul changed his mind?

Elizabeth Schüssler Fiorenza sees these household instructions as a reassertion of the old patriarchal order of the Roman Empire and a drawing back from the radical freedom offered women in Galatians 3:28.[39] The compromise occurs, she argues, because of tensions with the social environment and the need to make the early house churches more acceptable to their social context. Fiorenza then maintains that the Pastoral Epistles take this one stage further, with the result that the radical freedom women had in Christ is drastically curtailed and women cease to have a role in leadership.

There can be no doubt that historically this is the path the church took after the New Testament era. But whether Paul's household code in Ephesians 5 can be blamed for it is another matter. Paul certainly shows a respect for the social structures of his day and encourages Christian families to be sensitive to them. But 'for all the social conservatism in Paul's words, there is yet a subversiveness he dares not play down'.[40] Fiorenza's argument only holds water if the instruction to wives is isolated from that to husbands and seen, quite wrongly, as a one-sided call for subordination rather than a particular application of the call for all Christians, men as well as women, husbands as well as wives, to live in mutual submission to each other.

3. Authentic beauty (1 Pet. 3:1–7)

Peter's instruction to wives harmonizes with that of Paul but has a number of distinctive features that are largely determined by the circumstances of readers to whom Peter was writing. Within the general context of calling for submission, four features deserve attention.[41]

a. The motivation for submission (1–2)

Paul's reasons for instructing wives to submit to their husbands are theological but Peter's are pragmatic. Unlike Paul, he is not writing

---

[38] A. Lincoln, *Ephesians*, WBC (Dallas: Word, 1990), p. 386.

[39] Fiorenza, *In Memory of Her*, pp. 269–279.

[40] Keener, *Paul*, p. 157.

[41] W. Grudem's, 'Wives Like Sarah, and Husbands Who Honour Them' (*RBMW*, pp. 194–208) provides a complementarian's view of this passage which is helpful in several respects, but is so concerned with the meaning of 'submission' that it does not address either the context which Peter was addressing or some of the difficulties of v. 6.

to Christian couples, but to Christian wives, some of whom were married to unbelieving husbands. Greco-Roman households would usually find unity in observing the religion of the *paterfamilias* (the father of the family). It was expected that wives would follow their husband's religion, transferring their allegiance from the gods of their father's house to the gods of their husband on marriage. Plutarch advised newly-weds, 'is it becoming for the wife to worship and to know only the gods that her husband believes in, and to shut the front door right upon all queer rituals and outlandish superstitions?'[42] So it is significant that some wives have made the choice to follow Christ irrespective of their husband's religion. It may be that they were Christians before entering an arranged marriage. Or, perhaps it indicates some degree of independence on the part of women subsequent to marriage, of which we have some evidence in the region where Peter's readers live.[43] Either way, being in a mixed marriage posed serious problems.

Peter knows that any Christian woman would seek the conversion of her husband, but his advice is that she should not do so by preaching at him but do so *without words by [her] behaviour*. Peter knows that 'actions speak louder than words'. His concern is a missionary one and he instructs wives to avoid causing their husbands to build up defences against the gospel because of the way they treat them, but rather to behave in such a way as to remove any barriers. So, while they may have made an independent decision to follow Christ, in all other respects they should defer to their husbands and fulfil the role expected of a wife. Moreover they should do so not merely in terms of grudging obedience but of a submissive spirit. Peter's reference to *the purity and reverence of your lives* (literally, 'purity in fear') suggests, however, that their submission has a limit and should not go as far as reneging on their faith in Christ. Wherever else Peter speaks of *reverence* (literally, 'fear') in 1 Peter it is to speak of having reverence for God as opposed to fearing men.[44]

b. The nature of beauty (3–4)

Peter's mention of purity, which lays some emphasis on sexual purity but is not confined to sexual matters, leads him to discuss the nature

---

[42] Plutarch, 'Advice to Bride and Groom', 19, *Moralia* 140D, as quoted by P. H. Davids, 'A Silent Witness in Marriage: 1 Peter 3:1-7', *DBE*, p. 226.

[43] I. H. Marshall, *I Peter*, IVP New Testament Commentary (Downers Grove and Leicester: IVP, 1991), p. 98; B. Witherington III, *Letters and Homilies for Hellenized Christians: A Socio-Rhetorical Commentary on 1-2 Peter*, vol. 2 (Downers Grove, IVP and Nottingham: Apollos, 2007), p. 161.

[44] 1:17; 2:17; 3:6, 14. Davids, 'Silent Witness', p. 229.

of true feminine beauty. While some Christians down the years have thought that Peter was advocating that Christian women should dress in a drab or dowdy fashion, avoid cosmetics, and show little care for the way they present themselves, this is not Peter's point. The *outward adornment, such as elaborate hairstyles and the wearing of gold jewellery or fine clothes,* had particular meaning to his readers.[45] On the one hand, the manner of dress he describes involves an ostentatious display of wealth and his words are aimed at the social elite. Most would not have been in a position to afford such 'ornamentation'. On the other hand, the beautification he describes was frequently described by pagan moralists 'as an indication of sexual seductiveness' and was also the way in which women in some of the more sexually promiscuous cults were encouraged to dress. So, Peter is exhorting Christian women 'to avoid appearing morally improper by the standards of their culture'.[46]

He is not condemning the woman who gives attention to presenting herself beautifully or dressing well, but his words do stand as a rebuke to any woman who spends vast sums on clothes and who ostentatiously draws attention to herself by her wardrobe or coiffure. The attention such a woman gives to her wardrobe is better spent elsewhere since *the unfading beauty of a gentle and quiet spirit . . . is of great worth in God's sight.* Peter's desire is to be positive rather than negative. 'Virtue is the one garment that any Christian woman can wear with pride.'[47] A genuinely Christian woman will be committed to inner character rather than outward appearance, to eternal values rather than passing fashion, and to being attractive to God rather than being attractive to men. In contrast to the outward beauty that inevitably passes with the ageing process, the inner virtues of a Christlike character grow as time goes on.[48]

c. The example of Sarah (5–6)

In support of his appeal for their submission, Peter points to the example of how *the holy women of the past* would make themselves beautiful, using Sarah as an illustration whom he says *obeyed Abraham and called him her lord.* Peter's description of Sarah,

---

[45] The similarity of 1 Tim. 2:9 shows it was a common discussion point among early Christians. See further p. 260.

[46] Davids, 'Silent Witness', p. 230. Also, Witherington, *Letters and Homilies*, pp. 163–164.

[47] P. H. Davids, *The First Epistle of Peter*, NICNT (Grand Rapids: Eerdmans, 1990), p. 118.

[48] Christ described himself as 'gentle' (Matt. 11:29) and 'gentleness' is a fruit of the Spirit (Gal. 5:22).

however, raises questions because she is never said to have obeyed Abraham in Genesis and only once to have called him *lord* (in Gen. 18:12). Conversely, God did instruct Abraham to 'obey' Sarah, even if the instruction is usually softened in English translations.[49] And unfortunately the single example of Sarah calling Abraham 'lord' occurs when she expresses amused scepticism to herself about God's promise of a child, which hardly seems an ideal example to choose.

Peter's comments do not fit comfortably with Genesis but perhaps it was the very unusual occurrence of the title which 'catches Peter's attention', and perhaps we should not expect to find profound theology and contextually accurate quotations in Peter's simple instructions.[50] Peter's words do reflect the Jewish literature of his day, such as the *Testament of Abraham,* more than Genesis, and it could well be that Peter is simply echoing writings that would have been well known to his readers.[51]

Whatever he may have been alluding to in verse 5, Peter's point stands, and is reinforced by a further allusion, this time definitely from Scripture, in the next verse. Isaiah 51:2 instructs Israel to 'Look to Abraham, your father, and to Sarah, who gave you birth'. To be true daughters of Sarah, Christian wives need to model themselves on her by living morally upright lives with confidence, and *not give way to fear* of how their unbelieving husbands might respond.

d. The meaning of 'the weaker partner' (7)

From addressing wives, Peter more briefly addresses Christian husbands, commanding them to be *considerate* towards their wives and *treat them with respect as the weaker partner.* His instructions are again similar in substance to Paul's instructions to Christian husbands but his use of the distinctive phrase *the weaker partner* inevitably invites comment. In what sense are females *the weaker partners?* Since this is the only time Scripture speaks in this way there are no other obvious other scriptures to illuminate its meaning. Contemporary writers in the wider culture condescendingly spoke of the physical, social, intellectual and moral weakness of women.[52] But Peter is not adopting such views. Rather he is referring to the fact that a wife was physically weaker than her husband, especially 'before and after childbirth', even though they might live longer than

[49] Gen. 21:12. See comment on p. 78.

[50] J. R. Michaels, *1 Peter*, WBC (Waco: Word, 1988), pp. 164–165.

[51] For details see Davids, 'Silent Witness', pp. 231–234; Witherington, *Letters and Homilies*, p. 165.

[52] Davids, 'Silent Witness', p. 237. Witherington, *Letters and Homilies*, p. 167, gives examples.

their husbands.[53] What is weaker, says Peter, is the wife's *skeuos,* which means 'vessel' or 'instrument'. It suggests something physical and implies a 'frail mortal form'.[54] The word was also metaphorically used of a 'person' and so understandably gives rise to the NIV's use of *partner.*

In the flow of what Peter says to Christian husbands, the reference to *the weaker partner* comes between instructing them to *respect* their wives and a strong assertion of their equality *as heirs with [them] of the gracious gift of life.* Being the weaker sex, then, cannot in any way imply inferiority and none of the claims found outside of the Bible to women being weaker intellectually or morally apply here. As Davids concludes, 'The point is that the husband is in some respect "stronger" and needs to recognize this fact in his life with his wife, so that he does not exploit this disparity in strength, consciously or unconsciously'.[55]

4. Concluding comments

Twin tributaries flow into the New Testament's teaching on marriage to create one stream. One tributary emphasizes the equality of women and men in marriage, and the other the respect for the sense of order that is inherent in creation and the new creation, which was all too imperfectly reflected in the Greco-Roman world in which Paul lived. The tributaries flow happily into one, without opposing each other with cross currents. They run together because of Christ who, though 'head over everything' and 'head of the church', the community of the new creation, taught submission and modelled it. Where submission is mutual and where each partner defers to the other there is no tension between equality and accepting one's place in a structured order.

Streams flow on, often becoming fuller and creating more powerful currents as they do so. In like manner many see New Testament teaching as creating a current that pushes forward in the direction of equality beyond the narrow banks of the patriarchalism of his world.[56] Just as different styles of parenthood and different kinds of industrial relations are now accepted from those which were in

---

[53] Marshall, *1 Peter*, p. 103.

[54] Davids, *First Peter*, pp. 122–123; Witherington, *Letters and Homilies*, p. 166.

[55] Davids, 'Silent Witness', p. 237.

[56] The most extensive treatment of this argument is found in W. J. Webb, *Slaves, Women and Homosexuals: Exploring the Hermeneutics of Cultural Analysis* (Downers Grove: IVP, 2001) and more briefly in 'A Redemptive-Movement Hermeneutic: The Slavery Analogy', *DBE*, pp. 382–400. A critique of his position is found in W. Grudem, *Evangelical Feminism and Biblical Truth: An Analysis of 118 Disputed Questions* (Leicester: IVP, 2005), pp. 350–357, 600–645.

operation in Paul and Peter's day, and just as we no longer accept slavery as a legitimate arrangement of relations in the workplace, so we are no longer confined to a particular patriarchal arrangement of the family. The patriarchy of their day was one way of working out the principle of order in the family and it was natural for them to assume it.[57] Scripture itself, however, illustrates a number of ways in which families can be arranged so that the theological requirement of order is satisfied. While particular ways of applying biblical truth may pass, what remains is that order is created in the community of the new creation by mutual love, mutual submission, mutual deference and by giving up the will to power.

[57] See Marshall, 'Mutual Love', pp. 200–204; Davids, 'Silent Witness', p. 238.

1 Timothy 2:11–15
19. Women in leadership

No verses have exercised a greater influence on the debate about women in the church than these. The importance given to them has had a distorting influence on what the Bible teaches about women and the impression has sometimes arisen that its only concern is whether or not women can legitimately lead and teach in a church. Almost without exception when we have mentioned that we were writing a book about women in Scripture the responses have assumed we were writing about women in leadership in the church. How tragic that our debates have become so narrow in focus!

Nonetheless, 1 Timothy 2:11–15 are significant verses which are contained in authoritative Scripture; they need careful examination and cannot be dismissed by glibly saying, 'That was then, this is now'.

The meaning of the verses has been subject to minute analysis (and exhausting, as well as exhaustive literature) many times and given rise to strong disagreements.[1] Complementarians, while arguing for an equality of status in Christ, argue for a difference of function between male and female and see these verses as forbidding a woman from exercising a teaching role over men in the church for all time.[2]

---

[1] One of the most helpful introductions to the debate is *Two Views*. A judicious and even-handed discussion of the text is found in A. Perriman, *Speaking of Women: Interpreting Paul* (Leicester: Apollos, 1998), pp. 136–173.

[2] Among the representative expositions of complementarianism are: W. Grudem, *Evangelical Feminism and Biblical Truth: An Analysis of 118 Disputed Questions* (Leicester: IVP, 2005); J. B. Hurley, *Man and Woman in Biblical Perspective* (Leicester: IVP, 1981), pp. 195–233; G. W. Knight III, *The New Testament Teaching on the Role Relationship of Men and Women* (Grand Rapids: Baker, 1977) and *The Pastoral Epistles*, NIGNT (Grand Rapids: Eerdmans, 1992); D. Moo, 'What Does It Mean Not to Teach or Have Authority Over Men?', *RBMW*, pp. 179–193; W. D. Mounce, *Pastoral Epistles*, WBC (Nashville: Thomas Nelson, 2000); A. J. Köstenberger, T. R. Schreiner and H. S. Baldwin (eds.), *Women in the Church: A Fresh Analysis of 1 Timothy 2:9-15* (Grand Rapids: Baker, 1995).

Egalitarians agree about men and women's equal status in Christ and argue that the obvious differences between men and women do not lead to different functions within the church. They see these verses as forbidding a woman from exercising a teaching role over men as specific to the circumstances in Ephesus at the time, or equivalent circumstances today. They have continuing significance, however, in exercising a prohibition on anyone teaching who is in a similar position to the women to whom Paul is referring.[3]

Those who hold to the highest authority of Scripture are found on both sides of the debate, engaging in the complex discussion of both the original meaning of Paul's words and of their continuing significance today. In this volume we can only hope to introduce the key issues, albeit from a particular perspective.

1. What do the words mean?

We begin by examining the words Paul uses, which fall into nine sections, several of which raise questions because of the unusual expressions he uses.

a. A woman should learn (11a)

Having addressed 'women' in general in verse 9, Paul now switches to the single, 'a woman' (gynē), in order to lay down a general rule. The word gynē may either mean woman or wife. In 1 Corinthians 14:35, the other passage which instructs women to 'keep silent', the ambiguity is somewhat removed when Paul says 'they should ask their husbands at home'. There he clearly has wives in view. The difficulty may be more hypothetical than real since in the ancient world women would usually have been married. Here there are no definitive indications of whether gynē is used in the wider or more restricted sense but the context suggests that the wider sense of women, rather than just wives, are the ones addressed. In marriage they would have been essentially confined to the domestic sphere, at least until the rise of the 'new woman', so it is perhaps noteworthy

[3] Among the representative expositions of egalitarianism are: L. L. Belleville, 'Teaching and Usurping Authority: 1 Timothy 2:11-15', *DBE*, pp. 205–223; R. T. France, *Women in the Church's Ministry: A Test Case for Biblical Hermeneutics* (Carlisle: Paternoster, 1995); I. H. Marshall, *The Pastoral Epistles*, ICC (Edinburgh: T & T Clark, 1999); P. B. Payne, *Man and Woman: One in Christ* (Grand Rapids: Zondervan, 2009), pp. 291–463; P. H. Towner, *The Letters to Timothy and Titus*, NICNT (Grand Rapids: Eerdmans, 2006); A. Mickelsen (ed.), *Women, Authority and the Bible* (Downers Grove: IVP, 1986); B. Witherington III, *Women in the Earliest Churches* (Cambridge: Cambridge University Press, 1990), pp. 191–196.

that Paul begins positively in affirming the right of women to learn in a context where many would have denied them that opportunity. As France puts it, 'Paul's encouragement to the women of the Ephesian church to learn would have seemed uncomfortably avant-garde to many in the ancient world'.[4]

b. In quietness and full submission (11b)

The traditional wording of 'silence' is a legitimate translation of the word (*hēsychia*) but gives an overly-harsh impression. Paul is not imposing absolute silence or a 'no speaking' rule, for which there was another word (*sigaō*) that he uses elsewhere.[5] Rather than implying that a learner should never ask a question or engage in discussion, *hēsychia* carries the 'more normal sense'[6] of listening carefully and with respect, that is, of adopting a quiet demeanour rather than engaging in undisciplined or arrogant interventions in the classroom. In fact, Paul had used the word a little earlier to commend the living of 'peaceful and *quiet* lives' (2:2).[7]

Showing due deference and adopting a calm disposition rather than constantly challenging one's teachers was considered a prerequisite of learning. For women to learn submissively is the opposite of them attempting to dominate men through their (ill-informed) teaching, rather than being a reference to the husband/wife relationship.[8] Here submission must be to one's teacher, as would be expected of any learner. In any case, submission, as mentioned previously, is a widespread idea of accepting one's proper place without attempting to rebel against it. The emphasis on 'all' or *full submission* simply implies without mental reservation.

c. I do not permit (12a)

For Paul to write *I do not permit* (or, more accurately, 'I am not permitting') is an unusually personal way of addressing the subject and an unusual tense to use. Usually, as in 1 Corinthians 11:16 and 14:34–37, Paul points to the practice of the churches over such issues. The personal emphasis here is probably the result of Paul addressing a new situation and providing new guidance. It is mistaken to think

---

[4] France, *Women in Ministry*, p. 63.
[5] 1 Cor. 14:28, 30, 34.
[6] Marshall, *Pastoral Epistles*, p. 453.
[7] L. L. Belleville, *Two Views*, p. 80.
[8] Witherington, *Earliest Churches*, p. 193. But see K. E. Bailey, 'Women in the New Testament: A Middle Eastern Cultural View', *Anvil* 11 (1994), p. 20, who argues submission is to 'the sound doctrine' of 1:10.

that these words need not be taken as seriously as others simply because Paul writes personally. He writes as a 'true and faithful teacher' who has apostolic authority[9] and whose words, therefore, deserve to be given due weight. The relative novelty of the situation he is addressing,[10] however, combined with his use of the current continuous tense, which is never used to suggest a fixed and timeless principle,[11] suggests his words apply to that and similar situations rather than being an inflexible rule for all time.

d. To teach or assume authority over a man (12b)

As previous chapters have demonstrated, women certainly exercised a teaching function in the church earlier and Paul subsequently instructs 'older women' to adopt a teaching role towards younger women.[12] The key element that seems new, then, is a prohibition on women teaching men, as is highlighted by the conjunction between teaching and assuming *authority over a man.* These are the crucial words on which there is little agreement.

The first question is what the word *authentein (assume authority)* means. Is it a neutral expression, meaning 'to have authority', or does it carry some negative overtones of 'seizing' or 'wresting' authority or exercising it in a domineering, independent manner? The reason for asking is that the verb frequently carried implications of domineering or usurping authority. The related noun, *authentēs,* meant a murderer or the perpetrator of an act, and so had negative associations. Early Arabic translations certainly understood it as implying insolence, domination, and even that women were 'brutalizing' or 'battering' men.[13]

How one translates the word relates to a second question as to whether Paul is prohibiting two separate activities here – teaching and exercising authority – or one? Does the verse actually mean: 'I do not permit a woman to teach in a domineering manner over men', with the second phrase acting as a qualification of the first? If so, *authenteō* is more likely to have a more negative nuance. This is possible grammatically and fits the emphasis on learning quietly. It also reduces any tension between this instruction and the evident fact that women did teach elsewhere in the New Testament.[14]

[9] 1 Tim. 2:7; 1 Tim. 1:1. See also 1 Tim. 6:1; 2 Tim 1:11.
[10] The situation and argument is similar to that of 1 Cor. 14:33–34.
[11] Witherington, *Earliest Churches*, p. 193.
[12] Titus 2:3.
[13] Bailey, 'Women in', p. 21. The KJV translated it as 'to usurp authority'.
[14] The view is fully argued in Payne, *One in Christ*, pp. 337–360.

Köstenberger[15] argues that Paul is referring to two separate activities, (a) teaching and (b) having authority over men, and rejects the idea that *authenteō* has any negative overtones. When (*oude*) joins two infinitives together, he says, as here, they are always two separate activities, both of which carry the same tone. So, he concludes, since Paul is positive about teaching we cannot logically read *authenteō* as either qualifying teaching or as having the negative tone of 'domineering'. Paul is prohibiting both activities. While Howard Marshall finds the grammatical point 'convincing' he argues that 'the matter, however, is not quite so simple'.[16] Given that the word *authenteō* can have negative connotations, the context in which it is used becomes determinative and that suggests that Paul is not using it in a neutral fashion here.

The second question is who is the 'man' to whom Paul refers? Is it any man or might it specifically refer to a woman's husband, which would not only make it consistent with 1 Corinthians 14:34–35, but make the allusion which follows to Adam and Eve 'more appropriate'?[17] If it has a more limited reference it undermines the idea that Paul is drawing a general implication about the way genders are to relate.

e. She must be quiet (12c)

Literally, 'but to be in quietness'. This does not introduce anything new but serves as a succinct summary of Paul's instruction that women adopt a quiet demeanour, and does not imply that they should never speak.

f. For Adam was formed first, then Eve (13)

Paul now explains the reason for his instruction by reaching back to the story of Adam and Eve. The question here is what status Paul was giving to his explanation. The essential question is that by using the word *for* is he (a) giving a causal explanation, and so laying down an unalterable creation principle, or (b) justifying what he has written by reference to an illustration from way back at the time of creation? *For* (*gar*) could mean either and can be used in either way.

Complementarians argue this verse invokes the pre-fall creation order and so provides a principle for all time. They find the idea that

---

[15] Köstenberger, 'A Complex Sentence Structure in 1 Timothy 2:12', in *Women in the Church*, pp. 82–91.

[16] Marshall, *Pastoral Epistles*, p. 458.

[17] France, *Women in Ministry*, p. 38.

gar may simply be introducing an example 'singularly unconvincing'.[18] But *gar* is not always used in the sense of 'cause and effect' and here Paul may merely be introducing the incontestable fact that Adam was created before Eve before drawing out the implications of this in the following verse. 'The mere fact that it refers to Adam and Eve does not make it a "creation principle".'[19] Some suggest he may be referring to the natural advantages of going first, rather than an inflexible creation principle, as would be evident still in the educational advantages men had over women in Paul's day.[20] Still others think he is alluding to the common rabbinic view that 'first is best'.[21] Dogmatism is impossible and the most we can hope for is what makes best sense in the context.

g. It was the woman who was deceived (14)

Drawing further on the Genesis account of creation, Paul points out that Eve *was deceived and became a sinner* rather than Adam. Complementarians understand this to suggest that women are inherently more gullible and therefore less suited than men to exercising any authoritative teaching role in the church. George Knight, for example, writes, 'Paul now appeals to the fall as an event that demonstrates in the most absolute way the dire consequences of a reversal of leadership roles'.[22] If this is so, Paul's appeal raises more questions than it answers. Is he saying sin entered the world through a woman? Previously he has said Adam was responsible for its entry into the world.[23] Surely he is not saying that Adam was not deceived, even if he was not the first to be deceived? Is he saying all women are less rational and objective and more gullible by constitution than men?[24] If he had consistently believed this, why did his earlier practice seem so out of step with it?

The most likely explanation is that Paul reaches back to Genesis for support in addressing a specific issue among his readers (which

---

[18] T. R. Schreiner, 'An interpretation of 1 Timothy 9-16: A Dialogue with Scholarship', in *Women in the Church*, p. 134.

[19] France, *Women in Ministry*, p. 67. See also p. 68.

[20] Perriman, *Speaking of Women*, p. 166.

[21] Towner, *Timothy and Titus*, p. 226.

[22] Knight, *Pastoral Epistles*, p. 143.

[23] Rom. 5:12, 15, 17, 19.

[24] This view is expounded by Schreiner in *Women in the Church*, pp. 145–146, but as C. Blomberg (*Two Views*, p. 171) says, this conviction has 'rightly been abandoned by virtually all complementarians as well as egalitarians. [Since] there is simply too much physiological, social-scientific, and experiential to the contrary'. For a biblical feminist's view of the real differences see E. Storkey, *Created or Constructed? The Great Gender Debate* (Carlisle: Paternoster, 2000), esp. pp. 64–65.

we will explore further), but not that he is intending to suggest there is some fixed order of headship and subordination built into creation.

h. But women will be saved through child-bearing (v. 15a)

The questions do not lessen as Paul goes on to the next stage of his argument. The mention of Eve may naturally lead to him thinking of childbearing since she was 'the mother of all the living'.[25] But what precisely does Paul mean when he says *women will be saved through* [the][26] *childbearing?* Several explanations have been offered.

- Could it mean by the birth of *the* child, Jesus, who is born to be the Saviour? This may explain why Paul uses the definite article and writes about *the childbearing.* But this cannot be the right interpretation since Paul is speaking of the on-going role of bearing children rather than the past birth of one child.
- Could it mean that a woman would be 'kept safe' when having children since God's judgment after the fall decreed they would give birth in pain and since giving birth is always precarious and was even more so in Paul's day than today? The word *saved* (*sōthēsetai*) can mean kept well or healthy and does not always refer to eternal salvation. The use of the definite article suggests this meaning to some, and leads to understanding it as 'will be kept safe through the act of childbearing'. This makes sense because of the link to the story of the fall and once the wider religious context is taken into account (see below). However, is it really germane to Paul's argument?
- Could it mean that having children is the means by which women were to be saved? No, since this would be in flat contradiction to the united New Testament teaching that salvation is through grace by faith.[27] It would also mean, absurdly, that a childless woman could not be saved.
- Might it mean that women need not fear that they will miss out on God's salvation if they fulfil their role as mothers, bearing and nurturing children? This is the most relevant explanation in the context. Paul seems to be warning women not to stridently reject or abandon their primary role for some sought-after status as teachers in the church but to accept their procreative privileges with good grace. They need have no fear that they will be denied salvation if they fulfil the role that only they can play in creation. We shall discover that more might lie behind this than is

---

[25] Gen. 3:20.
[26] Omitted from NIV.
[27] Eph. 2:8.

immediately apparent to us once we look further into the context in which Paul's readers were living. It may, for example, have connections to the false teaching, which Paul refers to in 4:1–5 and which, among other heresies, forbade marriage. His comments here are a specific example of what he meant when he said that 'godliness *with contentment* is great gain'.[28]

i. If they continue in faith, love and holiness with propriety (15b)

Paul's concluding comment supports the interpretation given in the previous paragraph. Wrapping up the whole section that was addressed to women (9–15) which began with comments on the way they dressed and developed into comments on the way they behaved in church, Paul points out the need for them to persevere in a trio of godly virtues – *faith, love and holiness* – and to do so *with propriety,* that is in a manner which will not be misunderstood by people in the wider community in Ephesus. His teaching here fits exactly with what he taught in 1 Corinthians 11:1–16 and 14:34–40 and shares a similar concern for a credible witness to society and orderliness in the church. It also dovetails perfectly with Peter's instructions in 1 Peter 3:1–7.

2. Where do the words come?

Some years ago the *Guardian* newspaper ran a couple of television advertisements. In one a skinhead initially appeared to be mugging a businessman. As the camera drew back it became apparent that far from mugging the man, the skinhead was saving him by pushing him out of the way as a pile of bricks was making its rapid descent from above which would have almost certainly killed him. In another a 'yob' appeared to be attacking an old lady and pushing her to the ground. Again as the camera drew back we discovered that he was in fact saving her from the path of an on-coming car. To have drawn conclusions about these young men's actions on the basis of the initial close-up pictures would have been premature and totally to misinterpret what was happening. 'It is only when you get the whole picture you can fully understand what's going on,' the adverts concluded. A narrow focus can sometimes lead to a misinterpretation.

So it is with several of the issues raised in 1 Timothy 2:11–15, which can only be understood by drawing back somewhat and seeing them in their wider setting.

---

[28] 1 Tim. 6:6.

a. Specific context within 1 Timothy

As we begin to change the focus, the next wider lens immediately reveals that these verses come within a section of the letter where Paul is providing a number of instructions about worship. He begins by talking about prayer (2:1–7), then turns to the behaviour of men in worship (2:8), and only then turns to the behaviour of women (2:9–14). Like Peter, he instructs women not to dress ostentatiously but give attention to the virtues of 'decency and propriety' and of 'good deeds' (2:9–10). Only then does he turn to the question of women learning quietly and not usurping any teaching authority over men. This is not an isolated subject but one in a series which addresses inappropriate behaviour by men as well as women in worship. One wishes that those who are often very disputatious about verses 11–15 were as literal in 'lifting up holy hands' or as conscientious in prohibiting the 'anger or disputing', both of which are commanded in verse 8, as they are in forbidding women to teach in church.

b. General context of 1 Timothy

1 Timothy is written because the health of the church at Ephesus is threatened by 'false doctrines', taught by those who had become fascinated by 'myths and endless genealogies' and were promoting 'controversial speculations'.[29] With the exception of Hymenaus and Alexander (1:20), Paul does not identify them other than to say 'they want to be teachers of the law, but they do not know what they are talking about or what they so confidently affirm'.[30] He does not say that these false teachers were men and, in view of what we can glean about the nature of the heresies, it is more than probable that they included women. In this context it seems more than coincidental that he imposes strictures on women teaching and on their need to learn *in quietness and full submission* (11).

Some protest that Paul never links his prohibition on women to the issue of false teaching. Craig Blomberg, for example, writes, 'it is a big jump from men teaching women heresy to the conclusion, never stated in the text, that those women in turn became (false) teachers, so the *only* thing Paul is forbidding in 2:11–12 is the teaching of heresy'.[31] True, Paul is not *only* forbidding teaching heresy here but, as Craig Keener counters, it cannot surely be a 'coincidence that the one setting in the Bible where we *know* that false teachers were

[29] 1:3–4. The theme is found in 1:18–20; 4:1–5, 6:10, 20–21.
[30] 1 Tim. 1:7.
[31] Blomberg, *Two Views*, p. 166.

targeting women (5:13; 2 Tim. 3:6) provides the one passage that forbids women to teach?'[32]

The nature of the false teaching is complex[33] although, judging from the subjects Paul raises, a significant element of it related to the role of women. In addition to 2:11–15, with its intriguing references to Eve and childbirth, the false teachers forbade marriage (4:3) and the role of widows receives lengthy discussion (5:3–16). The activities of 'younger women' are causing special concern, some of whom are 'busybodies who talk nonsense, saying things they ought not to'[34] and they were 'talking nonsense' at the cost of neglecting their household responsibilities. Some of these 'younger widows' are said to 'have in fact already turned away to follow Satan'.[35]

It would be extraordinary if these wider issues were not all of a piece with Paul's words in 2:11–15 and do not explain the reason for his prohibition on women teaching. It is apparent that women were influenced by the false teachers. Their ignorance did not stop them talking or confidently teaching myths and heresies, and they needed silencing (5:13). They were not alone in broadcasting their ignorance to the detriment of the church but it appears they were particularly significant because of the nature of the issues on which they spoke. It is necessary, therefore, to dig further and see if it is possible to discover more about the nature of the false teaching they were circulating.

3. When were the words written?

If we widen the lens beyond the letter itself, we discover quite a lot about the context in which the church at Ephesus was living. Two particular aspects of the wider picture are significant.

a. The religious context in Ephesus

Although a pluralistic city, Ephesus was dominated by the worship of the goddess Artemis, a fertility deity who provided the city with a sense of security and was crucial to its economic well-being.[36] In the Artemis cult 'the female was exalted and considered superior to the male'.[37] She was also considered 'the protector of women' when

---

[32] C. S. Keener, *Two Views*, p. 188. See also p. 232.
[33] See full discussion in Towner, *Timothy and Titus*, pp. 37–53.
[34] 5:13; cf. 2 Tim 3:6.
[35] 1 Tim. 5:14–15.
[36] R. C. Kroeger and C. C. Kroeger, *I Suffer Not a Woman: Rethinking 1 Timothy 2:11-15 in the Light of Ancient Evidence* (Grand Rapids: Baker, 1992), p. 52–54.
[37] Belleville, *Two Views*, p. 89.

they were bearing children.[38] The high priestess had replaced the high priest as the chief functionary of the cult by the first century AD.[39] For these and other reasons, Kroeger and Kroeger reckon that 'Ephesus stood as the bastion of feminine supremacy in religion'.[40]

Thomas Schreiner objects that, 'there is no clear evidence in Paul's letter that the Artemis cult played a role. Paul does not mention the cult, nor is there any specific notion in the text that shows the influence of the cult'. To approach it in this way is, he says, 'an example of arbitrary mirror reading'.[41] But we rightly seek to interpret the biblical text as its original readers would have understood it, rather than treating its words as floating freely in a vacuum. Readers in Ephesus would have been immersed in the religious environment of the city and, however much they may have sought to be free from it, would have been affected by it, just as we are unconsciously affected by so much of our social environment today. 'No church is ever totally isolated from the sins of its culture.'[42] To ignore such a background is what leads to an arbitrary reading of the text.

Investigation by Richard and Catherine Kroeger into later Gnostic teaching at Ephesus has unearthed a plethora of ideas which were likely in some earlier form to have influenced the false teaching which Paul censures. Among the extreme views were that women were responsible for the creation of men[43] and that Eve had 'developed from that of deceived sinner to that of a powerful spiritual being who could enlighten those in need of salvation'.[44] Gnostic teaching, with its denigration of the body, also encouraged 'an aversion to childbearing'.[45] These ideas are reflected in embryonic form in the concerns Paul raises, and the use of the Gnostic terms[46] lends further support to the approach. It can be seen how such ideas would encourage women to commandeer a teaching role from men and also how fundamentally opposed to the Christian faith their teaching would have been. If this is the context, it is easy to understand why Paul commanded the women to learn in silence.

The obvious attraction of such an approach should not, however, lead us to throw caution to the wind. The Kroegers' research 'has

---

[38] Belleville, *Two Views*, p. 90.
[39] Kroeger and Kroeger, *I Suffer Not*, p. 71.
[40] Kroeger and Kroeger, *I Suffer Not*, p. 54.
[41] T. R. Schreiner, *Two Views*, p. 108.
[42] Bailey, 'Women in', p. 19.
[43] Kroeger and Kroeger, *I Suffer Not*, pp. 103–113.
[44] Kroeger and Kroeger, *I Suffer Not*, p. 160.
[45] Kroeger and Kroeger, *I Suffer Not*, p. 174. See also D. M. Scholer, '1 Timothy 2:9-15 and the Place of Women in the Church's Ministry', in *Women, Authority and the Bible*, pp. 196–200; France, *Women in Ministry*, p. 69.
[46] E.g., 1:4; 4:1–3; 6:4.

exceeded the evidence in reconstructing the Ephesian situation and Artemis cult'.[47] Much of it is based on later Gnosticism and we have no incontrovertible evidence about how influential it was in the Ephesian church in Paul's day. For all the cautions, however, the approach makes sense of both the general drift of Paul's words and the specific details, like Eve and child-bearing, he mentions.

b. The social context in the Roman Empire

The second contextual factor is more firmly based. The Roman Empire of the first century witnessed the emergence of 'new women'. These women threw off traditional values, rejected a secluded domestic role, spurned sexual modesty, scorned conventional dress codes, promoted marital infidelity, and sought freedom to participate in the public world of dinners and debates alongside men.[48] The appearance of these women greatly disturbed the social status quo and offended against ideas of respectability. From Augustus onwards a series of laws were passed to regulate dress, discriminate against the single, penalize childless marriages and criminalize promiscuity.[49]

All this, Bruce Winter justifiably claims, is reflected in Paul's teaching about women in 1 Timothy 2, both in what he commends and in what he forbids.[50] His insistence that women, or more specifically wives, 'dress modestly' and avoid 'elaborate hairstyles' or ostentatious clothes and jewellery directly relates to the discussion held in the wider world, where the way one dressed signalled the values one held. To dress in the manner Paul proscribes would not only advertise one's wealth and draw attention to oneself, but also imply one was hanging loose to one's marriage commitment and to what was generally considered morally respectable. 'The public perception of Christian wives was a critical matter in the community', Winter explains, 'they would play into the hands of the enemy of the early Christian movement in Ephesus if they dressed like high-class prostitutes'.[51] Paul's parting shot that women need to *continue in faith, love and holiness with propriety* (15) confirms this picture.

---

[47] Marshall, *Pastoral Epistles*, p. 466. For a somewhat overstated critique of the Kroegers' research see S. M. Baugh, 'A Foreign World: Ephesus in the First Century', in Köstenberger *et al.*, *Women in the Church*, pp. 14–50. Blomberg, *Two Views*, p. 165, and Witherington, *Earliest Churches*, p. 192, give more balanced evaluations of the influence of 'proto-gnosticism' in the Ephesian church.

[48] B. W. Winter, *Roman Wives, Roman Widows: The Appearance of New Women and the Pauline Communities* (Grand Rapids: Eerdmans, 2003), pp. 38–39.

[49] Details are found in Winter, *Roman Wives*, pp. 39–58.

[50] Winter, *Roman Wives*, p. 97.

[51] Winter, *Roman Wives*, p. 121.

The same context explains Paul's references to women learning in quietness rather than usurping men's authority in the church. The evidence of the 'new women' helps to determine the meaning of *authentein* in a way in which the endless listing of the word without its social context can never do. Both in the context of 1 Timothy and the context of the emergence of 'new women', the word not only means to exercise authority but to exercise it in an improper way. It indicates an attempt to exercise 'some form of social or intellectual control on the part of some' for which they are not equipped and which, in the social climate, was inappropriate and would be considered unseemly.[52]

The reference to women being kept safe in childbearing may equally be explained by the same social context. 'New women' increasingly wanted little to do with children and could avoid pregnancy, undergo abortions, or, if they did have children, distance themselves from their offspring by employing a wet nurse.[53]

It seems, then, that Paul was indeed addressing a new situation where women in the church, especially wealthy women, of whom we have hints later in 1 Timothy 6:6–10, were being influenced by the wider social trends of the emancipation of women which was taking place, especially in the cites of the empire like Ephesus. Such trends were controversial and, whatever the cultural currents dictated, embracing them would prove harmful to the gospel and the church's mission.[54]

4. Why were the words penned?

The interpretation that makes most sense of these verses, and the particular issues referred to in them, is one that gives full attention to the cultural and religious context of the Ephesian church. To read them in the abstract not only leaves a number of questions unsolved but runs the danger of misinterpreting them, just as a person's behaviour can be misinterpreted if too narrow a focus is used in seeking to explain it.

Paul's instructions do seem to have been addressed to a particular set of cultural circumstances. That, however, does not mean they can be safely dismissed as time-bound and ignored by later Christians. The point is rather, as Walter Liefeld has put it, that,

Paul *is* giving normative teaching. But the normative teaching is not women's silence, it is how God's people are to behave in the

---

[52] Winter, *Roman Wives*, pp. 117–119.
[53] Winter, *Roman Wives*, pp. 109–111.
[54] Paul's concern for the church's reputation is evident in 2:1–2; 3:7; 5:14; 6:1, 14.

world of the first century churches and therefore in other similar circumstances. The normative teaching is how to apply the various principles of God's word, in this case, the headship of man (properly understood), the avoidance of shame, and the avoidance of anything that would hinder acceptance of the gospel.[55]

Similarly, Klyne Snodgrass comments, 'Nothing may be labelled "cultural" and forgotten. All the Bible is culturally conditioned; that is, it arises from within a culture and is addressed to a culture. Still *all* the Bible is instruction for us.'[56]

Even the most conservative understand the need to interpret verses in their original cultural context when it come to verses 9–10, as is evident from the jewellery and pearls, to say nothing of the expensive clothes, which are seen in many conservative churches. Equally, the same process of applicatory translation is undertaken with reference to Paul's later instruction to put qualified widows on 'the list' of widows. I know of no church that maintains such a list. Why, then, are these verses treated differently?

The essential point is that the way people behave and relate in the church should do nothing that in the cultural circumstances of the time would bring the gospel into disrepute. The women of Ephesus were being unhealthily influenced by their culture and dressing and asserting authority in inappropriate ways, especially as they showed a marked ignorance of the doctrines of their faith and had succumbed to the false teaching found in the various pagan religions which surrounded them.

5. How do the words apply?

a. Complementarian approaches

Complementarians have taken these words as expressly forbidding women from occupying a teaching office in the church. While accepting that women can, and do, legitimately exercise a range of gifts, including those of sharing prophetic messages, a protective hedge is built around the 'formally designate leadership role', namely, that of the elder which, on the basis of 1 Timothy 3:2, must involve teaching.[57] 'God,' claims Schreiner, 'is not an equal opportunity

---

[55] W. L. Liefeld, 'Women, Submission and Ministry in 1 Corinthians', in Mickelsen, *Women*, p. 153. Although writing about 1 Cor. 11, the same argument holds for 1 Tim. 2.

[56] K. R. Snodgrass, 'Galatians 3:28: Conundrum or solution?', in Mickelsen, *Women*, p. 167.

[57] Blomberg, *Two Views*, pp. 152–153.

employer – at least as far as the installation into ministry is concerned'.[58] He and other complementarians have been at pains recently to argue this in no way implies the inferiority of women, as earlier hierarchalists might have believed. But the fact of 'equality of personhood does not rule out difference in role'.[59] So, Schreiner concludes, 'prohibiting a woman from teaching or exercising authority over a man applies to the task of an elder, for elders have a unique responsibility to teach and rule in God's church'.[60] Similarly, Hurley's understanding of 1 Timothy 2 and 3 leads him to 'conclude that Paul taught that the office of elder/bishop/presbyter was restricted to men'.[61]

This, it is said, was not a temporary measure but one which, because it was based on 'the order of creation'[62] which enshrined the headship of men, applies for all time.[63] Consequently, complementarians do not believe that women should be ordained, or occupy the pastoral office, or have teaching or governing authority in the church. Piper and Grudem go so far as to say 'We do not believe God genuinely calls women to be pastors'.[64]

There are at least three difficulties with this position. First, it assumes a particular interpretation of 1 Timothy 2:11–15 that, as we have set out above, is not by any means as well-founded as its proponents would suggest. Other interpretations are preferable.

However, even if one was to grant that interpretation, the application to contemporary ministry is certainly not obvious and incurs a second major difficulty. Quite apart from the fact that Paul does not link his prohibitions on women teaching to their filling 'offices' in the church, even though he does go on to talk of elders and deacons, this position requires the adoption of an anachronistic view of the

[58] Schriener, *Two Views*, pp. 288–289.

[59] Schreiner, *Two Views*, p. 288. Kevin Giles questions whether the recent emphasis on role differentiation is not foreign to Scripture and sees it as eisegesis not exegesis, since 'The Bible consistently holds that our maleness and femaleness are grounded in our God-given nature, not in the things we do' (*The Trinity and Subordinationism: The Doctrine of God and the Contemporary Gender Debate* [Downers Grove: IVP, 2002], pp. 177–194. The quotation is from p. 181.) There are differences but they are not differences of role. See Storkey, *Created or Constructed?*, pp. 64–87.

[60] Schreiner, *Two Views*, p. 311.

[61] Hurley, *Man and Woman*, p. 233. Similarly, Knight, *New Testament Teaching*, pp. 40, 65–67; Moo, *RBMW*, pp. 185–87; J. Piper and W. Grudem, 'An Overview of Central Concerns', *RBMW*, pp. 70–82; Schreiner, 'The Valuable Ministries of Women in the Context of Male Leadership', *RBMW*, pp. 218–221.

[62] For a critique of the 'order of creation' concept see Giles, *The Trinity*, pp. 170–179.

[63] Many complementarians curiously restrict their application of male headship to God's order for the family and the church and exclude society outside the church.

[64] Piper and Grudem, *RBMW*, p. 77.

'office of elder' or 'the pastoral office' on the text.[65] To relate Paul's words to contemporary patterns of ordination (which in any case are widely divergent across the denominations) or contemporary patterns of leadership as a 'settled office' is misguided. Significantly, the word 'office' is not used and the idea of Paul having the equivalent of contemporary fixed positions in mind is 'a figment of our modern imagination'.[66] Leadership in the New Testament church was much more fluid and radical than it is in contemporary denominations[67] and its 'most structured view of ministry' in the Pastorals, more charismatic than found in any contemporary denominations.[68] So to make a straight equation between Paul's instruction to women to keep silent and contemporary questions of ordination demands a leap over a wide canyon. Or, to change the analogy, the dogmatic superstructure that forbids women from being pastors and teachers today is built on a very flimsy foundation. To ask of the New Testament whether a woman should be 'ordained' is to ask the wrong question. The New Testament would ask whether anyone should be ordained in the contemporary sense.

The third problem is caused by reality, both historical and contemporary. Whatever we may believe about the place of women in authoritative teaching roles in the church, God has used women in such positions down the centuries and still does so today, in spite of discrimination against them in much of the church. He uses them not only to teach women, which complementarians would find acceptable, but also to teach men, which they do not. Craig Blomberg, himself a complementarian, sees this as a complicating issue:

> Countless women from Western cultures have been permitted to preach, teach, evangelize, and in general lead evangelical ministries in non-Western countries – 'on the mission field' – when their sending churches would never permit such practices 'back home'. Can this be anything other than a subtle racism that in essence says other cultures are so inferior that a double standard can be established for them?[69]

[65] Knight's use of 'Minister' in the outline of his commentary as in 'A Good Minister's Discipline' and 'How the Minister Should Exhort Others' is misleading and anachronistic. *Pastoral Epistles*, ix.

[66] Belleville, *Two Views*, p. 196–197. Elsewhere Belleville points out 'teaching was an activity not an office, . . . a gift not a position of authority . . . ' (*DBE*, p. 221.)

[67] See Derek Tidball, *Ministry by the Book: New Testament Patterns for Pastoral Leadership* (Nottingham: Apollos and Downers Grove: IVP Academic, 2008), esp. pp. 86–106, 142–145, 151–161.

[68] D. L. Bartlett, *Ministry in the New Testament* (Minneapolis: Fortress Press, 1993), p. 188.

[69] Blomberg, *Two Views*, p. 127.

Equally condescending, as mentioned previously, is the idea that women may play the role of teacher until the church is established and its institution formalized, at which time the women have to move over and submit to male authority.[70] It should be honestly acknowledged that many men have assumed positions of teaching authority who are far less able, gifted or informed than women, to the detriment of the church. One's authority to teach is not a matter of gender but of one's ability to faithfully explain and apply God's word to a congregation.[71]

In practice, complementarians 'are now doing their best to insist that women have many opportunities for ministry in the church and that they must be used in every possible way', short of a senior teaching role.[72] The area of restriction has been shrinking and is currently tiny, but significant for all concerned. The restriction is also 'arbitrary' or inconsistent, in the eyes of many, 'as churches that sing hymns to music written by women and read and publicly cite books, both devotional and scholarly, written by women must surely see'.[73]

Just as the early church re-examined its understanding of Amos' prophecy[74] and revised its practice at the so-called 'Council of Jerusalem'[75] in the light of what they saw God doing, so perhaps we should examine traditional interpretations of verses of Scripture that seem to be contradicted both by other passages of Scripture and by the way God is working in and through the church today, and has done since Pentecost.[76]

b. Egalitarian views

So how do those who do not see the teaching of 1 Timothy 2:11–15 as permanently forbidding leadership in the local church, especially when it involves a teaching responsibility, understand these verses?[77]

[70] See p. 203.

[71] Graham Cole, 'Women teaching Men the Bible: What's the Problem?', *Zadok Perspectives* 95 (December 2007).

[72] I. H. Marshall, writes, 'the Gospel does not change but our perception of it may need revision', in A. F. Johnson (ed.), *How I Changed my Mind about Women in Leadership* (Grand Rapids: Zondervan, 2010), p. 147.

[73] Marshall, in Johnson, *How I Changed*, p. 147.

[74] Amos 9:11–12.

[75] Acts 15:5–29.

[76] Those who fear this argument will lead to a revision of understanding about homosexual practice, which Scripture is unequivocally against, should read W. J. Webb, *Slaves, Women and Homosexuals: Exploring the Hermeneutics of Cultural Analysis* (Downers Grove: IVP, 2001). See also R. A. J. Gagnon, *The Bible and Homosexual Practice: Texts and Hermeneutics* (Nashville: Abingdon, 2001).

[77] On the hermeneutical principle see France's excellent *Women in Ministry*.

Here is a true apostolic command that needs, like all Scripture, to be interpreted in its context. Given the particular wording Paul uses and the fact that a flat understanding of these words would appear to be in conflict with earlier more 'permissive' (and clearer[78]) statements about the role of women, we must ask what the particular circumstances are which have provoked them. Cultural influences outside the church, both from Rome and in Ephesus itself, were causing some uneducated women to push better-informed men out of the way and introduce false ideas into the church. These ideas included the 'right' to wear inappropriate dress, to adopt uppity attitudes rather than live in mutual submission to one another, to have the freedom to talk nonsense, to spurn marriage and avoid bearing and nurturing children. This was bringing the gospel into disrepute in their society. At this stage, then, they should 'shut up and listen', taking warning from the story of Adam and Eve. Freedom in Christ was not a licence to do what they wanted but a freedom to live in *faith, holiness and love.* One day they would experience perfect freedom, although it would never be licence, but for the moment there was the need to be sensitive to the destructive cultural signals their behaviour was transmitting. They needed to realize that 'progress towards [the] goal of full equality cannot be made if either gender is asserting de-humanizing power over each other'.[79]

For women in Ephesus to teach and wrest authority from men was totally inappropriate for several reasons. This did not mean it would always be so or that Paul was laying down some fixed form of gender distinction that would determine a leadership structure for all time. What he was doing was:

- encouraging the uneducated to learn about the faith;
- forbidding the untaught (in this case women) from setting themselves up as teachers in the church;
- insisting that the common Christian virtue of submission be applied to learning as well as to marriage;
- instructing the church not to behave in ways which would undermine the gospel in the eyes of society;
- using Old Testament Scripture as a means of teaching endurance and providing encouragement to persevere;[80]
- assuring them they would not miss out on God's salvation if they contently accepted their place in an ordered society;
- and directing attention to the more important issues of *faith, love and hope with propriety.*

[78] France, *Women in Ministry*, p. 70.
[79] Bailey, 'Women in', p. 21.
[80] Rom. 15:4.

In a very different cultural context these same principles would need to be applied differently. First, the position of women in our society is very different. Secondly, the nature of teaching is very different than it was in Ephesus before the canonical Bible, which is what any Christian teacher should be explaining, was available. In the light of this J. I. Packer explains,

> I think it is an open question whether in our day Paul would have forbidden a woman to teach from the Bible. It is an open question whether he would have regarded what happened to Eve in the Garden of Eden as sufficient reason for forbidding a woman to teach from the Bible. When you teach from the Bible, in any situation at all, what you are saying to people is, 'Look, I am trying to tell you what it says. I speak as to wise men and women. You have your Bibles. You follow along. You judge what I say.' No claim to personal authority with regard to the substance of the message is being made at all. It seems to me that this significant difference between teaching then and teaching now does, in fact, mean that the prohibition on women preaching and teaching need not apply.[81]

Today, Paul is likely to argue that the refusal to permit women to exercise leadership in the church is what brings the gospel into disrepute. If Paul were writing now, he would surely be rebuking members of the church, both men and women, for compromising with the secular and self-obsessed values of our society and doing so by drawing attention to specific things he would not need to explain, for they would be understood as part of our cultural environment. And he would be instructing the church by reference to biblical illustrations, examples and warnings.

Given all that Paul writes elsewhere by way of positive appreciation about his female co-workers, who obviously were well instructed in the faith, we suspect he would be rejoicing at the many women who exercise their wonderful teaching and leadership gifts in the church, for the sake of the gospel and the glory of Christ.

6. Concluding comment

Examining the particular words Paul uses to prohibit women from exercising teaching authority over men in the church and reading them in the light of the contexts both of the rest of 1 Timothy and

---

[81] J. I. Packer, *The Proceedings of the Conference On Biblical Interpretation* (Nashville: Broadman, 1988), pp. 11–15.

the social changes of the day leads us to believe that Paul's prohibition was never meant as a fixed principle, built on a creation principle, for all time. Rather it was a wise prohibition in the circumstances, that needs to be taken seriously and applied and reapplied (not just to women) wherever such circumstances are repeated. There are many people, men and women, who, often with well-meaning but ill-judged enthusiasm, set themselves up as teachers and leaders who have not first been learners and who should be encouraged to adopt the humble and teachable attitude that Paul commands the women in Ephesus to demonstrate.

1 Timothy 5:3–16
20. Women in widowhood

'Christianity seems to have been especially successful among women', writes Henry Chadwick, historian of the early church.[1] And Rodney Stark, in a sociological study of the rise of Christianity, comments on the irony that, 'Amidst contemporary denunciations of Christianity as patriarchal and sexist, it is easily forgotten, that the early church was . . . especially attractive to women . . . '[2] All the evidence suggests that there was a great influx of women converts to Jesus Christ, because women were accorded greater respect, treated with greater dignity, and found greater freedom in Christian communities than in the other religions of the time.[3]

The success of the early Christians in winning women to Christ brought with it some practical problems. From the earliest days of the church in Jerusalem, as Acts 6 reports, there were a significant number of widows among the converts for whom the early church provided sustenance. Some widows were wealthy and contributed generously to the support of the Christian mission,[4] but many were not and needed support.

The church soon developed a reputation for offering practical support to needy widows. It was right that they should have done so, since the God whom Christians worshipped had a special concern for 'widows and orphans'[5] and the Christ whom they followed had

[1] H. Chadwick, *The Early Church* (Harmondsworth: Penguin Books, 1967), p. 58.
[2] R. Stark, *The Rise of Christianity: A Sociologist Reconsiders History* (Princeton: Princeton University Press, 1996), p. 95. The particular quotation relates to a later period but applies equally to the church of the New Testament era.
[3] Chadwick, *Early Church*, pp. 58–60; M. Green, *Evangelism in the Early Church* (London: Hodder and Stoughton, 1970), pp. 118, 175–178; Stark, *Rise of Christianity*, pp. 95–128; B. B. Thurston, *The Widows: A Women's Ministry in the Early Church* (Minneapolis: Fortress Press, 1989), p. 41.
[4] Luke 8:3.
[5] Exod. 22:22; Deut. 10:18; Pss. 68:5; 146:9; Isa. 1:17; Mal. 3:5.

demonstrated special compassion towards them.[6] Even so, the practice of the Jerusalem church, which was followed elsewhere, proved unsustainable without adjustment as numbers grew.[7] The support offered could be abused and seen as 'a soft touch', encouraging what later came to be known as 'rice Christians', that is those who converted for the material support they could derive from their new religious allegiance, rather than for genuine motives of faith.

So, late in the New Testament period, the apostle Paul issued ethical and practical guidance so that the church could apply its compassion wisely to the most needy, make the most of limited resources and avoid gullibility. Hence the last extended comment about women in the Bible and the most extensive treatment of any group in 1 Timothy, concerns the treatment of widows, old and young, needy and not-so-needy.[8] The subject may not be as exciting as debates about women in leadership but it testifies to God's care for people in the ordinariness of their lives.

Paul starts by instructing the church at Ephesus to *Give proper recognition to those widows who are really in need* (3). He actually tells them to 'honour' (*tima*) needy widows, using the same word as the fourth commandment uses about honouring parents.[9] His thinking is governed by that commandment, as becomes evident in his emphasis on filial duty, and his instructions are essentially an application of this general law to a particular situation. But to ensure appropriate honour was shown to widows in their varying circumstances, judgments had to be made about the genuineness of their need and so Paul carefully sets out a set of criteria by which to make that judgment. He also insists that the situation be clearly and openly communicated so that all in the church, givers and receivers, would understand the basis of their operation (7).

1. Widows who were already supported (3–4, 8)

The first step was to establish whether or not the widow had a genuine need for which the church should take responsibility or whether she had children or grandchildren who would have been expected to show respect to her by supporting her financially. This was the accepted social norm and, in fact, was required by the Roman law. This is why Paul says in verse 8, in what seems like harsh tones,

[6] Mark 12:41–44; Luke 4:26; 7:11–17.

[7] B. W. Winter, *Roman Wives, Roman Widows: The Appearance of New Women and the Pauline Communities* (Grand Rapids: Eerdmans, 2003), p. 128.

[8] P. H. Towner, *The Letters to Timothy and Titus*, NICNT (Grand Rapids: Eerdmans, 2006), p. 333.

[9] Exod. 20:12; Deut. 5:16 (LXX).

that any Christian who failed to take their responsibility seriously *has denied the faith and is worse than an unbeliever.*[10] Non-Christian families accepted their responsibilities, so Christian families who failed to do so were put in a very unfavourable light. But if non-Christian families had a reason to support their widows, Christian families had even greater reason for doing so since it meant they were *put[ting] their religion into practice* and as a result *pleasing God* (4). The genuineness of a person's faith was clearly not measured only by belief in right doctrine (a real concern of 1 Timothy) but also by evidence of right practice.

If widows had this means of support it was unreasonable and unnecessary to expect the church to show them honour by offering more. Where such support was available it was not the responsibility of the Christian church to provide for widows.

2. Widows who were in need of support (5–10)

Not all widows, however, would have received support from their families. For some the dowry left might have been inadequate to cover her needs, or they might simply be too poor to fulfil their duty. Others would not have shared the widow's faith and refused support. Still others might be negligent. Some widows might be entirely on their own. So, even discounting the widows who did not need support, there would be a good number left whose situation demanded consideration. How was the church to discern which of them to support, since it was unlikely that they would have the resources to support everybody who might ask for it?

Here Paul lays down a number of criteria by which to make the judgment.

a. Authenticate their spirituality (5–6)

Was the thrust of the widow's life one of devotion to God, or self-indulgent luxury, even, self-centred pleasure seeking?[11] The former deserved support whereas those pursuing the latter were paradoxically spiritually *dead* even while they were still alive (6) and had no claim on the church. The church's material provision was not to be used to fund the living of immoral or luxurious lifestyles.

The deserving widow would be marked by two characteristics: trusting in God and persistence in prayer. Perhaps their dire circumstances had driven them to intensify both their faith and their prayer

[10] Winter, *Roman Wives*, p. 126.
[11] The verb *spatalaō* (*lives for pleasure*) could refer to living luxuriously or immorally. See I. H. Marshall, *The Pastoral Epistles*, ICC (Edinburgh: T & T Clark, 1999), p. 588.

life.[12] Jeremiah had assured the widows of his day that they could depend on God[13] and these women were encouraged not to demonstrate anxiety or frantically try to fix things, as if they alone were concerned about their lives, but by a quiet spirit show that they truly believed a good and sovereign God would care for them. This would free them from a preoccupation with their own problems and release them to develop a ministry of intercession and prayer on behalf of others. Anna, the widowed prophet who 'never left the temple but worshipped night and day, fasting and praying', was a model for all such women.[14]

From the early church onwards older and single women have exercised this crucial ministry of intercession. Only eternity will reveal how much the success of those who are in the front line of ministry and mission was due to the committed prayer of those who regularly held their ministries up before God in prayer. I remember visiting an elderly female believer and discovering her uncharacteristically excited that a certain missionary was coming to preach the following Sunday. I assumed they were long-standing friends but discovered to my surprise that she had never met him before but had prayed daily for him for the last twenty-five years! She was a devout woman who, if the circumstances had demanded it, would have been truly worthy of support.

b. Check their age (9)

In our society it is considered impolite to ask a woman their age, but Paul says that *no woman may be put on the list of widows unless she is over sixty.* It becomes apparent later why he introduces this age restriction, when he addresses younger women. Sixty was recognized as 'elderly' in the ancient world.[15] The age is consistent with the duties that should be undertaken which Paul sets out in the next verse, that did not require much physical exertion. But Paul's words raise an intriguing question.

Paul speaks about enrolling widows on a *list,* which suggests that the support of widows was neither haphazard nor informal, with all the potential that had for favouritism, but openly done and properly organized so the church as a whole would consent to it. The word *katalegein* is a technical term for registration, used, for example, for enlisting troops. But what did such enrolment entail? The picture presented suggests that those 'enrolled' undertook special vows to

---

[12] Towner, *Timothy and Titus*, p. 341.
[13] Jer. 49:11. Thurston, *Widows*, p. 46.
[14] Luke 2:36–38. Thurston, *Widows*, p. 50.
[15] Thurston, *Widows*, p. 47.

eschew the search for another husband, and commit themselves to life-long singleness in the service of Christ.[16]

Some make much of the existence of an official list[17] and see within these words the foundations of the later religious orders where countless women have devoted their lives to doing good works. But whatever happened in subsequent history, it makes too much of it to see anything of the nature of a female order of ministry in Paul's words.[18] The point is simpler: serious attention should be paid to the way in which the church supported widows so that those who were worthy of it received the care they deserved. It was not to be undertaken in a hit-or-miss fashion, nor was it a one-way commitment. While the church committed themselves to the qualified widows, those widows, in turn, committed themselves to celibacy and to undertake ministries that demonstrated their devotion to Christ.

c. Examine their track record and behaviour (9–10)

If a widow passed these hurdles, further questions needed to be considered. It would be all too easy for a widow to enter 'a conversion of convenience' and become a Christian late in life purely for the sake of gaining material support, without any genuine evidence of having lived a godly life. To avoid gullibility,[19] Paul insists that consideration be given to their track record, a key element of which was whether they had proved a reliable partner to their husbands. *Faithful to her husband,* means she was not to have the reputation of being 'a flighty woman', who 'was an object of scorn' or guilty of sexual immorality.[20]

Their past record should also testify to the *good deeds* they had undertaken as a matter of course, not simply in order to gain support late in the day. These deeds should still be evident. Paul's illustrations are essentially acts of practical service, *such as bringing up children,*[21] *showing hospitality, washing the feet of the Lord's people, helping those in trouble,* before concluding with the catch-all phrase *devoting herself to all kinds of good deeds.*

[16] Thurston, *Widows*, p. 46.
[17] Thurston, *Widows*, p. 53.
[18] See Marshall, *Pastoral Epistles*, pp. 575–579; Towner, *Timothy and Titus*, p. 345.
[19] We once had a young man living with us for some months on bail as an alternative to his being remanded in custody. He spent those months, in the nicest possible way, educating us as to how gullible Christians were and how he and his friends could fleece us quite easily!
[20] Thurston, *Widows*, p. 47.
[21] The past tense suggests this is primarily a reference to bringing up her own children but it may not be restricted to that and could include caring for the children of others, such as orphans. Towner, *Timothy and Titus*, p. 347.

Later history came to particularly associate these acts with the diaconal order, but while there is a natural affinity between the two, Paul, as mentioned, does not have such an institutional order in mind here. In many respects, one would expect all Christians to have undertaken such deeds, since all were called to serve one another. When Jesus instructed his disciples to 'wash one another's feet' his words were not directed either originally or exclusively to widows![22] But Paul is making the more obvious point that widows were in a position to 'devote' themselves to such tasks and, rather than sitting around idly or expecting everyone to serve them, should occupy themselves usefully in doing so.

How grateful the church should be for countless widows (and other single women too) who have been living examples of what Paul commends here. It is remarkable how many women, free from their own family responsibilities, have generously provided hospitality and support to others, acted as surrogate aunts or grandmothers, and engaged in tireless acts of practical service. They should not be taken for granted but honoured for doing so and God praised for them. However, there are other strands of widowhood becoming evident in wider (at least) British society which the church should discourage. There are relatively wealthy widows living off their late husband's pensions who flit from one self-indulgent enjoyment to another, without any concern to invest in the lives of others. Others become pre-occupied with their own problems, or what they feel they deserve, and demonstrate quite the opposite attitudes and actions to the humility and servanthood Paul commends here. Not all widows are godly or outward-looking in their orientation; there is nothing in the status of being a widow that automatically makes them so.

Paul's concentration on the practical deeds widows might be expected to show is illustrative rather than exhaustive. When writing to Titus[23] about 'older women' (not just the more defined category of 'widows') he again encourages them to live godly lives but also draws attention to the vital role they can play in the training of younger women. How this was done is not specified, but however restricted one might argue a woman's teaching role might have been in the early church, no one dissents from the idea that older women played a significant part in training young women and children in the faith.

From this assessment with its concentration on 'age, sexual morality and attested good works',[24] a group of widows would emerge who

[22] John 13:1–17.
[23] 2:2–5.
[24] Marshall, *Pastoral Epistles*, p. 591.

had genuine needs and were deserving not of the grudging support of the churches but of their free and generous assistance. In making provision for them, the church demonstrates itself to be the true family of Christ, and binds itself together in love. It proved a powerful counter-cultural witness in a world that bred loneliness, was fractured by division, and treated many widows as insignificant (unless, of course, they were wealthy and likely to prove useful).

4. Widows who should not be supported (11–15)

Having ministered in Plymouth for some years we got used to conducting the funerals of elderly ladies who had been widowed for thirty or forty years. They had often only been married briefly when their newly-acquired military husbands were killed in action in the Second World War or lost their lives through the bombing that rained down on that city. Their opportunities for remarriage were restricted; given the war, men were in short supply. While we knew them as elderly widows, many had once been young widows and faced tough choices about their futures and the bringing up of their young children as single parents without too much welfare support.

Cities like Ephesus would have been familiar with the phenomenon of young widows. Forty per cent of those aged between forty and fifty were estimated to be widows in the Roman Empire. Probably a third of all women in the empire were widowed.[25] Women were widowed young for all sorts of reasons. Husbands tended to be older than wives and would usually die well before their spouses. Warfare and work-related accidents would have claimed a disproportionate number of males, although women faced their own challenges in giving birth. Epidemics swept many away, although would have been indiscriminate as far as gender is concerned.[26]

It was, then, anything but a hypothetical situation Paul addresses as he deals with the question of younger widows. Unlike those who were over sixty, Paul says that the church should not register them on the list of those who would receive support. He then explains his reasons and suggests an alternative way forward for them.

a. The temptations they face (11–12)

Being younger, the winds of sexual desire had not naturally moderated as with those who were sixty or more and those still of child-bearing age were likely to want to be sexually active or remarry. The image

[25] Winter, *Roman Wives*, p. 124.
[26] On the crucial role Christian compassion and nursing played during epidemics in the spread of the gospel see Stark, *Rise of Christianity*, pp. 73–94.

that young widows would be promiscuous was quite a common one,[27] but Paul seems to have something more specific in mind when he confronts their *sensuous desires* or, more accurately, their 'wanton behaviour'.[28] His focus is on their actions rather than their emotions as is plain from what follows. In remarrying, he says, they are reneging on *their dedication to Christ* and in so doing *bring judgement on themselves, because they have broken their first pledge.*

There was nothing wrong with their remarrying. In fact, that is the advice Paul gives them a few verses later. So what does Paul's strong denunciation of their behaviour mean here and why, in apparent contradiction to verse 14, does he write about them remarrying here in such harsh and unsympathetic terms? The clue lies in his references to *their dedication to Christ* and their having *broken their first pledge.* Being registered for support by the church, it seems, involved a commitment to stay single and be fully devoted to undertaking the sort of acts of service mentioned in verse 10 for all *the Lord's people.* Marriage would have been a betrayal of that pledge to remain single and, since the responsibilities of one's more immediate family would rightly take precedence, require a withdrawal from the life of service to others that such a register entailed.

Bruce Winter makes the further point that Paul may also be alluding to the fact that her desire to remarry may have caused her to abandon her faith because a prospective husband may not have chosen to marry her if she had remained committed to Christ.[29]

Younger widows faced some stiff challenges because of the tensions between their physical virility, emotional needs and their social isolation. And that was precisely why it was unwise for the church to support them through the widows' register. Enrolling them would either trap them into a life-long commitment they might come to resent or cause them subsequently to break their vow and remarry, possibly outside the faith altogether. Paul knows that it is better, as Ecclesiastes 5:5 advises, 'not to make a vow than to make one and not fulfil it'. So an alternative solution to their very real plight is suggested.

b. The influence they exercise (13)

Before providing the better solution to the problem faced by younger women, however, Paul realistically examines the influence they could have (or were actually having) on the church at Ephesus since as free agents, who had not entered into any covenant either in marriage or with the church, they were not carrying onerous responsibilities.

[27] Winter, *Roman Wives*, p. 123.
[28] Winter, *Roman Wives*, p. 132.
[29] Winter, *Roman Wives*, p. 137.

He sees them, with time on their hands, as idle, flitting about from house to house, interfering where they have no business doing so, and also talking *nonsense, saying things that ought not to be said.* Idleness was considered a vice in the ancient world and industrious domestic activity such as spinning and weaving held up as an ideal.[30] It is true to life that the less we have to do the less we want to do. The young widow, without responsibilities, was more than likely to fall into bad habits and it was not the responsibility of the church to enable them to live a life of 'subsidised leisure'.[31] Lying behind Paul's concern may equally be the specific influence of the new Roman women who prized the enjoyment of a social life above that of domestic industry.

Again, Paul is true to present-day life in pointing out the temptation to gossip about others in the church or what the leaders of the church are (or are not) doing when we have time on our hands and meet up with others. Our conversations can sometimes be anything other than 'full of grace [and] seasoned with salt',[32] even if we excuse them under the guise of saying 'I'm only saying this so you can pray about it'. But as with the reference to idleness, something deeper might also have been in Paul's mind. It may not simply be foolish chit-chat that he is condemning but a particular form of conversation. These young widows were probably the target of the false teachers in Ephesus and their idling the time away in silly conversation from house to house is one of the chief ways by which the false teaching was spreading. That too is not an unknown phenomenon in the contemporary church. Some exciting preacher breezes into town with a distorted, speculative or ill-founded Christian message, or something has been picked up on the internet which may have no real biblical foundation, but Christians excitedly gossip about it and it becomes viral in the church. In using the phrase, *saying things they ought not to*, Paul echoes what he says about false teachers in Titus 1:11, and links it to what he says earlier in 1 Timothy itself about false teachers who, 'do not know what they are talking about or what they so confidently affirm'.[33] So Paul may be particularly concerned to curtail the spreading of heresy by these excited but immature young women.

It is not, of course, only young widows (or only women) who have the potential to do damage to the Christian fellowship by gossiping and spreading of false ideas. Nor are all widows, whatever their age, guilty of living in the way Paul condemns. But, given the situation at

[30] Winter, *Roman Wives*, p. 134.
[31] Marshall, *Pastoral Epistles*, p. 577.
[32] Col. 4:6.
[33] 1:7. Towner, *Timothy and Titus*, pp. 354–355.

Ephesus, the young widows there seem to have been subject as a group to bad influences and to have a detrimental effect on the church, whilst having very real needs, which it was necessary to address.

c. The advice they received (14–15)

The church is sometimes very good at condemning the behaviour of people who have genuine needs but doing nothing to cure the problems that gave rise to their behaviour in the first place. Paul avoids that mistake and gives a practical way forward so that young widows will not find themselves with time on their hands to fill with idle gossip and free-wheeling lifestyles. He advises that they remove the problem by getting married.[34] If they have not pledged themselves to a life of singleness and service they are, as widows, free to do so. Doing so would fill their lives in meaningful ways as they fulfilled their marital responsibilities to their husband, looked after their children, and ran their households, which was often in itself a skilled and demanding managerial task. Within the context of marriage they would, in fact, be imitating the virtues of the older women.[35] This would mean they would *give the enemy no opportunity for slander*, since the opportunity to do so would be cut off at its source. Removing the source of temptation remains one of the best ways to combat it. Denying Satan the opportunity to tempt us is always wiser than allowing him to get a foot in the door in the hope we will prove stronger than him.

Paul does not lay this course of action down as a command but expresses his wish (*boulomai*) in strong terms. So this cannot be dismissed as merely his personal opinion for he writes as a wise apostolic pastor and justifies his reasoning, not by reference to the Roman law which penalized widows between twenty and fifty who did not remarry,[36] but by reference to spiritual realities. Satan must have no opportunity to bring the gospel into disrepute as would have happened if widows had broken their vows after being registered by the church, or by their promiscuity if they remained single, or by their gossiping and spreading of heresy if they remained idle. His objective was that the church should behave in such a way that 'no one will malign the word of God'.[37]

---

[34] The directions he gives here are perfectly compatible with 1 Cor. 7 where Paul expresses his personal preference for singleness because there (a) he states 'it is better to marry than burn with passion' (v. 9) and (b) his instructions are in the different context of 'the present crisis' (v. 26) which is absent in 1 Tim.

[35] G. Fee, *1 and 2 Timothy, Titus*, NIBC (Peabody: Hendirckson, 1984), p. 123.

[36] Winter, *Roman Wives*, p. 125. The law referred to is *Lex Julia* of 17 BC.

[37] Titus 2:5.

4. Women who were supporting widows (16)

In concluding his discussion of widows, Paul encourages believing women who were already caring for widows to continue to do so and not to pass off their responsibilities to the church. This is probably a reference to married Christian women caring for their own relatives, although it could be directed to younger widows who were caring for older ones. If the latter, Paul is telling them they need not remarry but should remain loyal in their service to the older widow.[38] It might also be addressed to some of the wealthier women householders and businesswomen, like Lydia,[39] Chloe[40] or Nympha,[41] who were perhaps personally supporting widows. Why should the collective resources of the church be drained when there were other ways in which needy widows could be supported? In a culture like ours where people regularly cry, 'The Government should do something . . . ' or 'They (often the church leaders) should do something . . . ', we need reminding, as they did, that we should not pass the buck to others but do what we can ourselves before calling on the resources of God's people.

5. Concluding comment

The Bible's last extended comment about women is full of compassion about the ordinary situations they face in life. The church should honour widows who faced financial difficulties by providing them with support, rather than neglecting them. But this final word calls for a discerning not a sentimental compassion. It neither idealizes solutions nor idealizes widows. Some widows needed more support than others. Some faced different temptations than others. And each should be treated with respect and dignity as appropriate. Genuine need calls for support. Those who can take other initiatives to resolve their plight should do so. The church is not in the business of creating a dependency culture that denies people the need to take responsibility before God for their own lives, or curtails the liberty they have in Christ. Rather it should seek to act in such a way as to enable a growth in godliness, whatever one's circumstances.

The church has a long track record of providing for unsupported women. In the Victorian era, Edith Smallwood was one of several who took up the challenge and in 1866 founded a 'Society for the

---

[38] G. W. Knight III, *The Pastoral Epistles*, NIGNT (Grand Rapids: Eerdmans, 1992), p. 229.

[39] Acts 16:13–15.

[40] 1 Cor. 1:11.

[41] Col. 4:15.

Assistance of Ladies in Reduced Circumstances'.[42] Few Western churches today, however, have a formal register of widows they support since the improved welfare systems in many developed countries render such a system largely unnecessary. Paul 'is not mandating a widow's organisation in the church'[43] but he is setting out the guidelines should one be needed. In doing so, he is also demonstrating the radical challenge of the gospel. Outside of the Jewish synagogue, no institution provided support for widows.[44] It was left to the family to do so. But the church demonstrated a new care, witnessed to a new set of values, and offered a new solution as the community of the new humanity created by Christ.

The contemporary church needs to demonstrate the same creative, yet realistic, thinking in responding to people's needs. Paul's advice was designed to ensure that the church did nothing that would bring the gospel into disrepute, and we too should aim to avoid doing anything that will cause the gospel to be dishonoured. For us this means that we should be looking to people who need support and, given our different circumstances, these may well not be widows or even within the church. Among those in need of our discerning compassion there will probably still be a disproportionate number of women, younger perhaps than the widows of which Paul writes; abused perhaps, and let down by men in their lives; struggling perhaps to bring up a family as a single mother or to cope with an unwanted pregnancy. Paul's command challenges us not only to look after widows, or 'our own', but others who are vulnerable and unsupported in our society. 'Therefore, as we have opportunity, let us do good to all people, especially to those who belong to the family of believers.'[45]

---

[42] Details of the present day society can be found at <http://www.salrc.org>.
[43] Knight, *Pastoral Epistles*, p. 223.
[44] Winter, *Roman Wives*, p. 127.
[45] Gal. 6:10.

Afterword

Earlier in the book we referred to the need to assemble the pieces of the jigsaw Scripture provides so that we can view a complete picture of its teaching before rushing to a particular conclusion about the place of women in God's plans. Having now placed well over twenty significant and varied pieces on the table it is reasonable to ask what sort of picture they make. The picture is a busy one, populated with many different people, each of whom makes a contribution to the total composition. As in any complex picture some figures and features are more prominent than others and there are also differences in depth and perspective. Yet for all the diversity and complexity, the picture is not an incoherent one, still less a discordant one.

Women are created in the image of God, of equal worth to men, and as sinners are redeemed in Christ, in the same way as men. They play their full part both in the created world and the new community of Christ, bringing their own distinctive gender characteristics to bear in doing so, resulting in the great enrichment of the world and the church. They exercise a unique place as wives, child-bearers and mothers, but are not restricted to these roles. Gender distinction relates to character and personality rather than role. God's creation design was that men and women should complement each other as equals. Once sin entered the world other elements of distinction and notes of hierarchy are introduced which are symptoms of humanity's fall. In the new community of Christ, the marriage relationship is one of mutuality and relationships in the church involve mutual submission. While radically challenging the hierarchical notions of gender relationships which had become enshrined in Judaism and the classical world, the early Christians are advised to make concessions to the contemporary culture in order not to bring the gospel into disrepute before it had a chance of being heard. Such concessions are part of many examples where we are reminded that we have not fully entered into the new creation, however much of it we have already begun to experience, but live inevitably with some limitations such as physical illness and mortality in the present. Nonetheless, we are required to live now as much as we can in anticipation of entering into our full inheritance, where everyone and everything will be subject to God the Father and his Son alone.

The path taken

Changing the analogy, we have completed a long journey which has taken us through some very varied terrain. At times the scenery has been familiar, but at other times less so. At times we have been in the valley and seen the awful abuse that can be done to women, the awful evil that they themselves can perpetrate and the self-centred assertiveness of which they are capable. Sometimes we have climbed the peaks and experienced the high points as they delivered Israel, took brave initiatives, brought God's word to bear on situations, expressed their emotions and gifts to the full, or played courageous and strategic roles in the birth, life and death of the Messiah. At other times, we have journeyed through the level plains and seen them in more routine situations as wives and mothers, using their gifts as members of the body of Christ, or as vulnerable widows in need of support.

The journey that began in the Garden of Eden is not yet finished. The route taken through Scripture is one on which even those who differ in their judgment on its teaching about women mostly travel together. They part company at a number of significant points. Near the start they differ over whether the gender distinction involved male headship at creation or whether that entered as a result of the fall. They part company over the significance of women in leadership and as prophets, as to whether the first was exceptional due to male failure and the latter more limited than their male counterparts or not. They see the significance of women being the first to receive and announce the good news both of the incarnation of Christ and his resurrection from different perspectives. They are at variance over whether there being no 'male or female in Christ' is limited to the spiritual status of men and women or whether it embraces their roles in the church as well. They diverge over whether male headship or mutuality is the predominant principle in marriage and the church. They separate over whether women's roles in the church are restricted for all time or whether Paul was teaching some significant timeless principles which might have different applications today.

These important divergences, however, should not obscure the extent to which Christians across the spectrum of complementarianism and egalitarianism travel together. All rejoice that women are made in the image of God, as are men. They rejoice in women and men having significant roles to play in bringing fruitfulness to God's world. They affirm that the creation of 'male and female' is an act of God in which the distinctiveness of each gender completes what is lacking in the other. They affirm that women, as well as men, are sinners in need of forgiveness. They affirm Jesus treated women with unparalleled dignity and accepted them fully as his disciples and worthy of being taught. They affirm there is only one way of salvation for both women and men. They affirm women have significant roles to play in the family and the church. They affirm that abuse of women is sinful and that when the social or economic arrangements of a society makes them vulnerable they are worthy of special care and attention.

We are not yet at our final destination. The journey continues. The new creation, begun in Christ, has not yet arrived in its fullness. In the meantime, we believe the teaching of Scripture directs us towards the path of equality between women and men in Christ. We cannot find what would be recognized as a contemporary equality agenda ready-made in the Bible. The Bible must be read within its own context before we use it to address ours. But, our review of Scripture leads us to believe that very significant progress was made towards egalitarianism in the course of the unfolding story of redemption and that the signposts point us unmistakably in that direction.

This is not to say that equality will or should eradicate all differences and we would be much the poorer if it did. Equality in Christ did not mean a Jew was any less a Jew, or a Greek a Greek. Ethnic and cultural diversity brought out the full flavour of reconciliation in Christ. What is true of Jew and Greek is even more true of male and female. God created them to be biologically different, with its attendant difference of character, for a purpose, and if we seek to deny this we will deny ourselves much human richness. Nonetheless there are many cultural interpretations which have been imposed on those differences which are not inherent in the creation distinction itself, such as those which mean women are ineligible for certain roles or not as worthy of education or respect as men. It is these cultural interpretations which should be removed in order that women might play their fullest part in the church and the world.

Current location

It is a sad but inevitable fact of life that Christians who uphold the authority of Scripture equally differ in its interpretation, not least on the subject of this book. If only it were as easy as expounding the texts and all coming to an agreement as to their meaning! Our intention in this book has been to expound the texts as honestly as we can – not in ways we have always seen them but in ways which in the light of further study and experience we now believe to be true – and to encourage our readers to study the texts again for themselves.

We need to recognize the limitations of such an exercise and the wisdom of Timothy Webber's words when he writes:

> Though the role of women in the church is usually debated in theological and exegetical terms, the argument frequently has little to do with the Bible or theology. Academic types may actually believe that everything is going to be determined by the parsing of Greek verbs or what we can discover about first-century Greek culture. But for most people, such matters are simply beside the point. More important to them are personal concerns such as self-image, sexuality and relationships. There are people on both sides of this question who will not change their minds no matter how cogent or persuasive the exegetical arguments because they personally have too much at stake in the outcome.[1]

The role of women is one that provokes strong emotions in the church, on all sides. For some the equality of women is a matter of biblical justice for which we should vigorously fight, and is not to be cast aside as a secondary issue. For those with whom they disagree the issue is sometimes felt to be the Maginot Line,[2] which if crossed will lead to the downfall of biblical Christianity. Heart, as well as head, need to be taken into account as we speak with each other about this topic.

What is important across the spectrum of opinion is the attitude with which we debate and disagree. We need to listen to others with respect, permit others to share their interpretations fully, as we trust they will allow us to share ours, and seek to correct by persuasion. There is no room for strident politicking, on either side. Nor is it a place for self-assertion, whether of the 'my rights' mentality of some strands of rampant feminism or the 'I'm right' mentality of some strands of equally arrogant scholarship. However important one considers the topic, it would be difficult to assert it is of such central importance to the faith that it should be a matter of separation and division on a par with that of Paul's denunciation of the

---

[1] T. Webber, in A. Micklesen (ed.), *Women, Authority and the Bible* (Downers Grove: IVP, 1986), pp. 281–282.

[2] The Maginot Line was a fortified wall built by France prior to the Second World War along its borders with Germany and Italy and was considered impregnable.

Galatians where the core issues of grace and faith were at stake. Our disagreement on this issue is the place where we should aim for our words to be 'full of grace, seasoned with salt'[3] and where we should 'serve one another *humbly* in love'.[4] Sadly we do not always live up to that calling, as many, especially hurt women, can testify.[5]

The future ahead

Whatever the present location and struggles, the Bible points us to the future of the church by using the metaphor of it as the Bride of Christ. The choice of metaphor may not be without significance. The prophets had long portrayed God as Israel's husband and used the metaphor to call for her to live faithfully and eschew adultery.[6] That imagery is redesigned in the New Testament to apply to the church.

The imagery first occurs in 2 Corinthians 11:2 where Paul writes of the Corinthians, 'I promised you to one husband, to Christ, so that I might present you as a pure virgin to him'. The marriage lies in the future but it is essential for the bride to keep herself for her husband and not flirt with those who would lead her astray from Christ. The Corinthians were being seduced by 'super-apostles' who were seeking to supplant the preaching of the cross with a preaching of false power, but the seduction can come in many other forms as well. The metaphor occurs again in Ephesians 5:25–27, in the context of speaking about Christ's self-giving love for the church as a model of the husband's love for the wife, where it makes a much more inclusive reference to the church seeking to be free from any form of imperfection in preparation for her wedding day:

> Christ loved the church and gave himself up for her to make her holy, cleansing her by washing with water through the word, and to present her to himself as a radiant church, without stain or wrinkle or any other blemish, but holy and blameless.

The final reference occurs in Revelation 19:7 where, at the climax of history, the invitations to the wedding supper of the Lamb are issued and the wedding day has at last arrived.

[3] Col. 4:6.

[4] Gal. 5:13. Italics ours.

[5] For a moving (and disturbing) insight into what many women have experienced see G. G. Hull, *Equal to Serve: Women and Men in the Church and Home* (London: Scripture Union, 1987).

[6] Isa. 54:3–8; 62:4–5; Jer. 3:1–25; Ezek. 16:1–63; Hos. 1:1 – 3:5.

> Let us rejoice and be glad
> and give him glory!
> For the wedding of the Lamb has come,
> and his bride has made herself ready.
> Fine linen, bright and clean,
> was given to her to wear.

Part of our preparation for that day must involve the way we debate the place of women in the world and the church. Both male chauvinism and arrogant feminism tarnish the bride, who needs to be characterized by the virtues of purity, grace and love. But the day is coming when the debates will fall silent, the misunderstandings and half-right interpretations will be behind us, and the bride will have her eyes fully focused on her groom. Since this is our destiny, perhaps we should be encouraged to focus more on him now and less on our own agendas.

Study guide

HOW TO USE THIS STUDY GUIDE

The aim of this study guide is to help you get to the heart of what we have written and challenge you to apply what you learn to your own life. The questions have been designed for use by individuals or by small groups of Christians meeting, perhaps for an hour or two each week, to study, discuss and pray together. When used by a group with limited time, the leader should decide beforehand which questions are most appropriate for the group to discuss during the meeting and which should perhaps be left for group members to work through by themselves or in smaller groups during the week.

PREVIEW. Use the guide and the contents pages as a map to become familiar with what you are about to read, your 'journey' through the book.

READ. Look up the Bible passages as well as the text.

ANSWER. As you read look for the answers to the questions in the guide.

DISCUSS. Even if you are studying on your own try to find another person to share your thoughts with.

REVIEW. Use the guide as a tool to remind you what you have learned. The best way of retaining what you learn is to write it down in a notebook or journal.

APPLY. Translate what you have learned into your attitudes and actions, considering your relationship with God, your personal life, your family life, your working life, your church life, your role as a citizen and your world-view.

Introduction (pp. 23–27)

1 Where have your ideas about women, God and the church come from? Reflect honestly about your culture, upbringing and the biblical teaching and experiences which have shaped you.
2 How do you expect reading this book to be helpful in your discipleship?

PART 1. FOUNDATIONS

Genesis 1:26–30; 2:18–25
1. Women as the image of God (pp. 31–43)

1 What do men and women share in common according to Genesis 1:26–27 and what is distinctive? Reflect on what that means for your identity, whether you are male or female (pp. 32–33).

2 Is the argument helpfully made that *'ādām* has both a specific meaning, the man Adam and the generic meaning 'humankind' (p. 34)? Does this explain something of our difficulty with understanding the creation of woman?

3 Note the different ways the term 'helper' is understood, and consider how far that is from the common view of a helper being subordinate (pp. 36–38). What added insight does Craig Blomberg's phrase 'corresponding to him' give to our understanding (p. 37)?

4 What are the important features of the creation of woman, (pp. 38–42)?

5 Explain the possible connotations of the naming of Eve (p. 40).

6 Intimacy and mutual relationship is built into the earliest themes of women's relationships with men. Does this surprise you (p. 42)? Is it the image usually portrayed by the church?

7 Do you agree with the authors' comment that with 'equality, unity and mutuality [t]he compass has been set for the journey ahead' (p. 42)?

Genesis 3:1–24
2. Women and the fall of humanity (pp. 44–53)

1 'Generally speaking, women are more relational and nurturing and men given to more rational analysis and objectivity. Women are less prone than men to see the importance of doctrinal formulations.' How far do stereotypes shape our thinking and are they always wrong (p. 45)?

2 How plausible is the authors' argument that the genre of wisdom literature helps us understand why Eve was approached and not Adam (p. 46)?

3 Trace in Genesis 3 how Eve was led into disobedience and mistrust of God. What principles are at work that are relevant for women and men (pp. 46–48)?

4 Why does the apostle Paul not apportion blame to Eve for the fall of humanity in Romans 5:12–19 and 1 Corinthians 15:22 (cf. 1 Tim. 2:14) (p. 49)?
5 'Hers is a sin of initiative. His is a sin of acquiescence': can a distinction be made in blameworthiness in this context (p. 49)?
6 For Eve, what are the consequences of the fall which women following on from her have faced (pp. 50–53)?
7 Meditate on the effect of the fall for God the Creator, who made everything good, and that creation was so quickly corrupted by human flaws.

Galatians 3:26–28
3. Women and the new creation (pp. 54–64)

1 The authors suggest the world was divided in Paul's day by ethnicity, social status and gender (p. 55). Is there a similar divide today?
2 What main emphasis is Paul making in these verses and what is the context which provokes such a focus (pp. 57–58)?
3 Are you persuaded of complete equality before God in terms of function and relationship with God? Or does it appear to you to support equality in the image of God but with differing social roles?
4 How far should a gospel lifestyle compromise, in cross-cultural mission, over issues such as the role of women? Is 1 Corinthians 9:19–23 relevant and how does it square with Galatians 3:28?
5 Can you imagine, for the women who first heard these words, who were second-class in their culture and religion, what the impact would have been?

'Under the blessed spirit of Christianity, women have equal rights, equal privileges, and equal blessings, and let me add, they are equally useful' (p. 64).

6 How helpful is Adam Clarke's quote, above?

PART 2. WOMEN UNDER THE OLD COVENANT

Genesis 24:1–67; 25:19–34; 26:34 – 27:46
4. Family women (pp. 67–79)

1 'Procreation is thus elevated from a mechanical act to a sacramental act.' Would you agree that giving birth is a sacramental act (p. 68)?
2 What biblical principles can be drawn from this chapter about motherhood specifically and parenthood in general (pp. 69–70)?
3 How far is the celebration of Mothers' Day in churches and society today a positive reflection of the biblical understanding of motherhood (p. 69)?
4 Is it true that Rebekah illustrates a wider truth that all mothers are flawed human beings (pp. 70–75)? What indicators of the flawed nature of mothers are evident in contemporary culture?
5 'Manipulative she was, but equally she was a conduit of God's grace' (p. 76): with this idea in mind, consider the strong women characters you know. You notice their flaws; do you also notice them being used by God?
6 Is the vow to obey, traditionally made by the bride in a wedding service, inappropriate in the light of the Forsters' insight (p. 78)?
7 What has been lost in contemporary understanding of women as mothers when compared with Old Testament models?

Judges 19:1–30
5. Victimized women (pp. 80–90)

'The Bible is nothing if not realistic. It presents the world as it is both in the splendour of human relationships and in their savage awfulness' (p. 80).

1 Women are often less powerful and therefore more vulnerable, than men, to being victims. Where does this place them in God's salvation plan (Isaiah 61:1–8)?
2 What would today's authorities make of the way Hagar was treated: Genesis 16:1–16; 21:9–21 (p. 81)?
3 Judges was a period of a breakdown of law and order. Consider contemporary contexts where a similar social context prevails and how far women are the most prominent victims.

4 Would the comment hold true today that the 'treatment of women serves as a thermometer' measuring the godliness of a culture (p. 82)?

5 As you read the narrative of the Levite and the concubine, outline the shocking elements of the story and consider why the victim's story is rarely heard in churches (pp. 81–87).

6 What shocked the Israelites when the concubine's body was distributed and what different things would shock a community today (pp. 86–87)?

7 How typical is it today that wrong done to a woman is understood as an affront to 'her man' and vengeance on other men's women is then legitimized (p. 88)? Do some women continue to be used as pawns in violent and abusive power struggles (pp. 88–89)?

8 What are the biblical lessons which can be gleaned from the 'texts of terror' – the stories of women such as the Levite's concubine, Hagar, Tamar and Jephthah's daughter, who are powerless before the abuse or corrupt use of power by others?

Judges 4:1 – 5:31
6. Leading women (pp. 91–99)

1 What are the key qualities which Deborah displays in her role a judge (pp. 93–94)?

2 In what ways was Deborah a model leader for women and men (pp. 93–96)?

3 Deborah calls herself 'a mother in Israel' (Judg. 5:7); what are the meanings embedded in this title (pp. 97–99)?

'Women were not usually in the public eye; they were, however, mightily used of God in the deliverance of his people and, whenever they appear in public roles, are readily accepted in them' (p. 92).

4 What do her mothering qualities contribute to Deborah's leadership?

5 Jael's actions, which are praised (Judg. 5:24–27), might be considered unfeminine. What insights into appropriate godly behaviour could Jael offer to women (p. 98)?

6 How does the mention of Sisera's mother add to our understanding of the experiences of women at the time of the judges (p. 99)?

7 In what ways can an application be made from the lives of Deborah and Jael to the role of women today when the social and cultural contexts are so different?

Ruth 1:1 – 4:22
7. Resolute women (pp. 100–114)

1 What does the inclusion of the four women, Tamar, Rahab, Ruth and Uriah's wife in Matthew's genealogy say about the mission of God (p. 100)?

2 The four women of Matthew's genealogy are described by the writers in the following way 'they took risks and held their nerve, demonstrating initiative and resolution. They were not afraid to act in an unconventional, irregular manner and to contravene the accepted practices of their day' (p. 101). In our risk-averse culture are we lacking such women and men today?

3 The narrative of Naomi and Ruth, according to Bauckham, is valuable because 'it renders visible' the 'invisible' (p. 103). Is there a problem across Scripture of women being invisible?

4 What do we learn from Naomi about *hesed* and the God of *hesed* (p. 104)?

5 What do Ruth's words to Naomi (1:16–17) indicate about godly faithfulness and commitment (p. 106)? Is it an example for all disciples of Christ?

6 'Two vulnerable women move centre stage'(p. 106); why might God choose to use vulnerable women?

7 Would Ruth be considered an overly assertive woman today (p. 107)? Would there be disapproval of her decisiveness and her proactive approach?

8 What emphasis of Scripture would be missing if the book of Ruth were not part of the Old Testament?

2 Kings 22:11–20
8. Prophetic women (pp. 115–123)

1 From your experience, what is the importance of prophecy within a biblical faith community?

2 Why might it be unexpected that Huldah is the one approached at this critical time in Israel's history (pp. 118–119)?

3 Should there be greater openness to unexpected prophets of God in contemporary Christian communities?

4 Note the six factors which bring significance to Huldah's prophecy as she responds to the king's advisers. Which of these factors most reinforce Huldah as God's 'visible spokesperson' (pp. 119–121)?

5 Consider the authors' question, 'If God uses a woman in the Old Testament, in a role which, it is argued, is equivalent to that of the apostles in the New, then how can women be prohibited from exercising a similarly strong gift in the post-Pentecost church'? (p. 122).

6 Why might the little-known Huldah be respected above the better-known Ruth, Esther and Hannah?

Song of Songs 1:1 – 8:14
9. Passionate women (pp. 124–135)

1 Reflecting on the views of Jerome, Origen and Bernard of Clairvaux, why does it appear that female sexuality has been such a problem to theologians down the centuries (p. 125)?

2 Read Song of Songs 5:2–8 and recall that it is the young woman speaking; do you agree with other commentators that the Song of Songs gives women their voice?

3 To what extent is the positive affirmation of the young woman's emotions contrary to how women's emotions are often evaluated (pp. 127–128)?

4 What part does the woman play as her relationship with the lover develops through the poetry of the song (p. 128)?

5 Women and men can be made to feel inadequate by comparison with the more refined and honed. How is the young woman's response in 1:6 a model for others and what is the source of her security (p. 129)?

6 Do women face discrimination in your culture (pp. 130–131)? What could be the church's response to discrimination of any kind?

7 Is the sensual joy of the young woman of the Song of Songs a lesson for worship and the godly life in general (pp. 131–134)?

8 How is the woman's sexuality portrayed in the Song and is it a helpful affirmation (p. 134)?

Proverbs 31:10–31
10. Capable women (pp. 136–147)

1 Is it a fair portrayal of women that some can be a risk or a temptation to men as in Proverbs 5:3–5, 6:25–26 or 9:13–18 (pp. 136–137)?

2 In what ways is the woman of Proverbs 31:10–31 exceptional (pp. 138–139)?

3 Verses 10–11 use words which imply the woman is like a warrior (p. 139). Is this language which could be helpful in the community of the church as a balance to the more prevalent images of sister, mother and wife?

4 'We know nothing of what she looks like.' On the whole, are women judged by more superficial values than men? What values are particularly emphasized in the woman's life (p. 139)?

5 What do we learn about this woman's commercial and business skill (pp. 140–141)?

6 Verses 19–20 are pivotal in the poetry – what profound truth do they convey for all who fear the Lord (p. 141)?

7 What strengths of character of the woman are listed in verses 20–27 (pp. 142–143)?

8 Reflect on what it means for you 'to fear the Lord' (pp. 142–143).

9 Differing perspectives on the woman of the passage are described as the chapter concludes: which is the most persuasive for you (pp. 143–146)?

PART 3. WOMEN IN THE KINGDOM

Luke 1:26–56; Mark 3:20–34; John 2:1–12; 19:25–27
11. Women in the life of Jesus (pp. 151–160)

1 Why is Mary's virgin status important (p. 153)?

2 Reflect on Mary's song (Luke 1:46–55). What can we infer about her from her words (pp. 154–155)?

3 Do Mary's words in Luke 1:46–55 amount to teaching as she presents profound truth for future generations?

4 At the wedding in Cana of Galilee, what insight did Mary show and what lack of understanding was revealed on her part (pp. 155–156)?

5 What does Mark 3:20–34 indicate about the confusion Mary faced over the ministry of her son (pp. 156–158)?

6 As the portrait of Mary in this chapter of the book draws to a close, how does Mary's transformed relationship to Jesus become a model for all disciples (pp. 158–159)?

7 Was Mary an exceptional woman or was she an ordinary woman called upon by an exceptional God?

Mark 5:25–34; Luke 7:36–50; John 4:1–42
12. Women in the encounters of Jesus (pp. 161–171)

1 How difficult would it have been for first-century Jewish males and females, born and bred in patriarchy, to consider the equality of women as suggested by the relationships Jesus had with women (pp. 161–162)?

2 Trace the ways in which Jesus gives significance to the woman who had been bleeding for many years (Mark 5:25–34) (pp. 162–164).

3 In what way might the encounter with Jesus of the woman who suffered a long-term health problem give hope today for the long-term unwell (pp. 162–164)?

4 What does the incident of Luke 7:36–50 tell us of Jesus' willingness to affirm those with whom the 'religious' might struggle (pp. 165–168)?

5 Could the immoral woman portrayed in Luke 7:36–50 be more different from the sick woman of Mark 5:25–34? Note the contrasts between them (pp. 162–167). What does this say about the inclusiveness of Jesus?

6 The authors speak of 'the extraordinarily unconventional nature of God's grace' when speaking of the encounter with the woman at the well in Samaria. Suggest the reasons for this comment about God's grace in relation to the encounter (pp. 168–170).

7 To an uneducated woman. Jesus speaks of worship (John 4:19–26). How might this challenge our assumptions when engaging with people (pp. 168–170)?

13. Women in the teaching of Jesus (pp. 172–184)

1 What is it about the quotation of Dorothy Sayers which opens this chapter that the authors find brilliant (p. 172)?

2 Does Jesus' inclusive use of women's and men's activities as illustrations in his teaching have an important point to make to Gospel commentators and preachers today (pp. 173–175)?

3 Bailey suggests Jesus possibly compensated for the gender gap in religious culture. With so few men in the church today should we actively seek to make Christian teaching more male friendly (p. 174)?

4 Are the domestic qualities and activities of women seemingly commended by Jesus something of which our current culture might disapprove (p. 175)?

5 Jesus is realistic about the flaws of women. Does contemporary Christian culture have unrealistic expectations of women's purity, and men's (p. 176)?

6 Identify how women are valued as significant in Jesus' teaching on parenthood, widowhood, marriage, sex and divorce. Why might that have been shocking in the first century (pp. 177–181)?

7 What two perspectives of Martha are presented in Luke 10:38–42 and John 11:17–37 (pp. 181–183)? What accounts for the difference between them?

8 Read the final two paragraphs of this chapter. Is there still a need for radical reform of the role of women in gospel communities today (p. 184)?

Luke 8:1–3; Luke 23:44–24:12
14. Women as disciples of Jesus (pp. 185–196)

1 What particular images of discipleship do the women of Luke 8:1–3 reflect (pp. 185–189)?

2 What is the evidence that suggests women were involved as preachers at the time of Jesus (pp. 189–90)?

'As disciples of Jesus, then, women listened and responded to his teaching, engaged in ministry alongside men, and served as ambassadors of the kingdom of God. Moreover, they illustrate how radical the kingdom of God was and how much it overthrew social conventions that insisted the woman's place was confined to the home. They epitomized the truth that the kingdom of God was an inclusive kingdom and had a particular place for the marginalized, powerless and vulnerable' (p. 190).

---

3 Is the portrayal of women in the authors' comment above one that is often or rarely heard in current preaching?

4 How significant is it for pattern of ministry today that the twelve apostles were men (pp. 190–191)?

5 The women at the cross are referred to as women of courage and endurance. How often are women within the Christian community today censured for courage and audacity, and does it result in the leading of the Holy Spirit being hindered (p. 192)?

6 Why was discipleship particularly attractive to women in the first century (p. 196)? Is it similar today?

PART 4. WOMEN IN THE NEW COMMUNITY

Acts 16:13–17; 18:18–28; Romans 16:1–16; Philippians 4:2–3
15. Women in action (pp. 199–209)

1 What part did Lydia play in the growth of the church? What does her role suggest about ways in which God uses women (pp. 200–201)?
2 Priscilla was an early church teacher. What difficulty have women found in following her example (pp. 202–203)?
3 What do we learn about Phoebe from the brief biblical reference to her (pp. 204–206)?
4 How does the recognition of Junia as a woman and an apostle affect your understanding of the role of women in leading the church today (pp. 206–207)?
5 What do Euodia and Syntyche add as we build a picture of women in action in the New Testament church (p. 208)?
6 How might we evaluate the role of women in the establishing of the early church from the women in action of this chapter?

1 Corinthians 11:2–16
16. Women in prayer (pp. 210–222)

1 Reflect on the four understandings of headship in this chapter and consider what meaning of it is most persuasive in context (pp. 211–213).
2 Are there gender-specific codes of dress or behaviour that are appropriate in worshipping communities today as in the first century (pp. 214–216)?
3 Do you agree that Paul instructs the Corinthians to affirm gender distinctions 'not as a matter of hierarchy or headship but as a matter of relationship' and what does this mean in practice (p. 218)?
4 What does the inclusion of angels add to the teaching about women and worship (p. 219)?
5 Men and women 'were equally free to contribute in worship, provided they were sensitive to both the created differences and the cultural signals they were transmitting in doing so'. Is this a helpful summary of how men and women should act in worship (p. 220)?

6 What cultural and social conventions should be taken into account in the context in which you are a witness and worshipper?

7 In your observation have women tried to be like men in worship? What different qualities do women bring to worship and leadership?

1 Corinthians 14:26–40
17. Women in worship (pp. 223–234)

1 Many questions are raised about the meaning of these verses and how they should be understood today. Does this suggest that we are usually too simplistic or overly complex when we seek to understand Scripture for today (p. 223)?

2 Why might Kenneth Bailey's analysis of 1 Corinthians 11–14 be a helpful way of approaching the text (p. 226)? Are there limitations to his approach?

3 Is there any gender-specific behaviour (male or female) which might deserve a particular rebuke within the church community today (pp. 228–229)?

4 Are there cultural parallels today to Plutarch's comments that a woman speaking in public is like her appearing naked (p. 231) or is contemporary culture devoid of similar issues?

5 What behaviour might be judged scandalous today, or is our level of tolerance so great that anything goes in church communities (p. 232)?

6 How do shame and honour reveal themselves in your social contexts today (pp. 232–233)?

7 Do you agree that the important question to be answered is not about male authority but how our practice of worship reflects the nature of God (p. 234)?

1 Corinthians 7:1–7; Ephesians 5:21–33; 1 Peter 3:1–7
18. Women in marriage (pp. 235–248)

1 Consider the radical nature of Paul's intimate teaching (1 Cor. 7:2–5) about the wife having authority over the husband's body. Imagine hearing this for the first time as the church gathers to hear the voice of the Holy Spirit; what might the initial response have been (pp. 236–237)?

2 How does 'out of reverence for Christ' (Eph. 5:21) apply in marriage or parenting (p. 239)?

3 Why have some Christians emphasized wives and members of churches submitting to husbands and leaders when Paul's words require us to submit to one another (pp. 239–241)?

4 In speaking of headship what do the authors mean by 'this is a new creation principle not just the old one' (pp. 241–242)?

5 Would you agree, as some have argued, that the radical freedom offered to women in the Gospels is compromised in the social setting of the church as reflected in the Epistles (p. 243)?

6 What should women and men note from Peter's comments on beauty in 1 Peter 3:3–4 (pp. 243–246)?

7 Why does a women's appearance cause so much discussion and men's so little both in and outside of the church (pp. 244–245)?

8 How is Peter's comment about women as the weaker sex to be explained (pp. 246–247)?

9 Summarize for yourself the conclusions the authors draw on marriage and the family and New Testament teaching from the comments on pp. 247–248.

1 Timothy 2:11–15
19. Women in leadership (pp. 249–268)

1 Read 1 Timothy 2:11–15 carefully. What questions does it raise for you?

'Paul's encouragement to the women of the Ephesian church to learn would have seemed uncomfortably avant-garde to many in the ancient world' (p. 251).

---

2 What deeper understanding do the authors reveal about the word *hēsychia* (often translated 'silence')?

3 What might we easily miss if we did not have a broad understanding of the context of these verses (pp. 256–258)?

4 Why is it suggested that the words 'I do not permit' are not a timeless principle? What is the difference between biblical texts which are bound by their context and those which are not (pp. 251–252)?

5 How would you explain verse 15 – 'women will be saved through childbirth' – within a Bible study group (pp. 255–256)?

6 On what basis might it be argued today that not allowing women to exercise leadership would bring the gospel into disrepute?

7 Why should 1 Timothy 2:11–15 not be the defining verses about the role of women in the church?

1 Timothy 5:3–16
20. Women in widowhood (pp. 269–280)

1 Do widows today face similar issues of need as the first-century widow (pp. 269–271)?
2 What responsibilities does Paul lay on widows if they are to receive support from the church (pp. 271–275)?
3 How might the picture painted of young widows in the first century apply today (pp. 275–276)?
4 How realistic is it today to expect people to care for widows or others in need?

'. . . this final word calls for a discerning not a sentimental compassion. It neither idealizes solutions nor idealizes widows. Some widows needed more support than others. Some faced different temptations than others. And each should be treated with respect and dignity as appropriate' (p. 279).

---

5 What is the difference between a discerning rather than a sentimental compassion (see the above quotation)?
6 Might the issue of support today relate far more to single-parent families or those who are divorced?

Afterword (pp. 281–286)

1 As you have read, what picture have you built of women in the biblical narratives?
2 What challenges has the exposition brought for you, and how will you respond?
3 What advice is given about the appropriate way to engage in conversations about the issue of women, or any other issue, when there is a difference of opinion (p. 284)? How frequently do we fall short of what is an appropriate way of discussing issues in the church?

The Bible Speaks Today: Old Testament series

The Message of Genesis 1 – 11
The dawn of creation
David Atkinson

The Message of Genesis 12 – 50
From Abraham to Joseph
Joyce G. Baldwin

The Message of Exodus
The days of our pilgrimage
Alec Motyer

The Message of Leviticus
Free to be holy
Derek Tidball

The Message of Numbers
Journey to the promised land
Raymond Brown

The Message of Deuteronomy
Not by bread alone
Raymond Brown

The Message of Judges
Grace abounding
Michael Wilcock

The Message of Ruth
The wings of refuge
David Atkinson

The Message of Samuel
Personalities, potential, politics and power
Mary Evans

The Message of Kings
God is present
John W. Olley

The Message of Chronicles
One church, one faith, one Lord
Michael Wilcock

The Message of Ezra and Haggai
Building for God
Robert Fyall

The Message of Nehemiah
God's servant in a time of change
Raymond Brown

The Message of Esther
God present but unseen
David G. Firth

The Message of Job
Suffering and grace
David Atkinson

The Message of Psalms 1 – 72
Songs for the people of God
Michael Wilcock

The Message of Psalms 73 – 150
Songs for the people of God
Michael Wilcock

The Message of Proverbs
Wisdom for life
David Atkinson

The Message of Ecclesiastes
A time to mourn, and a time to dance
Derek Kidner

The Message of the Song of Songs
The lyrics of love
Tom Gledhill

The Message of Isaiah
On eagles' wings
Barry Webb

The Bible Speaks Today: New Testament series

The Message of the Sermon on the Mount (Matthew 5 – 7)
Christian counter-culture
John Stott

The Message of Matthew
The kingdom of heaven
Michael Green

The Message of Mark
The mystery of faith
Donald English

The Message of Luke
The Saviour of the world
Michael Wilcock

The Message of John
Here is your King!
Bruce Milne

The Message of Acts
To the ends of the earth
John Stott

The Message of Romans
God's good news for the world
John Stott

The Message of 1 Corinthians
Life in the local church
David Prior

The Message of 2 Corinthians
Power in weakness
Paul Barnett

The Message of Galatians
Only one way
John Stott

The Message of Ephesians
God's new society
John Stott

The Message of Philippians
Jesus our Joy
Alec Motyer

The Message of Colossians and Philemon
Fullness and freedom
Dick Lucas

The Message of Thessalonians
Preparing for the coming King
John Stott

The Message of 1 Timothy and Titus
The life of the local church
John Stott

The Message of 2 Timothy
Guard the gospel
John Stott

The Message of Hebrews
Christ above all
Raymond Brown

The Message of James
The tests of faith
Alec Motyer

The Message of 1 Peter
The way of the cross
Edmund Clowney

The Message of 2 Peter and Jude
The promise of his coming
Dick Lucas and Christopher Green

The Message of John's Letters
Living in the love of God
David Jackman

The Message of Revelation
I saw heaven opened
Michael Wilcock